Heinemann
ASSEMBLY
Resources

MOMENTS

of

REFLECTION

JEAN HOWARTH & MIKE WALTON

Heinemann Educational Pulishers
Halley Court, Jordan Hill, Oxford OX2 8EJ
a division of Reed Educational & Professional Publishing Ltd

OXFORD   MELBOURNE   AUCKLAND
JOHANNESBURG   BLANTYRE   GABORONE
IBADAN   PORTSMOUTH (NH) USA   CHICAGO

First published 1995

99 98
10 9 8 7 6 5 4

British Library Cataloguing in Publication Data
A catalogue record for this book is available from the British Library

ISBN 0 435 30243 4

Designed by Linda Reed
Cover design by Threefold Design
Cover Photograph by Zefa-Mueller, W.H.
Typeset by Books Unlimited (Nottm), Mansfield NG19 7QZ
Printed and bound by Athenæum Press Ltd, Gateshead, Tyne & Wear

CONTENTS

FOREWORD

David Naylor
Former County RE Adviser and General Inspector for Hampshire

The teaching profession has reacted in a variety of ways to the 1988 Education Act with its requirement for daily acts of collective worship. The reaction has varied from an understandable but unhelpful cynicism to genuine attempts to fulfil the spirit of the Act. Perhaps the most common response has been to hold one or two Year or House assemblies each week, to lie low until OFSTED week and then hope that the one-liner in the report would only cause short-lived ripples amongst largely secular parents. Another popular device has been to try to initiate 'Thought for the Day' in tutor time. In many schools this has disappeared under the weight of general administration and homework diaries.

Jean Howarth and Mike Walton have seen beyond these difficulties with a vision of pupils' spiritual and moral development which transcends over-zealous religiosity and political posturing. Their vision focuses exclusively on the need to educate the whole child, the inner as well as the outer self. To achieve this they have used an imaginative variety of sources from within and beyond the religious traditions. The remarkable fact is that they have gained the willing co-operation of all their colleagues irrespective of their personal commitments.

In 1985 John Hull wrote a book entitled *School Worship: An Obituary*. *Moments of Reflection* could be sub-titled *School Worship: A Resurrection*. Like all resurrections it is more than a mere resuscitation; it embodies a wider view of spirituality which will appeal to all teachers with a concern for young people.

INTRODUCTION

Many adults today can remember starting their school day with an act of worship. This often consisted of a hymn, a prayer and a bible reading. Over the years this practice has become less frequent.

The 1944 Education Act required 'a daily act of collective worship', and the 1988 Education Reform Act reaffirmed this requirement, adding that it should be 'wholly or mainly of a broadly Christian character'.

In a talk on 'Religious Education and Collective Worship as seen through OFSTED inspection', an HMI said that 'very few secondary schools comply with the Act and that a particular problem afflicting secondary schools is the lack of accommodation': almost half of the schools inspected in 1994 had an accommodation difficulty. He followed this by saying, 'If there is a physical difficulty of accommodation, daily worship depends upon the participation of tutors.'

These words summed up the situation in our school as in many others. Two days a week were accounted for with a house meeting and a school meeting, but for three days it was the responsibility of the tutors to arrange daily worship. With their already demanding workload, we did not want to overburden the tutors so it was decided that they should be given a book with three daily readings per week that could be used in tutor time. Each week the readings would be on a set theme which supported the ethos of the school and complied with the demands of the Act. Each year group would have its own set of readings, maintaining the theme but making the content suitable to the age group.

We called this book *Moments of Reflection* because we wanted each pupil to spend this part of the day in a quiet frame of mind listening to the words and reflecting on their meaning. Each day's reading is divided into three parts:

A   a quote or comment appropriate to the week's theme
B   a reflective comment expanding or explaining the quote
C   a positive thought that the pupil can dwell on during the day.

For *Moments of Reflection* to work it needs to be taken seriously and a few ground rules laid down:

- calm and quiet atmosphere at the start
- silence during 'Moments of Reflection'
- sitting still in a comfortable position
- eyes closed or open and fixed on an object.

We suggest that the rule on silence is non-negotiable.

There are several ways that the readings can be presented using a structured, participative or individual approach.

Structured approach

Read each daily reading slowly. Allow pupils time to reflect silently on it and apply it to their lives before reading the reflective comment. Finally, leave them with a positive thought. A pause between each section can aid reflection.

Participative approach

Pupils can regularly be involved in the running of the act of worship by:

- reading one or more of the sections
- with guidance, writing and carrying out a 'Moment of Reflection' on the given theme

- members of the tutor group sharing their reflections on the reading. Thought might be stimulated by asking questions such as:
  - what, if anything, did you discover from listening to the reading?
  - did anything from the reading attract your attention?
  - did anything from it surprise you?
  - how did you feel as you listened to the words?
  - what, if anything, have you learnt about yourself?
  - some people would feel like the author of this reading; what would you feel or do?

After each question, a time could be given for quiet reflection.

Individual approach

There are several ways in which the material in this book can be adapted to suit individual needs and situations. For example:

- read the daily reading supplied but provide your own reflective comment and positive thought
- extend the 'Moment of Reflection' into a discussion
- use a piece of music in the act of worship.

Finally, after a year's trial, we can say that this is a workable book. Our staff have been very supportive in delivering the readings and their feedback has been very positive. We have also found that many pupils enjoy being involved. The book was purposely introduced into the lower school first, each year taking on another year, so it has become the norm for pupils as they enter the school and progress through the years. Other members of the school, like the non-teaching staff, have also requested books for their personal use.

Many schools are looking for ways to comply with the Education Reform Act in delivering a daily act of collective worship. This has been *our* response. We know that it is not perfect but it has been a help to us and we hope that you enjoy the same benefit.

We would like to express our thanks to our families and friends for all their love, help and encouragement during the writing of *Moments of Reflection*; to Sarah Evling-Walton for her written contributions and helpful reflections; to the pupils and staff of Bohunt Community School for their inspiration and co-operation; to Anneke Davey who quickly and carefully typed the manuscript; to our Headteacher, Dr Alan Leech, for reading every page, making constructive comments and supporting us from the very beginning of the project; and to Sue Walton and the staff at Heinemann without whose help the book would not have been published.

JEAN HOWARTH
MIKE WALTON

1 NEW BEGINNINGS

Year 7:1

A

There is a time for everything,
and a season for every activity under the heaven;
a time to be born and a time to die,
a time to plant and a time to uproot,
a time to tear down and a time to build,
a time to weep and a time to laugh.

ECCLESIASTES 3:1–4

B

Maybe we would add, 'A time to leave junior school, a time to begin secondary school, a time to say goodbye to some old friends, a time to say hello to new friends.'

As new things come into our life it is important to accept them and enjoy them. Our time at school is only a small percentage of our whole life. Let's make the most of it.

We could spend each day worrying about what is going to happen, or we could see it as an adventure and look forward to each new experience.

C

I am thankful for new opportunities and challenges in my life.

Year 7:2

A

A time to search and a time to give up,
A time to keep and a time to throw away,
A time to tear and a time to mend,
A time to be silent and a time to speak.

ECCLESIASTES 3:6–7

B

As we begin our time at secondary school, we will find that new things will be expected of us. We will meet new people and learn new skills. A school is a bit like a large family. We eat together, work together and play together. Sometimes we have quarrels as all families do, but we manage to sort them out and stay friends. There will always be new children joining the family, or older children leaving. When we share our thoughts and feelings, we will discover new things about others and ourselves.

C

Let us be responsible members of this 'family'.

Year 7:3

A

If you don't know where you're going, you'll end up somewhere else.

W. CLEMENT STONE, IN *CHANGES – BECOMING THE BEST YOU CAN BE*

B

'What do I want from life?' 'What am I going to be?' These are among the most important questions you can ever ask yourself. If you don't ask these questions, you can end up just drifting through life, like a leaf

blown by the winds. Alternatively, you can set goals for yourself and take charge of your life. You can be in control.

The most successful people are those who learn how to set goals. By thinking about goals – and then following them through with action – you can be a success in years to come. You can be the one who makes your future happen.

If you don't set goals, you're really making a decision to do nothing. Every successful person you've met or read about had a Definite Major Goal – every athlete, every entertainer, every great leader in the world.

Do you have a dream for the future? Is it something you're willing to work really hard for? That's what a goal is: something you want very much to do or be.

CHANGES – BECOMING THE BEST YOU CAN BE

C

Make this promise to yourself: 'I will try to learn things that will help me become the best I can be in order to achieve success in everything I do.'

Year 8:1

A

If I had my life to live over … I'd relax … I would take fewer things seriously. I would take more chances. I would climb more mountains and swim more rivers. I'd start barefoot earlier in the spring and stay that way later in the fall. I would go to more dances. I would ride more merry-go-rounds. I would pick more daisies.

NADINE STAIR, IN *TOUCHSTONES* (21 MARCH)

B

'Letting go' is a subject that has many variations. When we live with enthusiasm we are released to experience the full excitement of life, we are letting go. When we turn our lives and wills over to the care of God, we are freed of many cares. If we

3

direct our lives with a compass that always points to fear and insecurity, or to power and success, we are giving ourselves over to those forces. But we can direct our lives to God's care and support. That makes it possible to drop our guard, allow for some mistakes and delight in the pleasures of creation.

ADAPTED FROM *TOUCHSTONES* (21 MARCH)

C

Today let me forget my worries and enjoy the fullness of life.

ADAPTED FROM *TOUCHSTONES* (21 MARCH)

Year 8:2

A

Before the rain stops we hear a bird. Even under the heavy snow we see snowdrops and some new growth.

SHUNRYU SUZUKI, IN *TOUCHSTONES* (8 MARCH)

B

The signals that new growth is underway are often very small at first. It's sometimes discouraging when we are trying to improve our lives and all we can see for our efforts is minor growth. That is how the natural world works, and we are part of this world. When the little sprouts of growth first develop under the snow in spring, we don't even see them unless we search. Yet they signal the beginnings of a total transformation. Time will bring vast changes, but only little signs show first.

Today, we may be searching for signs of progress in our lives. The little things we see may signal bigger changes yet to come. To be true to them in the long run we must accept them – even welcome them.

ADAPTED FROM *TOUCHSTONES* (8 MARCH)

C

I will notice the gradual changes in my life. Welcoming them will encourage them.

ADAPTED FROM *TOUCHSTONES* (8 MARCH)

Year 8:3

A

Morning has broken like the first morning;
Blackbird has spoken like the first bird.

THE ILLUSTRATED FAMILY HYMN BOOK

B

All over Britain, children and young people are beginning the new school or college year. It is good to give ourselves a fresh start as we begin the year. All the things we did last year are in the past. We have no need to cling to that. The future is ahead of us, and how we are going to use it is up to us. We need to say, 'Let me be new, let there be a freshness in my life, let me be happy, let my work sparkle.'

C

Today is the first day of the rest of my life.

Year 9:1

A

Beginnings are apt to be shadowy.

RACHEL CARSON, IN *EACH DAY A NEW BEGINNING*
(4 NOVEMBER)

B

When we commence a new course, go to an unfamiliar place or make new friendships, we rarely see where the experience will lead us. At best we can see only what this day brings. We have to trust that we will be safely led through the 'shadows'.

To benefit in this life we must explore new places, contact new people and try new experiences. Even though we are frightened of what we do not know, we must go forward.

In our life we will experience many new beginnings. Each one adds to our growth as a person. Each one will help us learn a little more about ourselves.

ADAPTED FROM *EACH DAY A NEW BEGINNING* (4 NOVEMBER)

C

I will look to my new beginnings gladly. They are special to the growth I am now ready for.

EACH DAY A NEW BEGINNING (4 NOVEMBER)

Year 9:2

A

New life comes from shedding old skins and pressing through the darkness toward the light.

KAREN KAISER CLARK, IN *TOUCHSTONES* (20 MARCH)

B

Now we are beginning a new school year. It is a new beginning, but one that we can handle. We need new beginnings to develop ourselves, and we need to be ready for whatever comes our way. All of us have turning points in our lives. As yet we may not realize what changes lie ahead of us. Just as we watch a plant yet never see it grow, nevertheless we realize that day-by-day there is a change going on. So we might not see the change happening in ourselves, but one day realize that we are different people from the ones who started out this year.

ADAPTED FROM *TOUCHSTONES* (20 MARCH)

C

I am thankful for new beginnings in the world and the eternal spring within my being.

TOUCHSTONES (20 MARCH)

Year 9:3

A

A good beginning makes a good ending.

14TH-CENTURY PROVERB, IN *DICTIONARY OF QUOTATIONS AND PROVERBS*

B

Ahead of us this year lie choices. These choices will affect our future. Sometimes it can cause a lot of heartache wondering what to do and if we have done the right thing. However, each day is a new beginning, each day offers up new choices. Each day is the first day of the rest of our life. If we treat each day as special and take care with all the small decisions, when it comes to the larger decisions, they will fall naturally into place.

Each day is a precious gift, to be appreciated, enjoyed and respected.

C

I am thankful for the opportunities that are given to me each day and pray for guidance in the decisions to be made.

Year 10:1

A

This month shall be the beginning of months for you; it is to be the first month of the year to you.

EXODUS 12:2

B

At the beginning of year 10, we have the opportunity to build on what we have been studying, but we can also start with a 'clean slate'. We can let go of things that hindered us in the lower school and start afresh.

At the end of the examination courses the examiner is not going to say 'Ah! this is the pupil who forgot to do their homework in year 7'. What will show in the examinations is how much effort you have put into the course on which you are about to embark.

A new beginning – let's make the most of it.

C

Today I will look forward to the new opportunities offered to me.

Year 10:2

A

Though your beginning was insignificant,
Yet your end will increase greatly.

JOB 8:7

B

From the first time a teacher asks us for a piece of work we get the idea that we are working for the teacher. We feel that for some inscrutable reason the teacher has a need to mark our spelling test or our graph or whatever. The reality of the situation is that the teacher is checking our progress and assessing our capabilities.

When we reach Year 10 we realize that the work we are doing, whether research, coursework, or practical work, we are doing for ourselves. We are the ones to benefit from the work; no one else. The teachers already have their GCSEs, A levels and degrees.

This is the beginning of a new awareness, a realization that we are moving on from being a pupil – one who is taught by another – to being a student – a person who takes on responsibility for their own study.

We still need to be taught, we have a lot to learn, but this is a time when we begin to rely on ourselves for our motivation.

C

I am glad of the opportunity to show that I am a responsible person.

Year 10:3

A

True joy is one of the greatest gifts of life …
Joy is not confined to the religious or 'do-gooder',
but it comes to those who in a sense forget themselves
and become totally aware of the other.

D. RAE, *'LOVE UNTIL IT HURTS'*, IN *MANY THOUGHTS*

B

Year 10 can be an awkward time with relationships. We have just spent three years getting to know our tutor group, aware of each other's strengths and weaknesses, likes and dislikes, when we are thrown together with the rest of Year 10. Some will already be friends, others we will hardly know and there will be some that for some reason or another we don't like.

This was noticeable in a Year 10 GCSE group. Two opposing parties were in a small group and others in the group took sides; the tension built up. They discussed the problem openly, but it still was not resolved. Then one day one of the pupils said, 'This is silly, it is about time we got over this' and she apologised to the opposing party.

After mutual apologies and letting go of the past, the problem was over. They were able to work together, chat easily, laugh with each other and treat each other in a mature manner. It was a new beginning. Year 10 gives us the opportunity to build new friendships.

C

I will not take old prejudices into new situations.

Year 11:1

A

With each new day I put away the past and discover the new beginnings I have been given.

ANGELA L. WOZNIAK, IN *EACH DAY A NEW BEGINNING* (13 AUGUST)

B

We cannot alter the past, but we can spend a lot of time thinking about it. Life is full of 'If only's'. 'If only this had not happened'; 'If only I had spoken up'; 'If only I had not acted in this way'. And all the time we spend thinking about what might or might not have happened, we rob ourselves of the present. Each day gives us new challenges and opportunities. If we get too concerned over what happened yesterday, we will be too preoccupied to notice the opportunities of today.

C

I will notice the opportunities of each new day.

Year 11:2

A

Looking forward into an empty year strikes one with a certain awe, because one finds therein no recognition. The years behind have a friendly aspect, and they are warmed by the fires we have kindled, and all their echoes are the echoes of our own voices.

ALEXANDER SMITH, IN *THE DECADES BOOK OF BIRTHDAYS*

B

As we face a new school year we do not know what the coming year will bring. This is probably our last school year and by this time next year we could be in employment, at college or on a training course.

We know that we are going to face new situations, new routines, new expectations and new friendships. The important thing for us to do between now and then is to make the most of the opportunities that we face each day this year. Then we will have no regrets and our moving on will feel like a natural progression.

C

I will make the most of all the opportunities presented to me today.

Year 11.3

A

Change is the law of life. And those who look only to the past or the present are certain to miss the future.

JOHN F. KENNEDY, IN *THE DECADES BOOK OF BIRTHDAYS*

B

Change can be exciting, but it can also be frightening. Whatever we have to face each day we know that nothing stays the same. Our bodies change, our thoughts and emotions mature and our understanding develops. There is a certain security about the past, a familiarity, a cosiness, but if we cling to the past we will not be free to face the future.

In Year 11 we are becoming much more independent and

often have to face new challenges. We are not alone, because we are all going through the process of change, meeting the future together.

C

I will accept change as a part of life.

2 TEACHING AND LEARNING

Year 7:1

A

I am still learning.

MICHELANGELO'S MOTTO, IN *TOUCHSTONES* (28 AUGUST)

B

It is OK for a person to say 'I don't know'. How can we ever learn anything new if we can't look like beginners? That's the way to be an under-achiever. In our growing up, we can have the strength to admit we don't always know. To be learners, we need to be honest about what we already know as well as about what we do not know.

ADAPTED FROM *TOUCHSTONES* (28 AUGUST)

C

I will be honest about things I don't know so I can continue to learn.

TOUCHSTONES (28 AUGUST)

Year 7:2

A

Mistakes are teachers! Allow yourself to think of mistakes as a way of learning how to do things better.

PAT PALMER, *LIKING MYSELF*

B

Sometimes you may feel badly for making a mistake ... like

13

forgetting to come home on time, or pulling out the bottom can in a supermarket and causing a crash, or forgetting to do something you were supposed to do. BUT … the most important thing is to fix your mistakes! Help stack the cans again! Be home on time today! Mistakes are OK because they're learning opportunities. Remember, though, that it is not fair to others or to yourself to use 'I made a mistake' as an excuse for being careless or for hurting others.

ADAPTED FROM *LIKING MYSELF*

C

Today I will view my mistakes as learning opportunities.

Year 7:3

A

Feelings are good friends.
Feelings let us know …
what is happening,
what we want,
what is important to us.
Feelings are like a thermometer.

PAT PALMER, *LIKING MYSELF*

B

Listen to your feelings. They tell you when you need to take care of yourself, like finding a friend if you feel lonely, crying if you feel sad, singing and smiling if you feel happy and acting energetically if you feel good. We can pretend not to feel, but we still have feelings anyway. Holding them back and pushing them down inside just makes them stay … and stay … and stay … and keep hurting. Let out the hurt feelings as fast as you can. You don't need to hold on to them. Let go of them so they can leave.

Your feelings help you to know what is right for *you*. Feelings *are* good friends.

ADAPTED FROM *LIKING MYSELF*

C

Today I will get in touch with and experience my true feelings and learn from them.

Year 8:1

A

No person is your enemy, no person is your friend, every person is your teacher.

FLORENCE SCOVEL SHINN, IN *EACH DAY A NEW BEGINNING* (12 SEPTEMBER)

B

We can open ourselves to opportunities today. They are everywhere in our lives. Teachers are everywhere. And as we become ready for a new lesson, one will appear.

We can marvel at the wonder of our lives today. We can reflect on our yesterdays and be grateful for the lessons they taught. We can look with hope at the days ahead – gifts, all of them. We are on a special journey, serving a special purpose, uniquely our own. All experiences are simply to teach us what we have yet to learn.

ADAPTED FROM *EACH DAY A NEW BEGINNING* (12 SEPTEMBER)

C

I am a student of life. I can learn only if I open my mind to my teachers.

EACH DAY A NEW BEGINNING (12 SEPTEMBER)

Year 8:2

A

Pain is short and joy is eternal.

JOHANN SCHILLER, IN *DAYS OF HEALING, DAYS OF JOY*
(26 AUGUST)

B

Pain can be a teacher. And like many other teachers, pain deserves more attention than it sometimes gets. We can become so used to pain that we ignore it. Worse still, our pain may be so commonplace we don't even recognise it as pain.

Pain carries a message. Pain is telling us that something is wrong, that we need to behave differently, that what hurts must be fixed. It isn't normal to feel lonely, fearful, angry, or lost all the time. If that's the way it is for us, then we need to talk to a friend, or parent, or teacher.

ADAPTED FROM *DAYS OF HEALING, DAYS OF JOY* (26 AUGUST)

C

I am willing to reach out for help when I need it. I no longer accept hopelessness as a way of life.

DAYS OF HEALING, DAYS OF JOY (26 AUGUST)

Year 8:3

A

The time of discipline began. Each of us the pupil of whichever one of us could best teach what each of us needed to learn.

MARIA ISABEL BARRENO, IN *EACH DAY A NEW BEGINNING*
(25 JANUARY)

B

'When the pupil is ready, the teacher appears.' Life's lessons often come unexpectedly. Perhaps the teacher will be a close friendship, a difficult loss, or a time of illness. The time of learning can involve pain and questioning. But from these experiences and what they can teach us, we are ready to learn. As we are ready, they come.

To understand that all is well, throughout the learning process, is the basic lesson we need to learn. All is well. The teacher is the guide up the next rung of the ladder.

ADAPTED FROM *EACH DAY A NEW BEGINNING* (25 JANUARY)

C

Let me be grateful for my lessons today and know that all is well.

EACH DAY A NEW BEGINNING (25 JANUARY)

Year 9:1

A

An optimist expects his dreams to come true; a pessimist expects his nightmares to.

LAURENCE J. PETER, IN *DAYS OF HEALING, DAYS OF JOY*
(17 DECEMBER)

B

Sometimes the only thing we can change is our attitude – and that is enough.

One person who's stuck in traffic, fumes at fate, snarling, 'Why does this always happen to me?' Meanwhile, the person in the car just behind, stuck in the same jam, sees the first person's 'lost' time as 'found' time – the perfect opportunity to think through a problem without interruptions. One person sees only a problem; the other sees an opportunity. The traffic jam is the same for both of them, but their attitude about it is different – as are their blood pressures. The difference is all in the attitude.

ADAPTED FROM *DAYS OF HEALING, DAYS OF JOY* (17 DECEMBER)

C

I am learning to make the most of my opportunities.

DAYS OF HEALING, DAYS OF JOY (17 DECEMBER)

Year 9:2

A

The man who never alters his opinion is like standing water, and breeds reptiles of the mind.

WILLIAM BLAKE, IN *TOUCHSTONES* (30 SEPTEMBER)

B

We look for *the answer*. Sometimes we think we have found a central truth and later learn that beneath it is another truth. Or what seemed so important for our lives last year is still true but not as important.

We must continue forever to be eager learners. In stepping across a stream from one floating log to another, we must resist the temptation to become overcommitted to staying in an especially secure-looking place, or we will never reach the opposite shore.

ADAPTED FROM *TOUCHSTONES* (30 SEPTEMBER)

C

Today I will be open to new opinions – to things I had never thought of on my own.

ADAPTED FROM *TOUCHSTONES* (30 SEPTEMBER)

Year 9:3

A

They believed they could, and they could. I believe I can too.

DAYS OF HEALING, DAYS OF JOY (4 SEPTEMBER)

B

A positive mental attitude (PMA) means believing in yourself and your abilities. It means thinking to yourself, 'I can do it. Even if it takes a lot of hard work and a long time, I can do it.' PMA is like an engine inside you that keeps you going, keeps driving you on. With PMA you can do almost anything. It is so easy to have negative thoughts and so create more of what you don't want. Move away from negative thoughts and put your attention on what it is that you really do want to be or have. Learn to think in positive ways.

ADAPTED FROM *CHANGES – BECOMING THE BEST YOU CAN BE*

C

I look forward with enthusiasm to the adventures of the day.

Year 10:1

A

That is what learning is – you suddenly understand something you've understood all your life, but in a new way.

DORIS LESSING, IN *EACH DAY A NEW BEGINNING* (7 JULY)

B

As we are changed by our experiences, our knowledge and understanding of who we are also changes. We are forever students of life.

There is real excitement in knowing that learning has no end and that each day offers us a chance to move closer to becoming the persons we can be.

To understand something more deeply requires that we become open to the ideas of others; willing to part with our present opinions. School offers us many opportunities to trade in understandings we've outgrown.

Throughout our time at school, we can discover new interpretations of old ideas.

ADAPTED FROM *EACH DAY A NEW BEGINNING* (7 JULY)

C

Each moment offers me a chance to learn and to understand more fully who I am.

ADAPTED FROM *EACH DAY A NEW BEGINNING* (7 JULY)

Year 10:2

A

Though I have all science and all technology and have not considered the ethical ends to which they might be put ...

Though I have all keyboard skills and have not reflected on the uniqueness of my existence ...

Though I know all the continents, rivers and capitals and have not faced the question of my share of responsibility for the creation ...

Though I could list all the drugs, their uses and effects and have not been given access to any visions of the good life ...

Though I know all the physiological details of sex, yea even within the context of family life, and have never encountered the idea of the sacredness of the human body ...

I AM UNEDUCATED

DAVID NAYLOR

B

There are two educations:
The one that teaches how to make a living
and the one that teaches how to live.

ANTHONY DE MELLO, *THE HEART OF THE ENLIGHTENED*

C

Today as I am busy achieving things of outer value, I will not forget the things which are of inner value.

ADAPTED FROM *THE POWER OF MYTH*

Year 10:3

A

Some explorers found a beautiful undiscovered land. When they re-turned to their home, they told their friends about this country, describing the valleys, the hills, the rivers, the trees, animals and plants. They told them 'You must go there for yourselves, our words cannot do justice to that land.' Their friends were excited and keen to see the land for themselves. They asked the explorers to draw them a map to guide their journey and to show them exactly where the land was. They refused, saying 'No, you must set out and find the way yourselves'. There are many different routes and we only know one of them.' However, they insisted, and after a time the explorers gave in and drew a map for them. Their friends were excited by the map and spent days planning for the journey, discussing which route they would take, and what the land would look like. But they delayed, deciding that they had first better prepare thoroughly for the trip.

Perhaps too, they needed to know more about maps, how to read them, and how to understand what picture the map showed. Years passed, the map was studied, then copied and passed on to others. Schools were set up in map reading. The explorers were sad. No one visited the land.

NEW METHODS IN RE TEACHING

B

Maps are important. Without them you may get lost, or else stay at home, not fully aware that other places exist. However the map alone cannot reveal the true nature of the country.

Real learning can only take place if the map helps you to find that land and experience it for yourself.

ADAPTED FROM *NEW METHODS IN RE TEACHING*

C

Today I will distinguish between what I have learned through direct experience and what I've just learned from books.

Year 11:1

A

Try viewing everyone who comes into your life as a teacher ... Instead of judging others as people who should or should not be behaving in certain ways, see them as reflecting a part of you and ask yourself what it is you are ready to learn from them.

DR WAYNE W. DYER, *YOU'LL SEE IT WHEN YOU BELIEVE IT*

B

If, when we meet someone, we are caught up with judging them and finding fault with their ways, we may miss the chance to learn from them.

We can be so full of our own thoughts and opinions that there is no room to take on board what they may have to tell us or show us.

Whatever we notice about others can act as a mirror for us to look at ourselves, because the qualities that we most dislike and admire in others are also to be found in ourselves.

C

I will see every encounter as an opportunity to learn and grow.

Year 11:2

A

We are all teachers of each other …
I believe that in teaching what I want to learn … I can become more
consistent in achieving it for myself.

GERALD G. JAMPOLSKY, *LOVE IS LETTING GO OF FEAR*

B

Whenever we set out to teach, we also learn. We may be the most distinguished and eminent expert in a particular field of study, but we can never reach a point where we will know all that there is to know about a subject.

In passing on what we have learned, we put ourselves in a good position to find out even more about our interest. There is always a fresh way to look at what we think we know, and there is no end to the creative ways in which we can teach and learn.

If we can pass on to others what inspires and interests us, we will also increase our own understanding. So the next time a friend asks for help with schoolwork, remember, it may be a golden opportunity to understand more ourselves, and gain greater insight.

C

We are all teachers of each other.

Year 11:3

A

He who gives to me teaches me to give.

DANISH PROVERB, IN *PROVERBS FROM AROUND THE WORLD*

B

One of the best ways to teach others is by example. When we

show kindness and compassion towards our fellow human beings, we can be an example for others to follow. When other people treat us unkindly, we can change the way that they behave towards us by changing the way that we treat ourselves.

If we want others to treat us with respect, then it is important to start treating both ourselves and the people that we meet in this way too.

C

I will teach others by example.

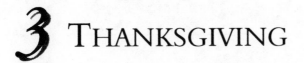

3 THANKSGIVING

Year 7:1

A

We must know how to say 'Thank you'. If we were in the habit of taking stock of all the good things we have each day, we would realise how rich we were.

ADAPTED FROM MICHEL QUOIST, *PRAYERS OF LIFE*

B

For health and strength and the gifts of seeing, hearing and enjoying so many good things,
For people who love us, care for us, even worry about us and want for us nothing but the best,
For the ones I love, for friends and all who mean a lot to me.
For music and laughter, reading and dancing, learning and sport,
For science and art, doctors and dentists, machines and gadgets,
For ordinary people who show courage and kindness,
For leaders, artists and those who uphold justice and protect us,
For those people who are special to us,
We say: 'Thank you'.

FRANK COOKE, *GET TOGETHER*

C

Today I will count all the good things that happen to me.

Year 7:2

A

'I thought there were ten of you altogether, where are the other nine?'

B

Leprosy is a terrible disease which even today is hard to cure. There is a story about Jesus and the ten lepers in the Bible. In those days there was no treatment for leprosy at all. People who had the disease had to keep away from everyone else, and were thought to be infectious. They could easily be recognised, because the disease wasted away their hands and feet. They shouted to Jesus from some distance away, 'Jesus, Master, please help us'. Jesus told them to go and show themselves to the priests. They hurried off immediately, because they knew Jesus could heal disease and because no leper could go back to his family until a priest had seen that the disease had gone.

Even as they hurried back to the village to find a priest, the skin on their hands and feet healed and they realised Jesus had cured them. They were all astonished as they looked at their fingers and toes which only minutes before had been covered with sores.

One of the ten turned back to find Jesus, thanking and praising God out loud as he went. He was so grateful that when he found Jesus, he knelt down at his feet to thank him. Jesus said to him, 'I thought there were ten of you altogether; where are the other nine?' Then Jesus told the man to go home to his family and that his faith in God had made him well again.

When we are ungrateful, we are just like the nine lepers, taking all the good things that happen for granted and not bothering to say, 'Thank you'.

C

I will be thankful for my health and for everything which makes me feel happy.

Year 7:3

A

It is good to have an attitude of gratitude, of giving thanks, of not taking anything for granted, but being thankful.

FRANK COOKE, *GET TOGETHER*

B

An American wanted to thank somebody on Thanksgiving Day. He began making a list of people and things for which he was thankful. He remembered a lady who had taught him in the infant school and he wrote a letter and thanked her. She wrote back:

'My dear Billy,
I cannot tell you how much your note meant to me. I am in my eighties, living alone in a small room, cooking my own meals, lonely and, like the last leaf of autumn, lingering behind. You will be interested to know that I taught in school for fifty years and yours is the first note of appreciation I have ever received. It came on a blue-cold morning and it cheered me as nothing has in many years.'

FRANK COOKE, *GET TOGETHER*

C

Being thankful for what we have means showing gratitude to people. Let's show our gratitude today.

Year 8:1

A

My life has been a tapestry of rich and royal hue,
An everlasting vision of the ever-changing view.

CAROLE KING, IN *EACH DAY A NEW BEGINNING* (26 OCTOBER)

B

I thank Thee, God, that I have lived

In this great world and known its many joys;
The song of birds, the strong, sweet scent of hay
And cooling breezes in the secret dusk,
The flaming sunsets at the close of day,
Hills, and the lonely, heather-covered moors,
Music at night, and moonlight on the sea,
The beat of waves upon the rocky shore
And wild, white spray, flung high in ecstasy:
The faithful eyes of dogs, and treasured books.
The love of kin and fellowship of friends,
And all that makes life dear and beautiful.
I thank Thee, too, that there has come to me
A little sorrow and, sometimes, defeat,
A little heartache and the loneliness
That comes with parting, and the word, 'Goodbye',
Dawn breaking after dreary hours of pain,
When I discovered that night's gloom must yield
And morning light break through to me again.
Because of these and other blessings poured
Unasked upon my wondering head,
Because I know that there is yet to come
An even richer and more glorious life,
And most of all, because Thine only Son
Once sacrificed life's loveliness for me –
I thank Thee God that I have lived.

ELIZABETH CRAVEN, IN *AN ANTHOLOGY OF HOPE*

C

Today I will look for things for which I can be thankful.

Year 8:2

A

Thank you for the tranquil night.

Thank you for the stars.
Thank you for the silence.
Thank you for the time you have given me.
Thank you for life.
Thank you for grace.
Thank you for being there, Lord.

MICHEL QUOIST, *PRAYERS OF LIFE*

B

Thankfulness is a way of looking at life, and it brings its own happiness, even in difficult situations. If we take all the good things of life for granted, when something is not so good it will confirm our suspicions that all is gloom. However, if we note all the good things of life this will help to balance out the unhappy things which occur.

C

Today I will appreciate the good things of life.

Year 8:3

A

I count it a privilege to share with others.

JONI EARECKSON

B

Joni Eareckson was a young woman who had everything, good looks, personality, intelligence, close friends and a loving family. She loved to ride her horse on the family ranch. Then one day it all changed. When she was 17 she had a diving accident and broke her neck. From then on she was confined to a wheelchair as a quadriplegic. At first she wanted to commit suicide, but she was so disabled she had no opportunity. Gradually she accepted her situation. She learnt to write and draw using her mouth. She wrote books, sang on records and her faith grew and grew. She spent a lot of time talking and writing to people who had suffered like her. Now she can say, 'So many people have helped me that I want to help others.'

C

Today I will accept, with thanks, all the help and support people give me.

Year 9:1

A

If the only prayer you say in your whole life is 'thank you', that would suffice.

MEISTER ECKHART, IN *TOUCHSTONES* (26 NOVEMBER)

B

'An attitude of gratitude', we sometimes hear, will help us on our way. There certainly are enough things for us to worry about, grieve over, and complain about. They have their place. But as we mature, we learn that joy can exist side by side with grief. Gratitude is a tonic for our self-pity. Saying 'thank you' actually opens us up to receive more of life's blessings which sit there waiting for us to notice. No matter how painful or worrisome a day may be, we can be thankful for our growth.

Gratitude is so simple we sometimes dismiss it while looking for a more complicated answer in our lives. We can say 'thank you' for all the simple things like trees, cool air, food to eat and love between people.

ADAPTED FROM *TOUCHSTONES* (26 NOVEMBER)

C

Let's be thankful for all that comes to me without my efforts.

Year 9:2

A

Gratitude isn't only an emotion to feel, it needs to be our incentive to act.

CLIFF RICHARD, IN *TEAR TIMES*

B

My first visit to Bangladesh was a life-changing experience. I was visiting a refugee camp where everyone seemed to be covered in sores. To tell the truth, I didn't want to touch anyone but then as I bent down towards one little baby lying on the floor someone trod on his fingers. He yelled out and I immediately gathered him up to cuddle him, forgetting all about the dirt and sores.

Since then I have seen work in Haiti, India, Nepal, southern Sudan, Kenya and Uganda. Statistics about hunger, homelessness and disease have changed from abstract numbers to actual people. In the poor countries I have been to it's the children that suffer most. I just feel grateful for what I have.

CLIFF RICHARD, IN *TEAR TIMES*

C

Let's fill our minds with thankfulness and our hearts with love.

Year 9:3

A

Situations that annoy us today may be the cause of thanksgiving tomorrow.

B

It was not until I left home at the age of 17 to join the forces that I realized how caring my parents were. Before I left I had regularly quarrelled with my father, but now I could see that it was only through his concern for me that we argued. I was mixing with plenty of young women who wished that they had parents who cared enough to question their actions.

Then I heard from home that my cousin had run away to Liverpool. The police eventually brought her home. I had always been close to my cousin, so I wrote to her, explaining that our families were not so bad. I told her how thankful I was for my family, that only now had I appreciated how good they had been to me.

My cousin must have shown the letter to my aunt, who must have shared it with my mother. The next time I was home, my mother shyly told me that she had seen the letter; her face looked so full of joy.

I realized then that I knew I was thankful. I had told my cousin that I was thankful but I had never shared it with the people to whom it mattered most.

J.A.H.

C

When I am grateful let me have the courage to say so.

Year 10:1

A

A thankful heart has a continual feast.

W. J. CAMERON, IN *GATHERED GOLD*

B

In America, Thanksgiving is almost the beginning of the Christmas celebrations. Thanksgiving Day takes place on the fourth Thursday in November. It is a national holiday; all the family get together for a huge meal. There is a big Thanksgiving Day football match and churches hold services of thanksgiving.

The first Thanksgiving celebration was observed in November 1621. The Pilgrims who had settled in America had survived a dangerous Atlantic crossing, a harsh winter and now they had gathered in their first harvest. Of the 102 that first arrived, nearly half had died in the winter, but the success of the harvest made them realize that they could survive as a community.

The United States of America has come a long way since 1621, but its early survival was very tenuous; sickness or a failed harvest could have changed its history. So just as the Pilgrims gave thanks to God in 1621, so all Americans join them today.

ADAPTED FROM *FESTIVALS AND SAINTS DAYS*

C

May I be mindful of the things in life for which I can be thankful.

Year 10:2

A

The greatest love a person can have for his friends
is to give his life for them.

JOHN 15:13

B

In the early days of June 1944, the first of a quarter of a million young men sailed across the English Channel at night to liberate Europe. They did not know if their mission would be a success or failure, whether they would live or die, whether they would be wounded or crippled.

Their mission was not a failure, although many died and many were wounded. Because of their success World War II drew towards its ultimate conclusion, and for many people on both sides suffering and killing came to an end.

It was decided that June 1994 should be a time to celebrate the 50th anniversary of this successful mission. But how should we celebrate when so many suffered; so many never returned? The

33

result was a great joining together of all the nations that had helped in the liberation, a gathering of the veterans who had survived the mission and many services of thanksgiving. Thanksgiving for the success of the 'D' Day landings, thanksgiving for those who sacrificed their lives to bring freedom to others.

C

May I never take my freedom for granted.

Year 10:3

A

During the time I lived in Canada the church I went to held an annual Gift Sunday. On that day the congregation would bring presents to be distributed to local hospitals. One year, much to my young son's consternation, I forgot to take a gift.

This clearly bothered him all week. The following Sunday, when I heard the people sitting behind me in church giggling, I was sure it had something to do with Sean. He meanwhile sat next to me, staring intently at the altar. Following his line of vision, I froze.

Right in the middle of the altar, in a place of honour between the two candlesticks, stood his favourite toy – an 18-inch Tyrannosaurus rex.

CHRISTINE GILLART, IN *READERS DIGEST*, JULY 1994

B

The little boy's gift was inappropriate, but that did not really matter. The fact that he was willing to give his favourite toy is all important. So often when we are asked to give, we give out of what we have left over, everything else we think we 'need'.

I sometimes wonder what it would be like if we had a major catastrophe in this country, and we were left homeless and hungry. We would be so grateful for people that cared enough to give something to help. The value of a gift is not what it costs, but what it costs us, to give it.

C

What does it cost for me to give?

Year 11:1

A

Thanksgiving is good but thanks-living is better.

MATTHEW HENRY, IN *GATHERED GOLD*

B

It is always possible to spot people who live with an attitude of thanks-living, because they are such happy people. They are grateful for everything they receive each day – food, clothing, shelter and friendship. They may be surrounded by the problems of ill health, family upsets or a lack of finances, but they do not allow themselves to focus on these. They focus on all the good things in life and the thankfulness just flows from their being.

C

I will practise being thankful today.

Year 11:2

A

He enjoys much who is thankful for little.

WILLIAM SECKER, IN *MORE GATHERED GOLD*

B

It is not always 'cool' to be thankful. We tend to accept all that comes to us as our due. Our eyes and ears are subjected to a barrage of images from the media that try to seduce us into believing that we need what the advertisement offers. A jacket is not the right jacket unless it bears the right designer label. There are hi-fi systems and hi-fi systems, but the most expensive one is the one to possess.

If we aim to own the most fashionable and most expensive items, we may disregard the little things in life that matter so much. When we forget to be thankful for everyday things, not realising how rich we really are, we become impoverished.

C

I will be thankful for every good thing in my life.

Year 11.3

A

He who forgets the language of gratitude can never be on speaking terms with happiness.

C. NEIL STRAIT, IN *GATHERED GOLD*

B

There is an old song which says, 'Count your blessings, name them one by one and it will surprise you what the Lord has done'. So often we do not realise what blessings we have until we lose them. We take our good health for granted until we are ill. Some children cope with permanent disabilities, while others take their ability to walk, run, jump and play games for granted.

We may not value our friends until they move away and we experience the loss. Nothing in life remains the same, so we need to be thankful for all the good things now, while they are there to be appreciated.

C

I will count my blessings.

4 SPIRITUAL AWARENESS

Year 7:1

A

One night I had a dream.
I dreamed I was walking along the beach with God,
and across the sky flashed scenes from my life.
For each scene I noticed two sets of footprints in the sand,
one belonged to me and the other to God.

When the last scene of my life flashed before us I looked back at the
footprints in the sand.
I noticed that at times along the path of life there was only one set of
footprints.

I also noticed that it happened at the very lowest and saddest times of
my life.
This really bothered me and I questioned God about it.
'God, you said that once I decided to follow you, you would walk
with me all the way, but I noticed that during the most troublesome
times in my life there is only one set of footprints. I don't understand
why in times when I needed you most, you would leave me.'

God replied, 'My precious, precious child, I love you and I would
never, never leave you during your times of trials and suffering. When
you see only one set of footprints it was then that I carried you.'

ANONYMOUS

B

There may be times when we feel abandoned and alone.

However, at these moments we may also become aware of a feeling of being supported by hidden hands and a loving presence.

C

My comfort is knowing that in times of need, I can feel supported.

Year 7:2

A

One night Rabbi Isaac was told in his dream to go to faraway Prague and there to dig for hidden treasure under a bridge that led to the palace of the King. He did not take the dream seriously, but when it recurred four or five times, he made up his mind to go in search of the treasure.

When he got to the bridge, he discovered to his dismay that it was heavily guarded day and night by soldiers. All he could do was gaze at the bridge from a distance. But since he went there every morning, the captain of the guards came up to him one day to find out why. Rabbi Isaac, embarrassed as he was to tell his dream to another soul, told the captain everything, for he liked the good-natured character of this Christian.

The captain roared with laughter and said, 'Good heavens! You a rabbi and you take dreams so seriously? Why, if I were stupid enough to act on my own dreams, I would be wandering around in Poland today. Let me tell you one that I had last night that keeps recurring frequently: a voice tells me to go to Krakow and dig for treasure in the corner of the kitchen of one Isaac, son of Ezechiel! Now wouldn't it be the most stupid thing in the world to search around in Krakow for a man called Isaac and another called Ezechiel when half the male population there probably has one name and the other half the other?'

The Rabbi was stunned. He thanked the captain for his advice, hurried home, dug up the corner of his kitchen, and found a treasure abundant enough to keep him in comfort till the day he died.

ANTHONY DE MELLO, *THE HEART OF THE ENLIGHTENED*

B

You don't have to travel to find the spiritual. The spiritual is where you've always been. To move from ignorance to understanding all you have to do is to see for the first time what you have always been looking at. Spirituality, after all, is only a matter of becoming what you really are.

ADAPTED FROM *THE HEART OF THE ENLIGHTENED*

C

Today I will explore the deeper knowledge I've always held within me.

Year 7:3

A

There is a Chinese story of an old farmer who had an old horse for tilling his fields. One day the horse escaped into the hills and when all the farmer's neighbours sympathized with the old man over his bad luck, the farmer replied, 'Bad luck? Good luck? Who knows?' A week later the horse returned with a herd of wild horses from the hills and this time the neighbours congratulated the farmer on his good luck. His reply was, 'Good luck? Bad luck? Who knows?' Then, when the farmer's son was attempting to tame one of the wild horses, he fell off its back and broke his leg. Everyone thought this very bad luck. Not the farmer, whose only reaction was, 'Bad luck? Good luck? Who knows?' Some weeks later the army marched into the village and conscripted every able-bodied youth they found there. When they saw the farmer's son with his broken leg they let him off. Now was that good luck? Bad luck? Who knows?

ANTHONY DE MELLO, *SADHANA – A WAY TO GOD*

B

Everything that seems on the surface to be bad may be good in disguise. And everything that seems good on the surface may really be bad. We don't exactly know what is good or bad for us or for anybody. All we can do is try to do what is right and fair, but with a light heart and a happy mind and trust that in the end, all will turn out well.

ADAPTED FROM *SADHANA – A WAY TO GOD*

C

Today I trust that all will be well.

Year 8:1

A

Oh, I have slipped the surly bonds of earth
And danced the skies on laughter-silvered wings;
Sunward I've climbed and joined the tumbling mirth
Of sun-split clouds – and done a hundred things
You have not dreamed of – wheeled and soared and swung
High in the sunlight silence. Hov'ring there
I've chased the shouting wind along, and flung
My eager craft through footless halls of air
Up, up the long, delirious, burning blue
I've topped the windswept heights with easy grace
Where never lark, or even eagle flew
And, while with silent, lifting mind I've trod
The high untrespassed sanctity of space,
Put out my hand, and touched the face of God.

JOHN MAGEE, 'HIGH FLIGHT'

B

John Magee was a fighter pilot in the Royal Air Force who was killed in action during World War II. Before he died he wrote this poem to express the sense of freedom and joy which flying gave him. The American astronaut, Michael Collins took the poem with him when he was a member of the crew which made the first landing on the moon.

When people recognise a source of joy, beauty or peace

they feel a sense of fulfilment in being a part of it. John Magee, Michael Collins and others like them have found their fulfilment in flying, in experiencing the majesty and freedom of space.

Many different things can give us this feeling: the natural beauty of the countryside, the hills and mountains, the open sea, music and art, human friendship and love. Many people find in such experiences a sense of union with something greater than themselves. They feel the presence of a power which is outside the material world but acts within it.

ADAPTED FROM J.P. TAYLOR, *FOCUS ON FAITH*

C

I will look for sources of joy, beauty and peace in my life.

Year 8:2

A

The guru, a religious leader, sat in meditation on the riverbank when a disciple bent down to place two enormous pearls at his feet, a token of reverence and devotion.

The guru opened his eyes, lifted one of the pearls, and held it so carelessly that it slipped out of his hand and rolled down the bank into the river.

The horrified disciple plunged in after it, but though he dived in again and again till late evening, he had no luck. Finally, all wet and exhausted, he roused the guru from his meditation: 'You saw where it fell. Show me the spot so I can get it back for you.' The guru lifted the other pearl, threw it into the river, and said, 'Right there!'

ANTHONY DE MELLO, *THE HEART OF THE ENLIGHTENED*

B

Do not attempt to possess things, for things cannot really be possessed. Only make sure you are not possessed by them,

41

because this will lead to feelings of 'I cannot do without it' and 'I am afraid in case I lose it' – which then leads to a troubled mind and unhappiness.

Peace of mind comes from learning to enjoy things without having to possess them. Peace of mind can be achieved by having the following attitude towards things: If I have it, it's OK and if I don't have it, it's equally OK!

The way to enjoy everything is to stick to nothing!

ADAPTED FROM *THE HEART OF THE ENLIGHTENED* AND *MASTERING SADHANA*

C

Today I will make a start at letting go of things.

Year 8:3

A

Every natural fact is a symbol of some spiritual fact.

RALPH WALDO EMERSON, IN *DAYS OF HEALING, DAYS OF JOY* (11 MAY)

B

Our spirituality doesn't show itself only when we pray, meditate, or go to church. Spirituality is much wider and deeper than that. Nearly everything we do is a reflection of the presence or absence of a spiritual dimension in our lives.

'Where is my security based?' is a spiritual question. If my security is based on status, or the approval of the crowd, this is also a statement about my spirituality. We act out our spirituality when we smile or gossip or tell racist jokes. We don't need to tell anyone how spiritual we are – if they're hanging around us, they already know.

ADAPTED FROM *DAYS OF HEALING, DAYS OF JOY* (11 MAY)

C

I seek to enrich my spirituality right now, but remember that it will be reflected in everything I do today.

DAYS OF HEALING, DAYS OF JOY (11 MAY)

Year 9:1

A

God be in my head,
And in my understanding;

God be in my eyes,
And in my looking;

God be in my mouth,
And in my speaking;

God be in my heart
And in my thinking;

God be at my end,
And at my departing.

FROM THE *SARUM PRIMER*

B

For some people living a spiritual life is about inviting the presence of God to be with them in everything they do.

Thomas Merton was a Trappist monk, a poet and writer on topics such as war, racism and social justice. His books are still read by and influence very many thousands of people, but his special gift was his ability to pray. He made regular spaces in his daily life for times of quiet and prayer. Before he died in 1968, he was asked by a nun why, when giving a talk, he had said nothing about converting people.

'What we are asked to do at present,' Merton responded, 'is not so much to speak of Christ as to let him live in us so that people may find him by feeling how he lives in us' (*Thomas Merton, A Pictorial Biography*).

Everything that we do however ordinary, can be an opportunity to lead a more spiritually aware life.

C

I will realize that how I live is important to those I meet.

Year 9:2

A

An American tourist in Beijing asked the waitress in a restaurant what religion was for the Chinese.

The waitress took him out to the balcony and asked, 'What do you see?'

'I see a street and houses and people walking and buses and taxis.'

'What else?'

'Trees.'

'What else?'

'The wind is blowing.'

The Chinese extended her arms and exclaimed, 'That is religion.'

ADAPTED FROM ANTHONY DE MELLO, *THE HEART OF THE ENLIGHTENED*

B

We're searching for spiritual awareness the way someone searches for sight with open eyes! It is so clear that it is hard to see. Normally, we don't so much look at things as overlook them. Our lives at school can be very busy and full. But are we stopping long enough to look, to take in experiences and grow from them?

ADAPTED FROM *THE HEART OF THE ENLIGHTENED*

C

Today I will slow down. I will absorb my experiences and give myself time to look.

Year 9:3

A

And Buddha said: '"This land is mine, these sons are mine" – such are the words of the fool who does not understand that even he is not his.'

ANTHONY DE MELLO, *THE HEART OF THE ENLIGHTENED*

B

You never really possess things. You merely hold them for a while. If you are unable to give them away, you are held by them. Your most prized possession must be held in the hollow of your hand as water is held. Clutch at it and it is gone. Hold it too close to yourself – you smother it. Set it free and it is forever yours.

ADAPTED FROM *THE HEART OF THE ENLIGHTENED*

C

Today, I will make a start at letting go.

Year 10:1

A

In the morning sunshine, in the evening twilight, a small Bear travels through a Forest.

Why did we follow him when we were so much younger? He is, after all, only a Bear of Little Brain. But is Brain all that important? Is it really Brain that takes us where we need to go? Or is it all too often Brain that sends us off in the wrong direction, following the echo of the wind in the treetops, which we think is real, rather than listening to the voice within us that tells us which way to turn?

45

The masters of life know the Way, for they listen to the voice within them, the voice of wisdom and simplicity, the voice that reasons beyond Cleverness and knows beyond Knowledge. That voice is not just the power and property of a few, but has been given to everyone. Those who pay attention to it are too often treated as exceptions to a rule, rather than as examples of the rule in operation, a rule that can apply to anyone who makes use of it.

BENJAMIN HOFF, *THE TAO OF POOH*

B

It is necessary to stop, be still and listen to the voice which is calling in our hearts. It may be hard to hear at times, but it is important just the same, because without it, we will never find our way through the Forest.

ADAPTED FROM *THE TAO OF POOH*

C

Today in the business around me, I will take time to stop and listen to the wise guidance within my heart.

Year 10:2

A

The disciples were full of questions about God.

Said the master, 'God is the Unknown and the Unknowable. Every statement about him, every answer to your questions, is a distortion of the truth.'

The disciples were bewildered. 'Then why do you speak about him at all?'

'Why does the bird sing?' said the master.

ANTHONY DE MELLO, *THE SONG OF THE BIRD*

B

Why does the bird sing? In his book, *The Song of the Bird*, Anthony de Mello answers:

'Not because it has a statement, but because it has a song.

The words of the scholar are to be understood. The words of the master are not to be understood. They are to be listened to as one listens to the wind in the trees and the sound of the river and the song of the bird. They will awaken something within the heart that is beyond all knowledge.'

C

Today I will reflect on the reading and let it speak to my heart, not my mind.

Year 10:3

A

Life is a Journey of Discovery, a journey that leads both outwards and inwards. What we believe affects how we live, and our experience affects what we believe. There are not two journeys but one, because they depend on each other. As we journey outwards, trying to build a loving society, we also journey inwards, seeking personal wholeness.

ADAPTED FROM *STATEMENT OF RE-AFFIRMATION OF TOC H*

B

We are all on our own individual journey. Each of us will start at a different point and travel at a different speed.

Every journey will be unique and special.

The journey inwards leads to the very core of you. Finding out what's in your heart is the inner journey.

When what you do on your outer journey is in harmony with what's in your heart, then – your journey is very special – it's an adventure.

C

Today I will see my inner and outer lives as one.

Year 11:1

A

The darkest hour is truly just before the dawn. When we finally give up the struggle to find fulfilment 'out there', we have nowhere to go but within. It is at this moment of total surrender that the light begins to dawn. We expect to hit bottom, but instead we fall through a trap door into a bright new world. We've rediscovered the world of our spirit.

SHAKTI GAWAIN, *LIVING IN THE LIGHT*

B

When we wake up to the idea that there is a spiritual life, fulfilment through enjoyment of what we own – like our personal stereo, bike, trainers or computer, can in fact leave us with an empty feeling inside. Knowing that whatever we buy will never be enough or give permanent satisfaction can be painful to face. But then at this darkest moment comes the light – the realization that it is possible to move away from emptiness by discovering our spiritual life – which can lead to inner peace and contentment. Whatever we do, whether it's praying, meditating or walking by a quiet seashore, we need to take time to withdraw from the hustle and bustle, connect with and develop our spiritual life.

C

I will look to my spiritual life for peace and contentment.

Year 11:2

A

I can remember a time when as a boy of four or five I was lying on the grass, looking at the flowers and the mountains and the sky and suddenly I felt God very close to me. I knew I was joined completely with everything I saw. This was a moment I had no doubt about spiritual reality.

GERALD G. JAMPOLSKY, TEACH ONLY LOVE

B

A spiritual experience can happen to anybody at any time and at any age. We don't have to be clever – just open to it.

We can make a spiritual life so complicated, when sometimes all it takes is the open heart and simplicity of a child.

C

May I have the openness of a child to let the spiritual life grow within me.

Year 11:3

A

We shall not cease from exploration
And the end of all our exploring
Will be to arrive where we started
And know the place for the first time

T. S. ELIOT, COLLECTED POEMS 1909-62

B

The spiritual journey can be seen as an exploration and search for truth. When we wish to lead a full life and fulfil our potential, our journey is from ignorance to awareness; from not knowing to knowing.

T. S. Eliot observes that at the end of all our searching, we will find the place where we started from, but it will be as though we are seeing it for the first time.

During our spiritual journey, we will come to see, for the first time, that which has been there for us all along.

C

May I journey from ignorance to awareness.

5 Food (Harvest Festival)

Year 7:1

A

Give a man a fish and you feed him for a day
Give him a net and teach him to use it and he will feed himself and many others for a lifetime.

B

In Europe and some other parts of the world people can always be sure of a harvest. It may be better in some years than in others and there are occasionally years when some crops are very poor or fail. But there is always something.

There are many parts of the world, however, where the harvest is not so certain. Sometimes it is not so good and sometimes it just does not happen at all. Maybe it is the drought that has stopped it, or floods, or war.

Fortunately today, we do not just 'Give a man a fish'. Charities like Tear Fund help with healthcare, agriculture and water, as well as emergency food distribution.

C

Let us appreciate all the varieties of food that we have in this country.

Year 7:2

A

As long as the earth endures, seed time and harvest, cold and heat, summer and winter, day and night will never cease.

GENESIS 8:22

B

Jewish people have celebrated Harvest for thousands of years. They were commanded in the Torah, 'Do not reap to the very edges of your field.' This command would please conservationists today, for although it is a very old command, only today do we appreciate how it cares for wild life and plants.

However, this command was given so that the crops that at the edge of the field could be left for the poor and the stranger. This meant that people who had no crops of their own, or had no money to buy food could quite safely collect what was left of the crops around the edges of a field. Maybe a similar situation today is where a charity organisation in America goes around the big food stores collecting food that is to be thrown out because it is a day out of date. They then use this food to make really good meals for the poor.

C

May we use the materials, talents and opportunities that we have wisely.

Year 7:3

A

Do all the good you can,
By all the means you can,
In all the ways you can,
In all the places you can,

To all the people you can,
As long as ever you can.

JOHN WESLEY, IN *DICTIONARY OF QUOTATIONS AND PROVERBS*

B

A young woman worked over the summer at a camp for young people. She noticed that whatever was on the menu for the day, the young holiday-makers took it whether they wanted it or not. Consequently lots of food was wasted as they emptied their plates into the bins at the end of the meal. One day there was not enough food to go around and the young woman suggested that they shared it out. Nobody would agree. They were going to take what they were entitled to, so those who were first in the queue got everything and those at the back of the queue got nothing! She was so disgusted she wanted to give up the job.

Doesn't this happen on a wider scale; some countries have everything and others have nothing? If there is plenty for everyone (and we know there is), why not share?

C

Let us be mindful of the needs of others and not waste food.

Year 8:1

A

Come, ye thankful people, come,
Raise the song of Harvest home,
All is safely gathered in,
Ere the winter storms begin.

HENRY ALFORD, IN *DAYS OF HEALING, DAYS OF JOY*
(22 NOVEMBER)

B

In the small community of Ikengeza in Tanzania the people are not rich, but the ground is good and they usually have a good harvest. Even so, some families will go hungry as the food crops begin to dwindle. However, the pastor of the church still expects his congregation to be generous to others.

'He explains that the harvest gifts before him are a sign of love for God, and a symbol of obedience. Later, the harvest gifts are sold to support the work of the church in the village. In previous years, for instance, the maize crop helped to buy the tin roof for their building. Sometimes food is given to poor people in the community.' (*Tear Times*, Autumn 1994)

For some people it costs a lot to give.

C

Today, I give thanks for the chance to give thanks.

DAYS OF HEALING, DAYS OF JOY

Year 8:2

A

We plough the fields and scatter the good seed on the land
But it is fed and watered by God's almighty hand.

THE ILLUSTRATED FAMILY HYMN BOOK

B

Except for those in a farming community we are very much removed from the words of this 19th-century hymn. In the past our health would have depended on the harvest, but now with tins of food, freezers and great storage silos containing grain, we do not depend on the vegetables and grain that are produced locally. What we cannot grow in this country we import from abroad. Modern farming methods often mean that we have a surplus supply of food.

However, somebody somewhere grows the food we eat, and although the harvest now does not carry the same importance as it did when the hymn was written, we should still be thankful that the food is still being produced, and we can get good quality food and that there is plenty of it.

C

Let us be thankful for all the good food we have. Let us be thoughtful for those who have very little.

Year 8:3

A

All good gifts around us are sent from heaven above;
Then thank the Lord, oh thank the Lord, for all his love.

THE ILLUSTRATED FAMILY HYMN BOOK

B

When we think of Harvest we usually think of wheat and barley, apples and pears. But there are other harvests too.

There is the harvest of the sea. At Colchester in Essex, there is a famous Oyster Festival, to give thanks for those shellfish. Many fishing towns and villages hold special thanksgiving services.

In a church in an industrial town the harvest display may not be one of fruit and vegetables but of bright shining pieces of machinery and of tools made in the local factories.

Harvest after all, is a time for people to give thanks for produce, whether it is from the fields, the garden, the factory or the sea.

ROWLAND PURTON, ASSEMBLIES

C

I will appreciate all the products that I am able to use each day.

Year 9:1

A

Love is not a vague emotion, but commitment to real people in a web of relationships in the midst of very concrete circumstances.

ANDREW KIRK, *TEAR TIMES* (SUMMER 1993)

B

If we go without food it is usually because of a diet, lack of time or a lack of money. In this country it is never because there is a lack of food. But often in countries where there is a famine the root cause there is not a lack of food. Famine is not always caused by a shortage of food! It is more a case of economics and distribution. In the 1984-5 famine, Ethiopia actually exported green beans to the UK! Much of the good land in developing countries is given over to growing crops like coffee which doesn't go to feed their own people, but earns them money to help pay foreign debts. Most people in the Third World grow their own food but when drought and civil war hinder them, their governments don't have the resources to buy and distribute spare food.

TEAR TIMES (SUMMER 1993)

If we were committed to spending more for the goods produced by such countries as Ethiopia they would have the resources to survive the difficult times.

C

May we be sensitive to the needs of others.

Year 9:2

A

Celebrate the Feast of Harvest with the first fruits of the crops you sow in your field.

EXODUS 23:16

B

For us the Harvest is all the year around. We are not dependent on the seasons. But it is good every year to think about the abundance that we have and be thankful for it.

In 1993 in southern Sudan, the villagers of the Nuer tribe were dying within sight of what they hoped would be a bumper harvest of maize. They had waited all year for this harvest, surviving on vegetables, then leaves and roots gathered from the forest. The day-long search for food was exhausting many. Then, just as the harvest was ready, the skies broke and torrential rains ruined much of the maize.

ADAPTED FROM *TEAR TIMES* (SUMMER 1993)

C

May we never become complacent with all the good things that surround us; may we always care about those who have less.

Year 9:3

A

Pull out some corn from the bundles and leave it for her to pick up.

RUTH 2:16

B

This is from the story of Ruth which tells of a young widow who had no means of support. A wealthy farmer instructed his workers to leave plenty of corn lying around for her to pick up, so that she and her aged mother-in-law could exist. It was leftovers to the farmer but to Ruth it was survival.

In the 1990s we seem to be hearing more and more about disasters – drought in Africa, earthquakes, floods and famines.

Real love reaches out a helping hand and gives people in need the opportunity to stand with dignity and hope.

Two pounds buys a year's course of Vitamin A for ten

children, preventing blindness. Seven pounds could give one hundred sick children the correct treatment. Our help may seem like just a drop in the bucket – but that bucket gets filled with lots of drops.

C

Today I will be aware of the needs of others.

Year 10:1

A

You shall observe the Feast of the Harvest, of the first fruits of your labours from what you sow in the field.

EXODUS 23:16

B

When things are going well it is easy to accept our food, our security and our freedom as being a matter of course. It is only when we feel that we are in danger of losing these necessities that we express our thanksgiving at their continuation.

Societies that rely on a good harvest to ensure that they do not go hungry celebrate when a crop is gathered in. They offer thanks to God for supplying their need and they rejoice that they are secure for another year. This is something that has happened for thousands of years and still goes on today. Sometimes it is difficult to enter into the celebration when we take for granted being fed every day, but we need to remember that we have not always been so lucky as to have food in plenty, and that there are societies where hunger and starvation are part of a way of life.

That is why often in this country Harvest is a time of sharing the good things with those who have less than the rest of us.

C

Let us celebrate and be thankful for the food we eat.

Year 10:2

A

And out of the ground the Lord God caused to grow every tree that is pleasing to the sight and good for food.

GENESIS 2:9

B

'The first time I planted some seeds and they grew I felt exhilarated. I had put these tiny dark brown dots of potential life into the soil and now there was a beautiful display of bright orange flowers. It was like a miracle. Inspired by this I planted a conker and a year later a small horse chestnut tree had begun to sprout. A few years later my father dug it up since, if it grew much more, it would undermine the house. I marvelled that such power could develop from such a small beginning.' (J.A.H.)

Planting seeds and bulbs are living experiments. On the one hand we are powerless to do anything because they already have the inbuilt capacity to grow and flower, on the other hand we have control in making sure they are in good soil and weed free.

C

Today, I will appreciate the wonder of nature.

Year 10:3

A

Season of mists and mellow fruitfulness!
Close bosom-friend of the maturing sun;
Conspiring with him how to load and bless
With fruit the vines that round the thatch-eves run;

JOHN KEATS, 'ODE TO AUTUMN'

B

Autumn is a beautiful time of year; it is no wonder that poets feel inspired to write about it. The trees change into fantastic colours, with brown, red, russet and golden leaves. The fields are golden with wheat and corn and the sun is low in the sky casting long shadows.

It is a time for picking and storing fruit, a time for turning soft fruit into jams, a time to freeze the vegetables, so all the crop will last through the winter.

The Psalmist wrote, 'Then he crowns it all with green, lush pastures in the wilderness, hillsides blossom with joy. The pastures are filled with flocks of sheep, and the valleys are carpeted with grain. All the world shouts with joy, and sings.' (*Psalm* 65:11–13)

C

I will appreciate the beauty of autumn today.

Year 11:1

A

When a man's stomach is full it makes no difference whether he is rich or poor.

EURIPIDES, IN *THE DECADE BOOK OF BIRTHDAYS*

B

When the gospel singer Nia visited Romania after the collapse of Communism, the country was undergoing economic hardship. Unsure of the food supplies, she took plenty of sweets, firstly as emergency rations, if she found herself short of food, and secondly as presents, as sweets were a luxury.

When her group performed at an orphanage, one young boy was really helpful in setting up all the musical equipment. As a thank you she asked him to help himself to some sweets.

Imagine it, this boy never has sweets and he has been told to help himself from boxes and boxes of sweets! When Nia returned to the van nothing was missing. She made enquiries and found out that the young boy had opened the case of Smarties, and had taken out a single Smartie from a tube. Not used to sweets but always used to sharing, the single Smartie was sufficient.

C

I will appreciate the wealth of food that we have in this country.

Year 11:2

A

If you love nature, you love people.

FATHER ANGELO REGAZZO, *TODAY*, 30 SEPTEMBER 1994

B

In 1984, when so many died in the Ethiopian famine, a tiny flower was planted in Matele by a nurse in memory of the many who had died. This tiny flower inspired Father Angelo Regazzo. He said, 'It was so beautiful. There, among the suffering of that terrible scene, was life. I thought that if we can plant a flower in the dirt, why not plant trees in memory of all those who died? So little by little we started. Those who were strong enough helped us and gradually hundreds of saplings grew up.

'Over the months, as we took down the tents and people drifted back to their homes, the scene that was left was a huge circle of trees. Then we built a dam and a pond, using solar pumps to get water up to the trees. And I taught people how to grow trees themselves, so they could do it in their own villages.'

'If you love nature,' he adds smiling, 'you love people.' (*Today*, 30 September 1994).

Using food aid biscuit tins to grow saplings from seed, Father Angelo continues to plant – hardy black pepper trees to help prevent soil erosion, fruit trees for food, eucalyptus trees for their wood.

Today wherever you go in Matele there are trees.

C

May I look for the good in dark situations.

Year 11:3

A

It is not what you have that matters,
It is what you do with what you have.

WILFRED GRENFELL, IN *MORE GATHERED GOLD*

B

So much of what we eat and drink in this country comes from abroad. Fruit like oranges and bananas, drinks like tea, coffee and cocoa. We can afford so much of this food because the people who grow it are paid so little, and consequently have a poor standard of living. When we buy a bar of chocolate we could be exploiting a family in the Third World.

The Fairtrade Foundation was launched in 1992 to fight for 'basic human rights for Third World workers who produce goods for our consumption.' (*Tear Times*, Spring 1995)

Now in supermarkets and delicatessens we can buy products with the 'Fairtrade Mark'. So we know that what we have bought has been fairly produced.

C

I will seek to be fair with everybody.

6 STEWARDSHIP

Year 7:1

A

Treat your body with respect, care for it, choose to eat and drink things that are good for it, exercise frequently and avoid chemicals which will hurt you.

B

Looking after your health involves caring and having respect for yourselfs. We put great store by friendships, money, hobbies and interests. But none of these can be fully enjoyed without good health. Making a bad health decision can hurt you for the rest of your life.

Your health is a very important resource. Health and quality of life can be very closely linked. In order to give yourself a chance to develop your full potential in life, you need to be making healthy decisions now.

C

Today I will make healthy and positive decisions for myself.

Year 7:2

A

A farmer had a big pond, for fish and ducks. On the pond was a tiny lily. The tiny lily was growing. It was doubling in size every day. 'Look,' said the people to the farmer, 'You'd better cut that lily. One day it'll be so big it'll kill all your fish and ducks.'

'All right, all right,' said the farmer, 'but there's no hurry. It's only growing very slowly.'

The lily carried on doubling in size every day. 'Look,' said the farmer several days later, 'the lily is still only half the size of the pond. No need to worry yet.' The next day the farmer was very surprised.

LEARNING FOR A CHANGE IN WORLD SOCIETY

B

The destruction of the environment, wherever it occurs, eventually affects us all. It is just as important to look after the environment on the other side of the planet as it is to look after our own environment. The air and oceans circulate around the earth like blood around a body. Must we wait until we face an environmental crisis which threatens our life on earth before we do something, or can we act now?

C

I will act *now* to keep our planet healthy.

Year 7:3

A

We are dirtying up your world, Lord.
Pollutants, Lord. Effluents and such.

Every spring you make it all new again, Lord,
Every summer it all grows.
Every autumn you show us colours to catch the breath, to swell the
    heart.
Every winter you remind us who's Boss.

We need reminding, Lord.
We litter the place.
We clash with the colours.
And worse, to be quite honest, Lord, a lot of us don't notice.

You forgive a lot of sin, Lord.
How do you keep your temper with indifference?

DAVID KOSSOFF, *YOU HAVE A MINUTE*, LORD?

B

The environment needs you as it has never done before. It must have your help to survive. Nearly every day, we hear more about the disasters that face us on this planet: seas and rivers are being filled with rubbish; the air is being poisoned with chemicals and smoke. But it's not all bad. People are making choices to live in a way that is less damaging to the planet by using recycling bins, buying environmentally-friendly products and making sure the countryside is free from litter. Governments and world leaders are now claiming that they have environment at the top of their lists. The world is your home. It's worth saving.

C

Today I will take a single, small step towards saving my planet.

Year 8:1

A

If the Earth were only a few feet in diameter, floating a few feet above a field somewhere, people would come from everywhere to marvel at it.

People would walk around it, marvelling at its big pools of water, its little pools and the water flowing between the pools. People would marvel at the bumps on it, and the holes in it, and they would marvel at the very thin layer of gas surrounding it and the water suspended in the gas.

The people would marvel at all the creatures walking around the surface of the ball, and at the creatures in the water. The people would declare it sacred because it was the only one, and they would protect it so that it would not be hurt.

The ball would be the greatest wonder known, and the people would come to pray to it, to be healed, to gain knowledge, to know beauty and to wonder how it could be.

People would love it and defend it with their lives, because they would somehow know that their lives, their own roundness, could be nothing without it.

If the Earth were only a few feet in diameter.

IT DOESN'T HAVE TO BE LIKE THIS – GREEN POLITICS
EXPLAINED

B

Part of the problem is that all of us are trapped in our own little worlds and so we only concentrate on the things that directly affect us. Sometimes we need to step back and survey the whole picture to see things how they really are.

ADAPTED FROM *IT DOESN'T HAVE TO BE LIKE THIS*

C

Today I will have a new respect for the Earth and try to see it as a small and fragile water planet – a blue jewel in space, which all people share.

Year 8:2

A

One. We should not so exploit natural resources that we destroy them … common sense you might think and yet look what we've done to the European herring and are still doing to other species.

Two. We should not interfere with the basic processes of life on which all life depends, in the sky, on the green surface of the Earth and in the sea … and yet we go on pouring our poisons into the sky, cutting down tropical rainforests, dumping our rubbish into the oceans.

And third. We should preserve the diversity of life not just because we depend upon it for our food, though we do, nor because we know so little about it that we don't know what we're losing, though that's the case as well. But it is surely that we have no moral right to destroy other living organisms with which we share the Earth.

As far as we know, the Earth is the only place in the universe where there is life. Its continued survival now rests in our hands.

DAVID ATTENBOROUGH, IN *IT DOESN'T HAVE TO BE LIKE THIS – GREEN POLITICS EXPLAINED*

B

These words were spoken by David Attenborough at the end of his TV series 'The Living Planet'. He said that on the evidence before us, human beings could clearly devastate the Earth. If we were not to do so, he said, we must have a plan of action.

In the next fifty years, unless we the people of Earth, change our policies and actions, then it is estimated that a quarter of the species of life on Earth will become extinct, not at the present rate of one a day, but one a minute.

In human terms, in the future, we must live more simply; so others may simply live.

ADAPTED FROM *IT DOESN'T HAVE TO BE LIKE THIS – GREEN POLITICS EXPLAINED*

C

I will do my best to make the Earth a secure and hospitable home for present and future generations.

Year 8:3

A

All of us have unique talents and gifts. No obstacle, be it physical, mental or emotional has the power to destroy our innate creative energies.

LIANE CORDES, IN *EACH DAY A NEW BEGINNING* (14 JUNE)

B

What each of us can contribute to the world is unlike every other contribution. Each talent is slightly different from every other talent. And they are all needed. We are all needed. Our talents are our gifts to the human race.

Do we know our talents?

Do we nurture, develop and make good use of our talents?

We all have a responsibility to ourselves to find our talents, and allow them to flourish.

ADAPTED FROM *EACH DAY A NEW BEGINNING* (14 JUNE)

C

I will recognize and enjoy my talents today.

Year 9:1

A

I do not want to die ... until I have faithfully made the most of my talent and cultivated the seed that was placed in me, until the last small twig has grown.

KATHE KOLLWITZ, IN *EACH DAY A NEW BEGINNING*
(9 SEPTEMBER)

B

We are each gifted with talents, similar in some ways to others' talents, but unique in how we'll be able to use them. Do we realize our talents?

We need to recognize, celebrate and cultivate our talents. Using our talents fully, may lead us to new opportunities; new friends; to places presently unknown.

We have many talents that are ours alone to offer the world. Perhaps we express ourselves very clearly or write particularly well? Listening when a friend needs it most may be our finest talent today.

ADAPTED FROM *EACH DAY A NEW BEGINNING* (9 SEPTEMBER)

C

I will appreciate and look after my talents.

Year 9:2

A

The Ministry of Agriculture decreed that sparrows were a menace to the crops and should be exterminated.

When this was done, hoards of insects that the sparrows could have eaten descended on the harvest and began to ravage the crops, whereupon the Ministry of Agriculture came up with the idea of costly pesticides.

The pesticides made the food expensive. They also made it a hazard to health. Too late it was discovered that it was the sparrows who, though feeding on the crops, managed to keep the food wholesome and inexpensive.

ANTHONY DE MELLO, *THE HEART OF THE ENLIGHTENED*

B

Everything that we do is interconnected. Every breath we take makes us part of this complex, living and breathing planet that we call Earth. Every act has a consequence. What we do today can rebound later, even if we are not around to see what happens. If we don't appreciate the interdependence of the natural world and our part within it, then we play a dangerous game. It is very important to look in detail at how any course of action affects people and the planet. If these *connections* are ignored, then the result can be damage and misery.

ADAPTED FROM *THE YOUNG PERSON'S GUIDE TO SAVING THE PLANET*

C

Today I will become more aware of what is happening in the world, by reading or watching the news.

Year 9:3

A

If we were to express all the time the planet has been in existence as a 24-hour day, then life began at around 8 p.m., the dinosaurs walked from 11.35 p.m. to four minutes to midnight and our ancestors only began walking upright ten seconds ago. The Industrial Revolution and all our modern age have lasted less than a thousandth of a second. During that time, people have ransacked, polluted, bombed, bulldozed and bruised the planet. Now something must be done to heal it.

The clock is still ticking. Over to you ...

B

Conservation and finding alternatives – trying to supply our needs in ways that are least damaging to the planet – are important parts of stewardship. Stewardship, in a global sense, is about keeping the world in a state where it is fit for us and future generations after us to live in. But as well as looking after things and using resources wisely, we need, where possible, to put back what we take from the planet.

As individuals, we can be aware of the power we have as consumers and reflect on our attitude towards the way resources are used and distributed.

C

Today I will choose to do something positive towards making my planet healthier.

Year 10:1

A

Said Somebody:
The trees, of course,
will have to be chopped down

and we'll build the road
across some farm land

Said Somebody else:
It would be easier to use the cricket field
We could build fifty houses there –
back to back, of course.
It's only used in summer anyway.

Said Somebody:
There might be objections,
and we've got our seats to consider

Well, said Somebody else:
How about that bit of scruffy Green Belt
or the National Trust Park
or with a wink in the right direction
something could be arranged.
And after all, we do need houses
and launderettes and pubs and streetlights…

Trouble is, said Somebody,
They've got their priorities all wrong
– think trees and fields and birds
are more important than rooves
over people's heads

If we're not careful, said Somebody,
we'll have the cranks out
with their placards again.
By the way,
Does anybody know what 'Ecology' means?

TINA MORRIS, IN *LEARNING FOR CHANGE IN WORLD SOCIETY*

B

Ecology is the study of living organisms in their environment.
Humans can change their environment; so that they can get
more food, fuel and living space from it.

Humans are remarkable creatures. They have sent people to the moon; they can send live pictures by satellite across the planet; they can explore the atom with powerful instruments, and they can transplant a human heart. They have achieved many brilliant things. However, they can also destroy things and people. Humans create wars, poverty, pollution and cause dreadful suffering to their fellow human beings, to animals and to the planet.

C

Today I will reflect on how I shape my environment.

Year 10:2

A

The question each of us has to ask time after time, as a community as well as individually, is this: will this purchase make our relationships more fully human in the context of our one human family and of one inter-related world?

JOHN V. TAYLOR, 'ENOUGH IS ENOUGH', IN *JOYFUL JOURNEY*

B

In the 1960s many people stopped buying South African fruit to show the South African government that they disagreed with their laws of apartheid.

More recently some people stopped buying Nescafé coffee to show the manufacturer, Nestlé, that they disapproved of their policy of selling baby milk to countries that had unhygienic water, causing the death of many babies.

You are a very powerful person. As a shopper, what you buy and where you buy it from triggers off a whole series of events which stretch across the world. Your choices can aid and abet an unfair trading system which leaves individual workers and entire nations poor and powerless – or they can support people struggling for freedom and justice …

C

Today I will consider my responsibilities as a consumer and aim at making informed shopping choices.

Year 10:3

A

TO HAVE, so it would seem, is a normal function of our life: in order to live we must have things. Moreover, we must have things in order to enjoy them. It would seem that the very essence of being is having; that if one HAS nothing, one IS nothing. Yet the Buddha teaches that in order to arrive at the highest stage of human development, we must not crave possessions. And Jesus teaches: 'For whosoever will save his life, shall lose it, but whosoever will lose his life for My sake, the same shall save it. For what is a man advantaged, if he gain the whole world, and lose himself?'

ERICH FROMM, *TO HAVE OR TO BE*

B

Erich Fromm was very influenced in his writing by Master Eckhart, a spiritual teacher in the Middle Ages, who taught that to have nothing and make yourself open and 'empty' was the condition for achieving spiritual wealth and strength. Another influence came from the radical humanist Karl Marx, who taught that the goal of living should be to BE much, not to HAVE much.

ADAPTED FROM *TO HAVE OR TO BE*

C

Today I will reflect on this:
'If I am what I have
and I lose all I have,
then who am I?'

ADAPTED FROM *TO HAVE OR TO BE*

Year 11:1

A

Viewed from the distance of the moon, the astonishing thing about the Earth ... is that it is alive ... Aloft, floating free beneath the moist, gleaming membrane of bright sky, is the rising earth ... If you could look long enough, you would see the swirling of the great drifts of white cloud, covering and uncovering the half-hidden masses of land. If you had been looking for a very long geologic time, you could have seen the continents themselves in motion, drifting apart on their crustal plates, held afloat by the fire beneath.

DR WAYNE W. DYER, *YOU'LL SEE IT WHEN YOU BELIEVE IT*

B

The 'living Earth' is a marvel to behold, which could, in an instant, be destroyed by nuclear warfare.

If all warring nations considering using nuclear weapons could view the Earth from the moon, surely their hearts would unite in wanting to preserve and cherish this planet.

C

May I marvel at the planet Earth I live on.

Year 11:2

A

Talk to yourself about your attitude toward ownership. How can you own a watch, a diamond, a house or anything? ... Things flow in and out of our lives just as frequently as we open and close our eyes ... Remind yourself that everything that serves you today – your home, your car, your jewellery – will some day soon be serving others.

DR WAYNE W. DYER, *YOU'LL SEE IT WHEN YOU BELIEVE IT*

B

We live on this Earth for a relatively brief period of time. We may legally own an allotment, a piece of land or even an island, but eventually it will be passed on to another.

We are only the caretakers of all our possessions. We are also the caretakers of the oceans, air and land – and it is our responsibility to take good care of them; so that future generations can enjoy the 'fruits of the earth'.

C

May I take care of the environment, for others in their turn, to enjoy.

Year 11:3

A

The lack of respect and attunement to our bodies is demonstrated on a global level by the way we treat the body of our planet. As we learn to trust and love our bodies, listen to their signals, give them food, rest, and nurturing ... I believe we will be able to treat our earth body with the same care and respect.

SHAKTI GAWAIN, *REFLECTIONS IN THE LIGHT*

B

Our Earth is like a living organism. The more we learn to look after ourselves, and to live in a balanced way, the more we can appreciate how to nurture and respect the Earth.

Regularly filling ourselves with 'junk food' is similar to dumping rubbish into the oceans, soil and air. After a while our bodies may not function properly and disease may develop under the stress of dealing with so much unwholesome food.

When we nourish our bodies and treat them well, we start to think highly of them. With this understanding and appreciation, it follows that we need to show the same tenderness and care towards the body of our Earth.

C

I will develop my awareness of what is needed by both my body and the Earth.

7 ONE WORLD

Year 7:1

A

'Tell me the weight of a snowflake,' a coaltit asked a wild dove. 'Nothing more than nothing,' was the answer. 'In that case, I must tell you a marvellous story,' the coaltit said. 'I sat on the branch of a fir, close to its trunk, not in a raging blizzard; no, just in a dream, without a sound and without any violence. Since I did not have anything better to do, I counted the snowflakes settling on the twigs and needles of my branch. Their number was exactly 3,741,952. When the 3,741,953rd dropped on to the branch – nothing more than nothing, as you say – the branch broke off.' Having said that, the coaltit flew away.

KURT KAUTER, *NEW FABLES, THUS SPOKE THE MARABOU*

B

Let there be peace on earth
And let it begin with us.
Let there be love on earth
And let it begin in our hearts.
Let there be miracles on earth
And let it begin with our faith.
Let there be a future
And let it begin with us –
Acting together – now.

ACT TOGETHER – ONE WORLD WEEK GUIDE, 1991

C

Today, I will remember that where two or three are gathered together … things can start to happen.

Year 7:2

A

There was this huge spaceship. It was travelling through space at 66,000 miles an hour. There were many thousands of people on board. They had all been on the spaceship for a very long time.

Indeed, they had all been born on the spaceship. The spaceship grew all its own food, and contained all the water and air and minerals that were needed to keep life going on for ever.

The people on the spaceship were in two main groups. First, there were the officers, and their wives and families. Their job was to steer the spaceship, and generally to control it. There were not many people in this group. They enjoyed their work, and also lived very comfortably.

But most of the people on the spaceship were not officers, but crew. These people, and their wives and children, did not have interesting work, and were not comfortable. They had to work very many hours every day, mainly growing food, or else making things to keep the spaceship running.

For many years the spaceship seemed a fairly happy place. The officers were particularly happy, and the crew did not complain. But as the years passed there were more and more problems.

For one thing, there were many deaths amongst the crew's children, because they were not getting enough to eat. Some of the officers' wives sent food parcels and some of the officers' children collected money and sent it down to the crew. But this help was not enough, and more and more children were dying.

Also, the ship's water was becoming dirty, its air was becoming poisoned, and the food-growing areas of the ship were being damaged. The apparatus causing all this was used entirely for providing various comforts for the officers.

Also there were many quarrels on the ship. The officers often quarrelled amongst themselves, and so did the crew. There were also various fights between the officers and crew, and these were getting worse.

'We'd better leave this spaceship,' said some of the people. 'It's terrible living here. Let's go away.'

But alas there was nowhere else, absolutely nowhere else, for them to go.

LEARNING FOR CHANGE IN WORLD SOCIETY

B

Everybody on the spaceship was affected by the environment. Our spaceship is planet Earth. There are no passengers – we are all crew, because we all have a responsibility to take care of our planet.

How uncomfortable do we have to become before we pull together and take care of each other and our world?

C

Today I will remember that there is only one world.

Year 7:3

A

When we arise in the morning, we go to the bathroom, where we reach for a sponge which is provided by a Pacific islander.
We reach for soap that is created for us by a European.
Then at the table we drink coffee which is provided for us by a South American, or tea by a Chinese, or cocoa by a West African.
Before we leave for our jobs, we are already beholden to more than half the world.

MARTIN LUTHER KING, JR, IN *WE COULD DO THAT! – ONE WORLD WEEK PLANNER'S HANDBOOK*

B

Who needs to be reminded that we live in one world – a small fragile planet whose past and future we all share? Yet we have made barriers all over it – barriers to separate rich and poor; east and west; north and south; Black and White; male and female; Christian, Muslim and Hindu. They are built on foundations of ignorance, prejudice and fear

– fear for ourselves and fear of one another. It takes courage and encouragement to cross those barriers, yet we are not fully human nor really free until we do.

WE COULD DO THAT! – ONE WORLD WEEK PLANNER'S HANDBOOK

C

Today I will do something positive and help to break down the barriers which divide me from others in school.

Year 8:1

A

We have numbed ourselves so that we do not feel the pain. We have to be asleep in order to protect ourselves from the horror of knowing that 28 people, most of them young children, are dying this very minute – 28 people no different from you or me, or our children, except that we have food and they do not.

We have closed down our consciousness and aliveness to a level where it doesn't bother us. So if you wonder if it costs us anything to allow millions to starve, it does. It costs us our ALIVENESS.

MARILYN FERGUSON, *THE AQUARIAN CONSPIRACY*

B

There is a price to pay for taking the stance: 'This is not my problem', or 'Let's not think about it'. We are all connected with each other and, therefore, are not free to ignore what happens to parts of 'our' world.

C

Today I will be responsible for what I think, feel and do.

Year 8:2

A

At one time in human history, everyone knew that ...
The world was flat,
the sun revolved around the earth,
slavery was an economic necessity,
a four-minute mile was impossible,
polio and smallpox would always be with us,
and no one would ever set foot on the moon ...
until courageous people challenged old beliefs and a
new idea's time had come.

All the forces in the world are not so powerful as an idea
whose time has come.

A SHIFT IN THE WIND 5, THE HUNGER PROJECT, (AN
ORGANISATION COMMITTED TO ENDING HUNGER IN THE
WORLD)

B

We can hold the belief that we can't stop hunger in the world
and that there is nothing we can do to make a difference. When
we recognize the truth – that hunger can be ended – we can
develop our own ideas on how we can stop it. By committing
ourselves to take action, we can change our ideas into reality.

The worldwide commitment to end hunger begins within
us. It expands as we tell others.

ADAPTED FROM A SHIFT IN THE WIND 5

C

We have the power to end hunger and starvation. Pass it on.

ADAPTED FROM A SHIFT IN THE WIND 5

Year 8:3

A

In the beginning was God,
In the beginning was the source of all that is,
God yearning,
God moaning,
God labouring,
God giving birth,
God rejoicing,
And God loved what she had made.
And God said
'It is good'
And God, knowing that all that is good is shared, held the earth
tenderly in her arms.
God yearned for relationship.
God longed to share the good earth,
And humanity was born in the yearning of God,
We were born to share the earth

ISABEL CARTER HEYWARD, 'BLESSING THE BREAD: A LITANY'

B

We build together with the bricks of tolerance – a better world.
We build together with the bricks of peace – a better world.
We build together with the bricks of understanding – a better world.
We build together with the bricks of sharing – a better world.
We build together with the bricks of hope – a better world.
We build together with the bricks of love – a better world.

ACT TOGETHER FOR TOMORROW'S WORLD

C

Today I will reflect on the part I can play in building a better world.

Year 9:1

A

Enjoy the earth gently
Enjoy the earth gently
For if the earth is spoiled
It cannot be repaired
Enjoy the earth gently.

YORUBA POEM, IN *PUTTING PEOPLE IN THE PICTURE*

B

Pollution threatens the survival of countries as distant as Bangladesh and Mexico. International greed and the desperation of the poor are leading to the destruction of the great Amazonian rainforests.

African farmland is being turned into barren desert. Throughout much of the world people go hungry every day. And the world's animals and plants are disappearing at an alarming rate. Famine in Africa, the burning of rainforests and pollution in Poland may once have seemed too far away to touch our lives. But now we know that pollution in Poland and forest destruction in Brazil affect not just their climate, but ours too. And we are beginning to realize that much of what we do in Britain affects the welfare of millions of people living thousands of miles away. We all belong to ONE WORLD.

ONE WORLD – TIME FOR ACTION

C

Now is a time for action – not just by governments, but by all of us.

ONE WORLD – TIME FOR ACTION

Year 9:2

A

This will be the week when the IRA plant flowers, not bombs,
When the prophet's children in Iran and Iraq grow up,

When Nicaragua and the USA resolve their contra-dictions,
When Ethiopians are in danger of being overfed,
And black South Africans are in danger of nothing,
When inner cities hold carnivals to celebrate their inner growth,
When rain passes the acid test by having none.
This will be the week when hostages are released and their captors
wish them well,
When nuclear weapons become exhibits in museums of ancient history,
When Blue Peter shows us how to make a useful ploughshare from
unwanted swords.

This will be the week which we will look back on and say:
That was the week.

RICHARD SKINNER, IN *WE COULD DO THAT – ONE WORLD*
WEEK PLANNER'S HANDBOOK

B

This is a poem whose time has yet to come.
It is possible.
What sort of world do we want?
Who creates the world in which we live?

C

Today I will be alert to how my actions contribute to the building of
'One World' in my school.

Year 9:3

A

First they came for the Jews, and I did not speak out, because I was
not a Jew.
Then they came for the Communists, and I did not speak out,
because I was not a Communist.
Then they came for the trade unionists, and I did not speak out,
because I was not a trade unionist.

When they came for me, there was no one left to speak out for me.

PASTOR NIEMOLLER – A NAZI VICTIM, FROM GEORGE BROWN,
FIRST THEY CAME FOR THE JEWS

B

There is a need to speak out for yourself if you are treated
unfairly; and to speak out for people who do not have freedom
of speech; and to speak out for people whose voices are ignored. When we do this we are helping ourselves and others
and building a better and fairer Tomorrow's World.

C

May I have the courage to speak out when appropriate.

Year 10:1

A

*In the long hundred years since the white man came, I have seen my
freedom disappear like the salmon going mysteriously out to sea. The
white man's strange customs which I could not understand pressed me
down until I could no longer breathe. And when I fought to protect my
land and home I was called a savage.*

CHIEF DAN GEORGE, IN *INTRODUCING MORAL ISSUES*

B

*Mines, dams, roads, colonization schemes, plantations, cattle ranches,
telegraph wires, televisions, motor cars – we call these things progress.
Yet they have destroyed and continue to destroy Earth's First Peoples,
or the indigenous peoples. These are the peoples whose ancestors were
the original inhabitants of the land and who lived on their original lands
peacefully. With European colonization, the indigenous peoples all over
the planet were killed, bullied, and their cultures were destroyed in the
name of progress. They were uprooted.*

Deforestation (cutting down forests), desertification (when soil is washed away, creating a desert where there was once fertile land) and destruction have ruined their land and their lives.

However, today, for the first time in 500 years of destruction, the indigenous peoples of the world are beginning to have their voices heard. They realize that they will never be able to return to their ancient ways of living, but they are protesting against progress which threatens their survival. They are opposed to the vandalism of the modern world which in some places destroys the Earth.

JOE JENKINS, *INTRODUCING MORAL ISSUES*

C

Today I will try to see beneath the surface appearance of events, withholding judgement until I have the facts.

Year 10:2

A

We are the lucky ones. Most of us do not know what it's like to be hungry for months or years on end. Most of us do not know what it's like to have our homes destroyed in war or see our loved ones murdered before our very eyes. Most of us do not know what it's like to have our freedom taken away, or to be maimed and tortured. But for millions of people, many of them young people like you, these things are happening at this very moment. These people are no different from you, your families or your friends. The only difference is that you are one of the lucky ones. You therefore, have the power and the ability to help them.

JOE JENKINS, *INTRODUCING MORAL ISSUES*

B

There are many people working today to make the world a better place. They are working to bring peace and justice (fairness) into a world full of war, famine and injustice. There are many organizations that are working to improve the world. You, the tutor group and the whole school have the power to help in some way. Now is the time to consider, for our own sake, for our fellow citizens' sake and for the children of the world, what we must do to get organised today.

ADAPTED FROM *INTRODUCING MORAL ISSUES*

C

Today I will act on behalf of a good cause that deserves my support.

Year 10:3

A

We have been called stewards or caretakers of our planet. This means that the earth does not belong to us, but that we belong to the earth. Compared to the age of the earth, our individual lives are very short. During our short stay here, we have a responsibility to look after the earth, and if we are able, to leave the earth a better place for the next generation.

JOE JENKINS, *INTRODUCING MORAL ISSUES*

B

During the last hundred years or so, the earth has been treated very badly. Our rivers and seas, our atmosphere, our fields and forests have all suffered terribly from pollution and destruction.

Many different species of animals and birds have been destroyed and many others have been taken to the brink of extinction. Happily, we are now beginning to understand that all things are connected. This awareness brings with it real hope: by caring for the earth and our environment, we are also caring for ourselves.

ADAPTED FROM *INTRODUCING MORAL ISSUES*

C

Today I will be aware that I am part of a living planet.

Year 11:1

A

Why should we love our enemies? The first reason is fairly obvious. Returning hate for hate multiplies hate, adding deeper darkness to a night already devoid of stars. Darkness cannot drive out darkness; only light can do that. Hate cannot drive out hate; only love can do that. Hate multiplies hate, violence multiplies violence.

MARTIN LUTHER KING, *STRENGTH TO LOVE*

B

Whilst film themes based on revenge may become box office hits, the idea of 'getting your own back' clearly doesn't work in reality. Violence does not cure a situation, it only makes it worse – two people have an argument, then a fight happens, then friends and families become involved and before long a small-scale neighbourhood war can be on the horizon.

Fear, hate and revenge only divide and destroy. The ultimate forces of love and forgiveness are the weapons of hope and peace for the future.

C

I will practise love and not hate.

Year 11:2

A

Today we are so interdependent, so closely interconnected with each other that without a sense of universal responsibility, a feeling of universal brotherhood and sisterhood, and an understanding and belief that we really are part of one big human family, we cannot hope to overcome the dangers of our very existence – let alone bring about peace and happiness.

THE DALAI LAMA, A HUMAN APPROACH TO WORLD PEACE

B

If the human race is to survive then the people of the world have to pull and work together. But co-operating and getting on with each other is not easy because our survival instincts are rooted in competing and winning.

Greed, selfishness and the need to control others can end up in a conflict situation and when this involves whole nations, widespread destruction can so easily occur. What we do and how we behave, both as individuals and as nations affects many others.

The Dalai Lama calls upon each member of the human family to choose between living in a united world which is compassionate, loving and peaceful or a divided world where conflict, suffering and oppression dominate our lives.

Christopher Gibb describes The Dalai Lama's argument like this 'If we adopt a selfish approach to life and constantly try to use others for our own gain, we may achieve temporary benefits, but in the long run we will not succeed in finding even personal happiness, let alone world peace' (*The Dalai Lama*).

C

I will work with others for the good of all.

Year 11:3

A

Let us look at the world as if it were a village – a village with a population of 1,000. In this village there would be 140 North and South Americans (60 of them representing the United States); 210 Europeans; 86 Africans; 565 Asians. There would be 300 white people, 700 non-white people, 300 of the thousand would be Christians. Half of the total income of the village would be in the hands of 60 people, representing the USA. Almost all the affluent part of the village would be composed of Christians from Europe and North America. Over 700 of the 1,000 villagers would be unable to read. Over 500 would be suffering from malnutrition. Over 800 would live in what we call sub-standard housing. No more than 10 would have a university education.

STEPHEN F. BAYNE, JR, IN *PRAYERS FOR PEACEMAKERS*

B

As long as people in the world are poor, we can never be rich.
As long as people in the world cannot read or write, we can never call ourselves educated.
As long as people in the world are ill through lack of food; we can never be completely healthy.
As long as people in the world do not have adequate shelter, we can never be comfortable and warm. We can never become what we can be until everybody has the freedom to do likewise. This is because we belong to one world. This is the way our world is made. We are interdependent, interconnected and related to each other – we all belong to the human family.

ADAPTED FROM *PRAYERS FOR PEACEMAKERS*

C

We belong to one world, one family – the human family.

8 SELF-KNOWLEDGE

Year 7:1

A

Pay attention to your health, Camera, and do not take it for granted. Whatever else you learn in school, I would like you to master at least two 'life sports', those you can play long after you are out of school. Sports are wonderful; they can bring you comfort and pleasure for the rest of your life. Sports can teach you so much about yourself, your emotions and character, how to be strong in moments of crisis and how to fight back from the brink of defeat. You quickly discover your limits but you can also build self-confidence and a positive sense of yourself.

ARTHUR ASHE, FROM A LETTER TO HIS DAUGHTER, CAMERA, *DAYS OF GRACE*

B

Success in sport is measured not so much by the position reached but by the effort and progress made and the knowledge we have gained about ourselves. The achievements we make are special and unique to us.

C

Today I will not worry about who's ahead or who's behind. I will run my own race.

Year 7:2

A

Allow yourself to be you. You can be different from everyone else and still be OK.

LIKING MYSELF

B

Allow yourself to be you. You don't have to pretend to be someone else ... or act like someone else ... or copy someone else ... or talk like someone else ... or look like someone else. You can just relax and be you!

LIKING MYSELF

C

Today, I'm glad I'm me and you're you.

Year 7:3

A

Opportunities to know about the wider world are also opportunities to know more about ourselves.

B

Watching and listening to the news; reading newspapers and books; visiting museums and art galleries; travelling abroad; taking part in pupil exchange visits and participating in lessons at school – can increase our knowledge and help our understanding of other people's values and cultural practices. These experiences will probably bring up questions within ourselves such as: Who am I? What do I really care about? What do other people see when they look at me?

C

Today I will be open to opportunities which come my way.

Year 8:1

A

The simplest questions are the deepest. Where were you born? Where is your home? Where are you going? What are you doing?

ADAPTED FROM RICHARD BACH, IN *TOUCHSTONES*
(27 NOVEMBER)

B

As we examine our personal answers to these simple questions we find deep truths about ourselves. We may have been born in more places than the place of our biological birth. Some of us might say, 'I truly was born the day I first felt the love of another person in my life,' or 'My life began the day I stood up to a bully'.

If we think about where our home is or where we are going and what we are doing as spiritual questions, we may find some comforting answers. Perhaps the place where we find rest, peace and comfort is our home. That may be found in a moment of reflection rather than in a physical place.

ADAPTED FROM *TOUCHSTONES* (27 NOVEMBER)

C

Today I will keep my attention on the basics in my life.

TOUCHSTONES (27 NOVEMBER)

Year 8:2

A

Any idea, person or object can be a mirror for us. The tiniest flower can be such a mirror, as can a wolf, a story, a touch, a religion or a mountaintop.

ADAPTED FROM HYEMEYOHSTS STORM, IN *TOUCHSTONES*
(1 APRIL)

B

The ancient spiritual teachings of the Cheyenne Indians tell us that we meet ourselves in almost everything we confront. A group of people spending a night on a mountaintop will each have a different experience. One may be overcome with a sense of awe, another may spend every moment gripped by fear, and another may sleep the night away. While the mountain is the same, each has had a different experience. When we meet an animal, feel a touch, or take a walk down the street, we see a reflection of ourselves.

This day is a mirror for each of us. Our response to today's circumstances will tell us more about ourselves. We need not waste energy judging ourselves harshly, but learn from our feelings and reactions. Our reflections point the way for further growth.

ADAPTED FROM *TOUCHSTONES* (1 APRIL)

C

Today I will look for my own reflection in what I meet.

ADAPTED FROM *TOUCHSTONES* (1 APRIL)

Year 8:3

A

All people should strive to learn before they die what they are running from, and to, and why.

ADAPTED FROM JAMES THURBER, IN *TOUCHSTONES*
(13 NOVEMBER)

B

We are getting to know ourselves each day. When we have come face-to-face with ourselves, surrendered and stopped running, nothing else ever need be so frightening again.

ADAPTED FROM *TOUCHSTONES* (13 NOVEMBER)

C

I will let myself know where I am going today.

TOUCHSTONES (13 NOVEMBER)

Year 9:1

A

Who's not sat tense before his own heart's curtain?

RAINER MARIA RILKE, IN *TOUCHSTONES* (19 SEPTEMBER)

B

Looking at ourselves, squarely in the mirror, may feel as frightening as anything we do. For some of us, this is a necessary step which leads to self-knowledge and inner peace. We feel unique, different, alone, maybe even crazy. For the first time, we are listening to our inner truth rather than outside messages.

Let's think for a moment about today's tensions and strains. Are we really aware of their source? Perhaps they are created by the disturbing honesty of our hearts? We may find our spiritual growth in yielding to the truth. When we dismiss our spiritual experience or when we ignore the importance of our soft-spoken inner wisdom, we are avoiding the truth from our hearts. And we miss the possibility of becoming strong from within.

ADAPTED FROM *TOUCHSTONES* (19 SEPTEMBER)

C

Today, I will live through the tension and fear of my honesty to reach the point of peace with myself and increase in self-knowledge.

ADAPTED FROM *TOUCHSTONES* (19 SEPTEMBER)

Year 9:2

A

When I was young and free and my imagination had no limits, I dreamed of changing the world.

As I grew older and wiser, I discovered the world would not change, so I shortened my sights somewhat and decided to change only my country.But it too seemed immovable.

As I grew into my twilight years, in one last desperate attempt, I settled for changing only my family, those closest to me, but alas, they would have none of it.

And now as I lie on my deathbed, I suddenly realize:

If I had only changed myself first, then by example I might have changed my family.

From their inspiration and encouragement I would then have been able to better my country, and who knows,

I may have even changed the world.

WORDS ON THE TOMB OF AN ANGLICAN BISHOP IN THE CRYPT OF WESTMINSTER ABBEY, 1100 CE

B

There are many things in this world you might like to change to make it a better place – but where do you start?

The words of Michael Jackson's song 'Man in Mirror' put forward a powerful message:

'If you want to make the world a better place
Take a look at yourself, and then make a change,'

So where do you start?
You start with yourself.

C

Today I will look at changes I can make within myself.

Year 9:3

A

If you follow your joy, you put yourself on a kind of track that has been there all the while, waiting for you, and the life that you ought to be living is the one you are living. Wherever you are – if you are following your joy, you are enjoying that refreshment, that life within you, all the time.

ADAPTED FROM *THE POWER OF MYTH*

B

When you are true to your inner feelings, when what you are doing is in harmony with how you feel deep inside, then you are doing something special – you are following your joy.

You'll find your joy at the very centre of you – at the very heart of you. It is the thing that stirs you. No one can tell you what it is going to be. You have to learn to recognise your own joy. When you do – grab it – and don't let anyone pull you off course.

ADAPTED FROM *THE POWER OF MYTH*

C

Today I will stop and think about something I really want to do in my life.

Year 10:1

A

We all wear masks, and the time comes when we cannot remove them without removing some of our skin!

ANDRE BERTHIAUME, IN *TOUCHSTONES* (9 MARCH)

B

The masks people wear are as varied as those who wear them, but their purpose is quite simple. We wear masks to hide our real faces from those around us and even from ourselves. There are 'tough people' masks; 'victim' masks; 'nothing bothers me' masks; 'give me attention' masks; 'I don't need anybody' masks; 'joker' masks and many more.

Sometimes we want to hide behind masks so others won't see our fears and insecurities. Or we may think that putting on a particular mask will make people like us better or give us power over others. Or perhaps by wearing a mask, we can escape ourselves.

The cost of wearing a mask can be that we forget who we really are.

ADAPTED FROM *TOUCHSTONES* (9 MARCH)

C

May I have the courage to drop my pretend masks in order to grow stronger in self-knowledge.

ADAPTED FROM *TOUCHSTONES* (9 MARCH)

Year 10:2

A

Learned people who don't know themselves are really unintelligent; they don't know what thinking is, what life is. Self-knowledge is the beginning of wisdom. In self-knowledge is the whole universe; it embraces all the struggles of humanity.

THE PENGUIN KRISHNAMURTI READER

B

Observing how we talk with others; observing our relationships with others can help us to get to know ourselves better. How do we treat others in the tutor group? How different are we when we're with different people? Which people in the tutor group have the most influence on us?

The moment we begin to see ourselves in these situations,

we begin to know ourselves more. As we allow our relationships to reflect more of who we are, we can go deeper and
deeper into knowing ourselves. There is no end to self-knowledge. Through self-knowledge we get to know the workings
of our minds and hearts and grow more wise.

C

Today I will watch how I treat others and so learn more about myself.

Year 10:3

A

'Who are you?' said the Caterpillar.

*This was not an encouraging opening for a conversation. Alice re-
plied, rather shyly, 'I – I hardly know, sir, just at present – at least I
know who I was when I got up this morning, but I think I must have
been changed several times since then.'*

*'What do you mean by that?' said the Caterpillar sternly. 'Explain
yourself!'*

LEWIS CARROLL, *ALICE IN WONDERLAND*

B

If we continually ask ourselves the question: 'Who am I?', the
answers can go beyond the external details such as: name,
birthdate, birthplace, names of our parents, the things we own;
and can touch on the mystery of human experience – 'Who are
we?'

We know more about ourselves than anyone else, yet how
often do we reflect on the question 'Who am I?'.

C

Today I will ask myself: 'Who am I?'

Year 11:1

A

The most elusive knowledge of all is self-knowledge.

MIRRA KOMAROVSKY, IN *EACH DAY A NEW BEGINNING*
(28 OCTOBER)

B

When did you last spend some time with yourself? It's now possible to fill the 24 hours in a day, tuned into a radio station or television channel. It's easy to cram our heads with other people's thoughts, at the expense of listening to what our hearts have to say. Keeping a diary or journal of our innermost thoughts and feelings is one way of bringing what is going on deep within us, to the surface; so that we may know ourselves better.

As we develop and mature, change and grow, it's valuable to keep in touch with what is important to us; so that we become aware of our own thoughts and feelings, sorrows and joys, confusions and discoveries.

C

I will strive to know myself better.

Year 11:2

A

So many of us are in the habit of looking 'out there' for our answers, invalidating our own inner wisdom by assuming that, in some magical way, others must be wiser than we are – even about what is good for us. We become other-directed rather than self-directed.

SUE PATTON THOELE, *THE WOMAN'S BOOK OF COURAGE*

B

Part of the joy of increasing our self-knowledge is the opportunity to take more responsibility for ourselves and our lives.

It takes courage to enquire within and find our own answers. We may also need courage to act upon our own advice. We may be afraid that we'll make a mistake, but nevertheless, we can learn to listen to our inner guidance and learn to trust ourselves, by being still and enquiring within.

C

Today I will listen to my own inner wisdom.

Year 11:3

A

I love and accept myself just as I am.

GILL EDWARDS, *LIVING MAGICALLY – A NEW VISION OF REALITY*

B

The more that we know about ourselves, the more fully we can love and accept ourselves. Self-knowledge and self-acceptance are about recognizing and embracing both our 'positive' and 'negative' qualities.

We may discover that we can be unkind or deceitful or behave aggressively. These qualities are just as valid and part of us as our kindness, truthfulness and peaceful ways.

Our wholeness is to be found in acknowledging the negative and positive in us – recognizing that within us are both light and dark aspects.

From this point of self-knowledge, self-acceptance and love, we can begin to make choices about how we behave.

C

Today I will love and accept all parts of myself, just as I am.

9 INTERNATIONAL CO-OPERATION AND PEACE

Year 7:1

A

Peace I leave with you
My peace I give;
I do not give to you as the world gives;
Do not let your hearts be troubled and do not be afraid.

JOHN 14:27

B

We do not always choose the peaceful way of life. We can pass on gossip, make unhelpful remarks, do something that we know will offend.

Two small sisters had an argument, that developed into a fight. Their mother pulled them apart and sent them to separate rooms. Later that day when one of the sisters saw the television news and saw the awful pictures of people injured in a war, she asked why countries fought one another. Her mother replied, 'For the same reason you and your sister fight.'

C

Today I will be honest about my angry feelings towards others.

Year 7:2

A

Since wars begin in the minds of men, it is in the minds of men that the defences of peace must be constructed.

UNESCO CONSTITUTION

B

There are some people who are always boasting or letting others know how clever they are. They will insist that they are right and will not listen to others. Some will insist that they are right even when they are wrong. We may call them 'pig-headed', on the other hand those who are always right we tend to call 'big-headed'.

We cannot change others but we can change ourselves. We can accept and respect people who think and act differently from ourselves, and we can make sure that we do not think too highly of our own opinions.

C

In my mind are thoughts which can hurt me or help me. I can choose the helpful thoughts.

Year 7:3

A

Be of one mind, live in peace. And the God of love and peace will be with you.

2 CORINTHIANS 13:11

B

So often when people are asked what would be a perfect world for them, the reply is 'Peace' yet the behaviour of individuals does not work for that. It is as if peace is something that is outside ourselves, something that will come upon the world and everything will be peaceful. But it is not from outside, but from within. If every one of us set out to act and speak in a peaceful manner then surely we would have a peaceful community.

C

Today I will look for peace in myself and the world.

Year 8:1

A

Lord, calm me down. Be with me now when I need your help more than ever. Help me to say the right things.

MARTIN LUTHER KING

B

It is easy to give an angry response when someone says or does something against us. It is easy to tell everyone how we have been wronged, and get them to take sides.

Martin Luther King had plenty of hurtful things done and said to him. Born in Atlanta, Georgia in 1929, he suffered many insults throughout his childhood and adult life because of the colour of his skin.

As a leader and a great speaker he could have stirred up the crowds to riot, but he was a pastor of a church and believed in non-violence.

C

Today I will give my energy to creating peace around me.

Year 8:2

A

Love your enemies and pray for those who persecute you.

MATTHEW 5:44

B

The movement that Martin Luthur King led took an old cotton-workers' hymn called 'We shall overcome' as its signature tune. It was sung whenever they met, whether they were marching or demonstrating peacefully for their rights. And they did overcome in many ways. They overcame a lot of pride, hatred, prejudice and other attitudes which keep people apart when they should have been living happily together.

C

Today I will choose to see love and peace instead of fear and hate.

Year 8:3

A

I have a dream that one day this nation will rise up and live out the true meaning of its creed: We hold these truths to be self-evident, that all men are created equal.

MARTIN LUTHER KING

B

In August 1963, Dr Martin Luther King delivered a great speech in which he said: 'I have a dream that one day on the red hills of Georgia the sons of former slaves and the sons of former slave-owners will be able to sit down together at the table of brotherhood ... When we allow freedom to ring from every town and every hamlet, from every state and every city, we will be able to speed up the day when all God's children, black men and white men, Jews and Gentiles, Protestants and Catholics, will be able to join hands and sing in the words of the old Negro Spiritual, 'Free at last'.

We have only to read in our newspapers to see what is happening in many of the countries of the world, where people are not free and many suffer at the hands of others. Martin Luther King did great work but it is not finished.

C

Today I will look beyond the outward appearance to see all people for what they are.

Year 9:1

A

Blessed is the man who finds wisdom, the man who gains understanding ...

Long life is in her right hand; in her left hand are riches and honour. Her ways are pleasant ways, and all her paths are peace.

PROVERBS 3: 13-17

B

In this day of man's highest technical achievement, in this day of dazzling discovery, of novel opportunities, loftier dignities and fuller freedoms for all, there is no excuse for the kind of blind craving for power and resources that provoked the wars of previous generations. There is no need to fight for food and land. Science has provided us with adequate means of survival and transportation, which make it possible to enjoy the fullness of this great earth. The question now is, do we have the morality and courage required to live together as brothers and not be afraid?

MARTIN LUTHER KING, JR

C

I have the strength to face my fears today. I will not release them as hatred.

Year 9:2

A

Peace must be based on truth, built on justice, supported by love and created in an atmosphere of freedom.

POPE JOHN XXIII

B

What is needed is the renewal of truth, if we are to avoid a situation where individuals, groups and nations begin to doubt the power of peace and to accept the forms of oppression. To reinstate the truth means first and foremost to call by name any act of oppression, whatever form it takes. One has to name a murder by its name – murder is always a murder; political and ideological motivation cannot change its nature ...

To promote the truth as the foundation of peace means to make every endeavour to avoid the use of the lie even in a good cause. The gospel strongly underlines the link existing between the lie and violence ... The living source of the peace of the gospel is truth. We should therefore live by truth, and then it will reveal to us unexpected lights and energies, thus opening new possibilities for peace in the world.

JERZY POPIELUSZKO

C

Today I will allow myself to have the single goal of inner peace. I will be less judgmental of myself and others.

ADAPTED FROM *LOVE IS LETTING GO OF FEAR*

Year 9:3

A

The way of peace is the way of truth ... Truthfulness is even more important than peacefulness. Indeed, lying is the mother of violence. A truthful man cannot long remain violent. He will perceive in the course of his research that he has no need to be violent, and he will further discover that so long as there is the slightest trace of violence in him, he will fail to find the truth he is searching.

MAHATMA GANDHI

B

Our concern with the past and always bringing it into the future defeats our aim of present peace. The past is over and the future is yet to be. Peace cannot be found in the past or future, but only in this instant.

ADAPTED FROM *LOVE IS LETTING GO OF FEAR*

C

I am determined to live today without either past or future dreams. I will remind myself: this instant is the only time there is.

ADAPTED FROM *LOVE IS LETTING GO OF FEAR*

Year 10:1

A

The powers of evil appear to be on the rampage, but in the end they will not be able to prevail against the force of order, of love, of peace.

ARCHBISHOP DESMOND TUTU

B

*I had a paint box
but it didn't have the colour red
for the blood of the wounded,
nor white
for the hearts and faces of the dead.*

*It didn't have yellow either
for the burning sands
of the desert.*

Instead it had orange

for the dawn and the sunset
and blue
for new skies
and pink
for the dreams of young people.

I sat down and painted peace.

BY A CHILD OF 10, IN *MANY THOUGHTS*

C

What colours do I want in my paintbox?

Year 10:2

A

Lead me from Death to Life
from Falsehood to Truth
Lead me from Despair to Hope
from Fear to Trust
Lead me from Hate to Love
from War to Peace
Let Peace fill our Heart
our World, our Universe
PEACE   PEACE   PEACE

PRAYERS FOR PEACE

B

Most people want peace, but few do anything about actually achieving peace. We all know of peace talks as various factions in the world fight their corner, but the same countries that negotiate in talks continue to develop weapons for nations to destroy each other. On a personal scale, how many of us would like to be at peace with those around us?

Peace is not a passive thing. Peace needs to be made, peacemakers are needed, not only to help us in our own relationships but also to help others. Peace is not easy to achieve, but it is worth striving for.

C

I will be aware of the times when I can act as a peacemaker.

Year 10:3

A

There are times when we can rise above our own needs and concentrate on the needs of those around us.

J.A.H.

B

Lord, make me an instrument of thy peace.
Where there is hatred, let me sow love.
Where there is injury, pardon.
Where there is doubt, faith.
Where there is despair, hope.
Where there is darkness, light.
Where there is sadness, joy.
O divine Master,
grant that I may not so much seek to be consoled
as to console;
to be understood as to understand;
to be loved, as to love;
for it is in giving that we receive,
it is in pardoning that we are pardoned,
and it is in dying that we are born to eternal life.

THE PEACE PRAYER OF ST FRANCIS

C

Today in helping others, may I bring more peace into the world.

Year 11:1

A

Destruction.
Homeless people, walking the streets,
Young children crying with nothing to eat.
Starving families nowhere to go,
Is this our fault? I do not know.

Why should they have to live in this way,
If we can do something about it today?

JOANNA SMITH, AGED 14, IN *GO GREEN*

B

Many cities are growing fast, especially in poor countries where they act like a magnet, drawing those looking for better jobs, good facilities and new opportunities. The country people leave their areas due to shortage of land, poor pay and jobs being taken over by machinery. Unfortunately the cities also have high unemployment and poor housing. The people end up in shanty towns with no running water or waste disposal. The problems appear enormous but it is possible to bring about change.

A young couple in Mexico City set to work in a particularly bad area. They provided activities for the children, they approached the city mayor about sanitation, and with the help of volunteers they built safe homes. With compassion, a willingness to work for others and physical and financial help from around the world, whole communities can be transformed.

C

I too can help others.

Year 11:2

A

The Hurt World.

The mystery of death rules our lives,
We can hear the horror in children's cries.
While mothers look on with sad expressions,
At their children who have sung their last song.
The barren lands are alive with groves,
While our country lives to save,
So help this world we beg,
For the world will soon be dead.

DEBORAH WILSON, IN *GO GREEN*

B

One of the results of war is the fact that children become orphaned. This was most evident in the civil war in Rwanda in 1994, where it is thought that 150,000 children were left on their own. Whatever we think about war, the children are the innocent victims.

It is good that there are people who are not prepared to stand by and watch, but become fully involved with the situation. Organizations like *Food for the Hungry International*, search for the relatives of the abandoned children or try to find foster homes. They also give the children practical, emotional and psychological help.

By giving to such organizations, we too are helping the abandoned children.

C

I will look for opportunities to contribute to peace in the world.

Year 11:3

A

O Lord, open my eyes
that I may see the need of others,
open my ears that I may hear their cries,

open my heart so that they need not be without succour.
Let me not be afraid to defend the weak
because of the anger of the strong,
nor afraid to defend the poor
because of the anger of the rich.
Show me where love and hope and faith are needed,
and use me to bring them to these places.
Open my eyes and ears that I may, this coming day,
be able to do some work of peace for thee.

ALAN PATON, IN *PRAYERS FOR PEACE*

B

Those who watched the television in 1984 can never forget the harrowing pictures of the famine in Ethiopia. We watched, seemingly helpless, at babies with extended stomachs, twig-like limbs and large hollow eyes. Drought and civil war killed half a million people.

Journalists and TV crews sent their pictures around the world, and the world responded. In this country, the singer Bob Geldof set up *Band Aid*, and many others were moved to help. Food was sent immediately, but there was also long-term action like the building of dams, the pumping of water and planting of hardier crops.

It will take many years for Ethiopia to recover fully from that awful famine, but already we can see healthier babies, a greener landscape and a more self-sufficient people. What a dividend for all those people around the world who gave in 1984.

C

May I see the need of others around the world and respond.

10 Joy

Year 7:1

A

When I was younger, I wanted many things: a computer, a TV, a stereo, clothes with fashionable labels, holidays abroad and opportunities to see my favourite pop group. The list went on and on. Each new 'want', I was sure, would make me happy and feel satisfied. All it did was make me want more and more. The things that seemed so important lost their specialness after I'd experienced or had them for a few weeks.

M.W.

B

We live in a material world, in which we try to find material pleasures. Such pleasures can give us thrills and make us feel very satisfied – for a time. But such things don't bring joy. Real joy, a kind of glow inside, is not achieved through having or possessing things. Joy, at its fullest, is not found in the material world – outside us – but experienced in a place within us.

We can create joy by accepting and appreciating ourselves more. We can live with joy by experiencing more, celebrating more often and daring to love ourselves and others.

ADAPTED FROM *DAYS OF HEALING, DAYS OF JOY* (28 JUNE)

C

Each and every day there are opportunities to discover real joy.

ADAPTED FROM *DAYS OF HEALING, DAYS OF JOY* (28 JUNE)

Year 7:2

A

I saw him enter the world, get turned upside down, cry a little and then stop, get cleaned off, wrapped up, and put into my arms. For an hour I held him and he was warm and close and peaceful. I kept thinking that this time might be the most important of his life. What a way to begin, by giving joy to parents!

WILLIAM SCHUTZ, *JOY – EXPANDING HUMAN AWARENESS*

B

For little children the joy continues. They wake up each morning eager for new adventures. Maybe today it will be a piece of string, the telephone or pots and pans, or – more rarely – a new toy. Little children are joy. They can enjoy each part of their lives with their whole being, giving joy to those near them. Their joy is contagious.

ADAPTED FROM *JOY – EXPANDING HUMAN AWARENESS*

C

Today I will try to recapture and share the joy I once felt as a child.

Year 7:3

A

Perhaps this very instant is your time …

LOUISE BOGAN, IN *EACH DAY A NEW BEGINNING* (5 NOVEMBER)

B

The only lessons that matter for our lives at this time will come to us today. Just as what we needed and were ready for yesterday came yesterday.

All we need to do is be aware of and react to this moment now. What has gone is gone. Yesterday's problems are in the past. What doesn't come our way today, will come when the time is right. We need not worry about the future.

Living one day at a time brings a sense of joy to our own life and the lives of our friends and family.

ADAPTED FROM *EACH DAY A NEW BEGINNING* (5 NOVEMBER)

C

There is wonder and joy waiting for me each day.

EACH DAY A NEW BEGINNING (5 NOVEMBER)

Year 8:1

A

If people only knew the healing power of laughter and joy, many of our fine doctors would be out of business. Joy is one of nature's greatest medicines. Joy is always healthy. A pleasant state of mind tends to bring abnormal conditions back to normal.

CATHERINE PONDER, IN *EACH DAY A NEW BEGINNING* (12 JUNE)

B

Feeling joy may not come naturally to us most of the time. We may not even recognize genuine joy in the beginning. A way for finding it is living fully in the present and with thanks for all we can see, touch and feel. Joy is catching. Joy is freeing. Greeting life with joy changes every experience for us and for those we share it with.

ADAPTED FROM *EACH DAY A NEW BEGINNING* (12 JUNE)

C

I will bring joy wherever I go today. I will give the gift of joy to everyone I meet.

EACH DAY A NEW BEGINNING (12 JUNE)

Year 8:2

A

People need joy. Quite as much as clothing. Some of them need it far more.

MARGARET COLLIER GRAHAM, IN *EACH DAY A NEW BEGINNING* (13 MARCH)

B

Life is not without pain. Pain brings new awareness which brings growth. And the gift of growth is joy. Pain and joy are, therefore, closely related. It is possible to feel only pain and not the joy, however.

Joy does await each of us today. We must open our eyes to it, just as we must open our hearts to one another. We must be willing to peel away the layers of pain to discover the core, the seedling of joy. And we need joy in our lives, just as surely as we need rest and a good diet.

ADAPTED FROM *EACH DAY A NEW BEGINNING* (13 MARCH)

C

The knowledge that joy is present, within every experience, is mine, now and forever.

ADAPTED FROM *EACH DAY A NEW BEGINNING* (13 MARCH)

Year 8:3

A

'What kind of weather are we going to have today?' asked the traveller.

'The kind of weather I like,' answered the shepherd

'How do you know it will be the kind of weather you like?' asked the traveller.

'Having found out, sir, I cannot always get what I like, I

have learned always to like what I get. So I am quite sure we will have the kind of weather I like,' replied the shepherd.

ADAPTED FROM ANTHONY DE MELLO, *THE HEART OF THE ENLIGHTENED*

B

In your mind are thoughts that can hurt you or help you. You can choose the thoughts of your mind. You can choose to experience joyful thoughts.

Joy and sadness are in the way we meet events, not in the nature of those events themselves.

ADAPTED FROM *THE HEART OF THE ENLIGHTENED*

C

In every situation, I have an opportunity to discover real joy.

Year 9:1

A

True philosopher that he was, Socrates believed that the wise person would naturally lead a simple life. He himself would not even wear shoes; yet he constantly fell under the spell of the marketplace and would go there often to look at all the goods on display.

When one of his friends asked why, Socrates said, 'I love to go there and discover how many things I am perfectly happy without.'

ADAPTED FROM ANTHONY DE MELLO, *THE HEART OF THE ENLIGHTENED*

B

Spirituality is not knowing what you want but understanding what you do not need. People have been known to make a rich life for themselves and others, with very few possessions.

Often people need to buy things because their hearts are empty and there is a lack of joy in their lives.

ADAPTED FROM *THE HEART OF THE ENLIGHTENED*

C

Today I will think about the difference between the satisfaction of a desire and joy.

Year 9:2

A

Joy is the feeling that comes from fulfilling your potential. Joyful fulfilment helps you to feel good about yourself; gives you a sense of confidence and a feeling of being able to cope with and handle situations.

B

Joy can come from realizing your potential – the potential for being more of a person than you thought you could be.

When you experience yourself anew and are able to cope better with negative feelings; and come to accept, respect and love yourself more, then the glow of joy can flood your entire being.

Joy then is what you experience in the process of growing nearer to the goal of becoming your true self.

C

Today I will become more accepting and loving of myself and release the joy within me.

Year 9:3

A

Your joy is your sorrow unmasked.

And the selfsame well from which your laughter rises
Was often times filled with your tears.
And how else can it be?
The deeper that sorrow carves into your being,
the more joy you can contain.

KAHLIL GIBRAN, *THE PROPHET*

B

In order to live fully you have to embrace all that life brings and allow yourself to experience all of your feelings, whether joyful or painful, and be glad and accepting of both.

Life's difficulties can be seen as opportunities for enriching your joy – because the rough and hard times deepen your understanding and this can help to bring joy to others.

C

Today I will be glad for all of life's experiences.

Year 10:1

A

We are on a journey in this life. And our travelling is bringing us closer to a fuller understanding of joy with every sorrowful circumstance.

B

We live both in the material world and the spiritual world. In the material world, we seek material pleasures, but real joy lies beyond the material world and lives fully within us in the secret, small place inside where we always know that all is well. Each circumstance in the material world is an opportunity for us to rely on the spiritual world for direction, security and understanding.

As we look within to our spiritual nature we will know joy.

ADAPTED FROM *EACH DAY A NEW BEGINNING* (28 JUNE)

C

Every day I have an opportunity to discover real joy.

ADAPTED FROM *EACH DAY A NEW BEGINNING* (28 JUNE)

Year 10:2

A

Some people walk in the rain. Others just get wet.

ROGER MILLER, IN *DAYS OF HEALING, DAYS OF JOY*
(23 DECEMBER)

B

How do we enjoy ourselves? Is it to have a party or to get away?
For some it could mean getting smashed – but that's only an
escape from reality – an imitation of celebration.

Real celebration is not so much escaping but more about
coming back and 'touching centre' and so heightening awareness. To celebrate is to refresh and remake the spirit. It is to do
with inner growth.

How much happier and joyful our lives will become when
we can say, 'Come and celebrate – let's talk. Come and celebrate – let's walk together. Come and celebrate – let's listen to
the wind and watch the night fall.'

The joy which follows such celebrations touches our very
centre giving a sense of wholeness and well-being.

ADAPTED FROM *DAYS OF HEALING, DAYS OF JOY* (23 DECEMBER)

C

Today I will celebrate in ways which allow joy to enter my heart.

Year 10:3

A

Joy comes from the capacity to feel deeply, to think freely, to enjoy simply, to take risks in life.

ADAPTED FROM *DAYS OF HEALING, DAYS OF JOY* (31 DECEMBER)

B

Wise people have likened joy to a butterfly – try to catch it and it flees; sit quietly and it will light on your shoulder.

Do you know any joyful people? Joyful people are those who are fully human – they are able and willing to feel, to celebrate, to challenge old ideas and to risk. Do you know any joyful people?

The good news is that we have the power to change. We can be like butterflies ourselves, but we've got to leave the cocoon behind if we want to fly.

ADAPTED FROM *DAYS OF HEALING, DAYS OF JOY* (31 DECEMBER)

C

I can't pull back from and reach out to life at the same time. Today I choose to reach out.

DAYS OF HEALING, DAYS OF JOY (31 DECEMBER)

Year 11:1

A

The lack of joy makes it necessary to seek ever new, ever more exciting pleasures.

What is the difference between joy and pleasure? It is not easy to appreciate the difference, since we live in a world of 'joyless pleasures'.

ERICH FROMM, *TO HAVE OR TO BE*

B

Pleasure is about satisfying our senses and desires. It may be being 'in' with the right crowd, wearing the latest fashion, winning the lottery, eating and drinking to our heart's content.

Although all these activities may be pleasurable, they are 'joyless pleasures' because they do not last. Joy is not the thrill and excitement of the moment, but is a lasting spiritual glow that is felt deep within. We need models to show us what is of value in life. For Christians, Jesus is the model they want to imitate; and when they do, they experience everlasting joy.

C

May I too find everlasting joy.

Year 11:2

A

The joy of discovery is delicious. I know of no explorer who once having reached his or her goal has not wanted to go out and explore some more … Joy is the result of using our powers to their fullest, and for that reason, joy, not happiness, is the goal of life.

SUSAN JEFFERS, *FEEL THE FEAR AND DO IT ANYWAY*

B

We say YES to life by fully participating in the world and fulfilling our potential. We can do this by developing our interests, pursuing our goals, growing and maturing.

We can take time to: read, write, enjoy a hobby, learn new skills, develop friendships, have fun, laugh and cry – and feel the joy in our lives.

C

I will make joy the goal of my life.

Year 11:3

A

From belief in God's love comes a sense of security, an unshakable faith that (in the words of Julian of Norwich) 'all will be well, and all will be well, and all manner of thing will be well'. It may look all wrong; but all will be well.

WILLIAM JOHNSTON, *SILENT MUSIC*

B

There can be times in our lives when things seem difficult or maybe even hopeless and impossible, making us feel anxious and afraid. But dark and dismal times such as these can also be opportunities for discovering joy, building inner confidence and trusting in what the future holds. If we can open ourselves to the possibility that things will turn out well, then our fearfulness can diminish and be replaced with a sense of security, comfort and joy.

C

Whatever happens today, I will remember that all will be well.

11 A FORGIVING SPIRIT

Year 7:1

A

Forgive and you will be forgiven.

LUKE 6:37

B

So often we hear the words, 'I will never forgive you for this', and we store up in our minds the thing that has upset us. Every time we hear the name of the person who has upset us we remember what they did to us. Sometimes we have a long list of complaints against one person. Meanwhile the person is probably totally unaware of our feelings.

As long as we hold a grudge, as long as we harbour resentment, we become victims. We cannot be set free until we forgive.

When we upset someone we expect to be forgiven, let's do the same for those who upset us.

C

What is done is done! When I forgive someone I don't let anybody off the hook but myself.

DAYS OF HEALING, DAYS OF JOY (22 JULY)

Year 7:2

A

Be kind and compassionate to one another, forgiving each other, just as in Christ God forgave you.

EPHESIANS 4:32

B

Forgiveness should be a continuing process. It will daily help our relationship with others and encourage us to appreciate ourselves.

Firstly we should forgive ourselves for all those things we wish we had not said or done. When we can forgive ourselves we can then forgive others. Forgiveness can free us. It will change the way we look at our life and see others. It gives us greater happiness.

ADAPTED FROM *EACH DAY A NEW BEGINNING* (10 DECEMBER)

C

The forgiving heart is special. My whole life could change if I develop a forgiving heart.

ADAPTED FROM *EACH DAY A NEW BEGINNING* (10 DECEMBER)

Year 7:3

A

Forgive us the wrongs we have done, as we forgive the wrongs that others have done to us.

MATTHEW 6:12

B

Between the wars in Kenya there was a lot of unrest and tension. There were horrendous attacks on different racial groups. Jomo Kenyatta was accused of taking part in some of the uprisings and was imprisoned. Later on it was found that false evidence had been given against him.

In 1960 Kenya gained independence and in 1963 Jomo Kenyatta became President. He was determined to make Kenya a multi-racial nation. He said, 'There is no society of angels, whether it is white, brown or black. We are human beings, and as such we are bound to make mistakes.'

He urged that there should be forgiveness on both sides and that everyone should work together for the good of Kenya so that people of various races and beliefs could live together.

ADAPTED FROM ROWLAND PURTON, *ASSEMBLIES*

C

I love and forgive myself as I would a close friend.

Year 8:1

A

Forgiveness is another word for letting go.

MATTHEW FOX, IN *TOUCHSTONES* (6 OCTOBER)

B

Learning forgiveness – both giving it to others and accepting it for ourselves – is one of the basic means of a person's spiritual recovery.

Simply going through the motions of forgiving or accepting forgiveness will not get us very far. We must squarely face our feelings and tell someone so we are no longer alone with our guilt. Then, if there is the possibility for repair without further hurt, we must make repair. In this concrete way we can be genuinely forgiven and fully accept forgiveness. When we have a spiritual experience like this, we mature and gain the ability to forgive others.

ADAPTED FROM *TOUCHSTONES* (6 OCTOBER)

C

I am grateful for the relief of being forgiven and letting go of past mistakes. I will genuinely let go of my guilt and resentment.

ADAPTED FROM *TOUCHSTONES* (6 OCTOBER)

Year 8:2

A

Judge not, that you be not judged.

MATTHEW 7:1

B

If we put ourselves down, we will also put other people down.
If we reject ourselves, we will reject others.
If we judge ourselves we will judge others.

We know that we are not perfect, so we need to forgive ourselves.
We sometimes need to be forgiven by others and we also need to forgive those who hurt us.

To forgive is not weakness but strength.

We may reject some aspects of a person's behaviour, but we should never reject the person.

C

Today I am willing to forgive the hurts of the past.

Year 8:3

A

They may not deserve forgiveness, but I do.

ANNE P, IN *DAYS OF HEALING, DAYS OF JOY* (14 APRIL)

B

Forgiveness is an act, not a feeling. Though it may bring about feelings, forgiveness is an exercise of the will. When we forgive, we refuse to be further damaged by the wrong-doing of others.

A refusal to forgive is called a resentment. And the victim of resentment is always the one who carries it. The people we refuse to forgive may neither know nor care about our resentment.

To hang on to a resentment is to harbour a thief in the heart. By the minute and the hour, resentment steals the joy we could treasure now and remember forever. It steals our energy to celebrate life – to face others as messengers of grace rather than ambassadors of doom. We victimize ourselves when we withhold forgiveness.

ADAPTED FROM *DAYS OF HEALING, DAYS OF JOY* (14 APRIL)

C

Today I will remember that forgiveness is a giver and resentment is a taker. Because I deserve it, I will forgive old hurts. I will see forgiveness as a gift to myself.

ADAPTED FROM *DAYS OF HEALING, DAYS OF JOY* (14 APRIL)

Year 9:1

A

A man who studieth revenge keeps his own wounds green.

FRANCIS BACON, IN *TOUCHSTONES* (23 FEBRUARY)

B

How do we use our energy? Are we spending time and thought on how we have been wronged? On the unfairness of life? Those who use up their energy in this way have little strength left for growth and development. Their wounds stay open for years, and they block the healing.

What do we need to set aside our resentments and hateful attitudes? Perhaps we have been passively waiting for the other person to put things right. That only puts our enemies in charge of us. It would be better if we could say, 'I am going to move on. The change that is needed for me to heal will come from within me. I will not put my happiness in another's hands.'

More than revenge, we want a life worth living – for ourselves and the ones we love. We can give our energies to that.

ADAPTED FROM *TOUCHSTONES* (23 FEBRUARY)

C

I will let go of the desire for revenge. Each day I am more and more able to love and forgive.

ADAPTED FROM *TOUCHSTONES* (23 FEBRUARY)

Year 9:2

A

Forgiveness is a process.

HULBERT L, IN *DAYS OF HEALING, DAYS OF JOY* (20 OCTOBER)

B

Sometimes we think of forgiveness as an all-or-nothing kind of thing – once done, forever done. But forgiveness is most often a process in which we make progress one step at a time.

Willing is not the same as wanting. We may be willing to forgive but not want to. The injury done us may be so painful and fill us with such rage that forgiveness just can't be all-or-nothing. What we can do, however, is start. We can start thinking one forgiving thought a day. We can resist one hateful, resentful thought a day. We can continue further by acting out, however small that action may be, a forgiving action every day. The process can continue as we make a list of all the reasons why not forgiving is hurting us more than it hurts others. It can go on as we learn to pray for those we are trying to forgive.

All of a sudden we will find that the unattainable forgiveness has been accomplished. But, of course, it wasn't all of a sudden at all.

DAYS OF HEALING, DAYS OF JOY (20 OCTOBER)

C

Today I pray for courage to begin the process of forgiveness and faith to believe in it.

DAYS OF HEALING, DAYS OF JOY (20 OCTOBER)

Year 9:3

A

Any man can seek revenge, it takes a king or prince to grant a pardon.

ARTHUR J. REHRAT, IN *DAYS OF HEALING, DAYS OF JOY* (11 DECEMBER)

B

Revenge is the simplest and easiest of quests. But it is a self-defeating action. It doesn't get the job done. Forgiveness, on the other hand, is the gesture of a healthier mentality and power. By not forgiving we are, in fact, injuring ourselves. As long as we fail to forgive, we condemn ourselves to be fixed on the cause of our pain.

Carrying our anger, rage, and revenge from the past into the present can become an automatic response. We will probably need to work overtime to maintain and justify our outrage at what happened to us in the past, and at the price we have paid since. We can become so single-minded that it becomes a holy mission to carry this blind resentment to the grave.

But then we become like a grave, and the lack of pardon is the corpse within, contaminating everything we touch.

ADAPTED FROM *DAYS OF HEALING, DAYS OF JOY* (11 DECEMBER)

C

As I grow in understanding, I will grow in forgiveness.

ADAPTED FROM *DAYS OF HEALING, DAYS OF JOY* (11 DECEMBER)

Year 10:1

A

Love your enemies, and pray for those who persecute you.

MATTHEW 5:44

B

I think that one of the most controversial lessons that I have been in was on the subject of forgiveness.

Seeing examples of people being deliberately hurt by others, few pupils could see the value of forgiveness.

Forgiveness does not mean ignoring what has been done, it does not mean preventing justice. It *does* mean not allowing the evil act to remain a barrier to a relationship. It allows Michael Saward, who was robbed and beaten in his home, to visit his attacker in jail. It allows Nelson Mandela to work with the people who once imprisoned him for 27 years.

J. Vanier, in *Many Thoughts*, wrote:

'Forgiveness is the cement that bonds us together;
it is the source of unity;
it is the quality of love;
that draws together out of separation.'

C

Forgiveness is peace-making.

Year 10:2

A

Love your enemies, do good to those who hate you, bless those who curse you, pray for those who ill treat you.

LUKE 6:27–28

B

Captain Gordon of the Argyll and Sutherland Highlanders was captured during World War II and for three and a half years he suffered in the notorious Changi prison camp. The prisoners were brutally treated in foul conditions and many died.

When they were released and on the train to freedom they saw a train full of injured enemy soldiers who were in a very bad state. Without hesitation they went to help them and give a little comfort. Someone exclaimed, 'But they are our enemies.' They were also people who needed help.

Jesus told a story of a Samaritan who helped his enemy who was injured, and he said to his followers, 'Go and do likewise.' Captain Gordon and his fellow ex-prisoners were doing just that.

ADAPTED FROM ROWLAND PURTON, *ASSEMBLIES*

C

May I be ready to forgive, keen to help and willing to give.

Year 10:3

A

Forgiveness is peace-making:
struggling to create unity,
to build one body,
to heal the broken body of humanity.

J. VANIER, IN *MANY THOUGHTS*

B

If we are honest we know in our heart of hearts that we are not as good as we could be, we could be better, gentler, more peaceful. We can all remember times when we have hurt somebody else, by what we have said or done.

Knowing this about ourselves we can conclude that it is true of everybody else. So we should not be surprised when we get hurt by others.

We have a choice when we get hurt; to fight back or forgive. The hardest choice is to forgive, but it is the choice that helps to build a peaceful community. Maybe, if we start forgiving others, they might start forgiving us.

C

I will practise forgiveness in order to bring more peace into the world.

Year 11:1

A

It is the person who most knows himself liable to fall that will be most ready to overlook any offences from his fellow men.

ALEXANDER AULD, IN *GATHERED GOLD*

B

When we know that we have done something wrong, and others, maybe our friends or family have given us a fresh start, we can appreciate what it means to be forgiven.

We all do things that are unacceptable, but so often we justify what we have done. Maybe we put the blame on somebody else, or we blame the circumstance. Sometimes we minimize the extent of our misdemeanour. We may hurt our friends but pretend that they do not really mind.

There are times in our life when we all need forgiveness, and there are times in our life when we need to show forgiveness.

C

I will be aware of the failings in my life and use these to be compassionate and forgiving towards others.

Year 11:2

A

Those who say they will forgive but can't forget, simply bury the hatchet but leave the handle out for immediate use.

D.L. MOODY, IN *GATHERED GOLD*

B

When we have been hurt by a friend it can be difficult to let go of the incident. We may eventually forgive and renew the friendship, but the depth of the forgiveness will determine the depth of the friendship. If every time there is a quarrel the issue is thought about or raised again, it will weary the relationship. In fact it may be easier to dissolve the friendship rather than keep being reminded of the past.

Forgiveness is needed in all relationships, and if we want good friendships we must learn to forgive and forget.

C

I will practise letting go of old wounds.

Year 11:3

A

Everyone says that forgiveness is a lovely idea until he has something to forgive.

C.S. LEWIS, IN *GATHERED GOLD*

B

Forgiveness is often difficult because it conflicts with our sense of justice. If we feel that someone has done something wrong to us the automatic response is to get our own back – to give as good as we get. We feel justified in behaving like this.

If, for instance, someone destroys your personal stereo, it does not miraculously repair itself just because we say, 'I forgive you'. We still need to sort out the problem of compensation. Justice must be done – but forgiveness allows the friendship to continue despite the damage.

If we did not learn to forgive, there would be no friendships, no peace, and no community. Forgiveness is the oil that keeps the wheels of society turning.

C

I will choose to forgive.

12 LIVING AS A FAMILY

Year 7:1

A

God sets the lonely in families.

PSALM 68:6

B

'For us to rejoice means to eat together in happiness. Not alone. We want the whole family there. Mother and father, grandmothers and grandfathers, brothers and sisters – and if it is a big celebration, uncles and aunts and cousins, too. In fact, when we celebrate we celebrate with the Jewish community. They are not merely our people but sort of our family spread very wide. And there are always ceremonies, candles and wine, blessings and prayers. For we are not alone in time. We are linked with God in our lives and in the life of our people. We celebrate His being with us now and His having made the celebration possible for us.' (Harry Gersh)

Some people find their family more important than others, but there are always occasions in life when we are glad to have our family around. As time goes on we may value different members of our family, we may come to appreciate those we once had no time for. We do not choose our family, but they are special because they belong to us.

C

Let us put more into our families than we take out.

Year 7:2

A

In order to build good relations with parents, brothers, and sisters, begin by putting yourself in their shoes. Treat them as you would like to be treated.

CHARLIE W. SHEDD, IN *CHANGES, BECOMING THE BEST YOU CAN BE*

B

Everything was OK for 13-year-old Jimmy until his mother got married again. Up to that point he'd had his own room to himself, and he and his mother got along fine.

Jimmy felt happy for his mum when she started to spend time with Gary. But now that Gary is his stepfather, things are different. Gary was part of a package deal that included Gary's children from his first marriage. The girl is Jimmy's age; he doesn't like her because he thinks she's a snob. The boy is five years younger, and Jimmy thinks he's a spoiled brat. Worst of all, now that Jimmy's mum and Gary are married, Jimmy has to share a room in their new house with his stepbrother.

Many families today are made up of stepbrothers and stepsisters. It's not so unusual. And because it involves a change from how things used to be, it takes some getting used to.

CHANGES, BECOMING THE BEST YOU CAN BE

C

May I see change as a challenge.

Year 7:3

A

Everyone in your family needs love, kindness, and appreciation – just like you.

CHARLIE W. SHEDD, IN *CHANGES, BECOMING THE BEST YOU CAN BE*

B

Saying 'thanks' is an important key to building respect for one another. It will give you a sense of pride by making family members feel good and will help them feel appreciated for their efforts to be good parents.

At least once a week do something nice for family members. Any little thing will do, as long as they weren't expecting it and you get the message across that you'd like to make life a little easier for them.

One girl during her teenage years, would say to her parents now and then, 'This Friday I'm going to stay at home and baby-sit. You're going to go out and have a good time.' What do you suppose that did for their feelings towards her?

CHANGES, BECOMING THE BEST YOU CAN BE

C

Let us promise to say 'thank you' to family members at least once every day.

CHANGES, BECOMING THE BEST YOU CAN BE

Year 8:1

A

Everyone in your family deserves respect – just like you.

CHARLIE W. SHEDD, IN *CHANGES, BECOMING THE BEST YOU CAN BE*

B

Learn to talk and listen.
Yelling, pouting and running to your room in anger are not ways to improve your relationship with your parents. Just as you learn to accept and adjust to your friends, the same is true about your parents. You need to accept them and make adjustments for your differences. This probably won't happen without some honest and open talking – and listening.

Learn how to disagree.

Expect some disagreement. Don't be ashamed of anger. It's a natural part of being a thinking person. The only thing you need to regret is when you handle it badly. Learn how to keep your temper during a disagreement by staying in control and not raising your voice. Learn how to compromise and, above all, learn to say 'I'm sorry. I apologize.'

CHANGES, BECOMING THE BEST YOU CAN BE

C

All families have their good qualities. Focus on the good things in your family.

CHANGES, BECOMING THE BEST YOU CAN BE

Year 8:2

A

'I only talk to my friends. My parents don't understand me. Or they don't want to. They hassle me over decisions, choices, friends and everything. So I won't talk to them about important things.'

CHARLIE W. SHEDD, IN CHANGES, BECOMING THE BEST YOU CAN BE

B

To avoid some arguments, make a few agreements in advance. You could settle some questions, such as: Where can you go? What time will you be in? How much pocket money will you get? What work will you do around the house? How much privacy will they give you? Dozens of things can be settled in advance, rather than fought over later. Smart teenagers think ahead.

Ask for your parents' advice now and then on something big enough to make them feel important. There isn't a parent alive who wouldn't react favourably to the four words 'I need your help'. Parents really do know some things worth knowing. They would be flattered. And just think how that would improve feelings at home!

CHANGES, BECOMING THE BEST YOU CAN BE

C

Today I will look at things through the eyes of my family.

Year 8:3

A

'This may sound strange, but I really like it when I'm alone with my mum, the TV and radio are off, it's completely quiet and we're in the kitchen. We have to be in the kitchen. I don't know why, but I feel so comfortable just sitting late at night, chatting with my mum. You'd have to meet her to understand. She's the most honest, open, loving, sincere person that I know. And even when I'm mean and rotten and evil to her, I know she will always be there.'

CHARLIE W. SHEDD, IN *CHANGES, BECOMING THE BEST YOU CAN BE*

B

Families are changing today, but no matter what kind of family you have, it's one of the most important things in making you the person you are. One of the main ideas in this section is the need to appreciate our families – to love and support each other no matter what the family's problems may be.

No question about it – getting along with our families can be a real challenge. Some days everything seems OK, and other days it feels like a war zone. But that's normal. The key is to help make family relationships as good as they can be. Create more sunshine than thunder.

Trying to be understanding is a good start to improving any relationship. What it means is that you try to see things through the other person's eyes.

CHANGES, BECOMING THE BEST YOU CAN BE

C

If someone in my family needs a listening ear – let me be there.

Year 9:1

A

Always be honest. It's the best way to build trust in your family.

CHARLIE W. SHEDD, IN *CHANGES, BECOMING THE BEST YOU CAN BE*

B

There are many things that might become sore spots between parents and their children: money, jobs around the house, clothes, hair, homework, friends and lots of others. In fact, almost anything you mention could be a battleground. This can be especially true in families that are going through certain kinds of stress that are common in families today. It's even more important when your family is under stress for you to think about each other's needs and to be extra careful of each other's feelings. Otherwise, problems and conflicts are bound to arise.

Sometimes it may seem easy to lie our way out of trouble but it only puts up barriers. The first time you lie to your parents, you have put your foot on a dangerous road. It may be difficult to understand this until you are a parent. When your family loses faith in you and it's your fault, you have lost more than you would want to lose.

CHANGES, BECOMING THE BEST YOU CAN

C

Let me never do anything to betray their trust or make them question my honesty.

CHANGES, BECOMING THE BEST YOU CAN BE

Year 9:2

A

I like the family that can joke, have a good time together, communicate and love.

CHARLIE W. SHEDD, IN *CHANGES, BECOMING THE BEST YOU CAN BE*

B

Remember, there are times when you're not easy to live with either! If there is one thing as tough as being a teenager, it's having one. So when things get rough between you and your family, suppose you go and look in the mirror. You'll do a great thing for your future if you learn to start thinking about your 'people' problems by asking the question 'Where am I wrong?'

You can't always get everything you want. There are other people in the world besides you! You're at the age when you begin wanting more. You want to try new ideas, to feel more grown-up, to impress more people. But maybe you had better back off now and then to see the whole picture. Your family wants what's best for you. And they may be right, even if you can't see it.

The wise teenager doesn't try to win every argument. If you show your parents you're willing to give at times, you're being smart. They'll be more likely to co-operate when it's something that you really care about.

CHANGES, BECOMING THE BEST YOU CAN BE

C

Today I will listen to advice.

Year 9:3

A

Even parents need someone to listen to them, and an understanding child can be a great comfort.

B

Most families have times of stress and tension. Maybe there is a shortage of money, resulting in worry about the future, so parents are under pressure. Perhaps there has been an argument with insults and so far no one has made up. The wound just festers and gets worse, and those who have been hurt don't talk to each other.

Maybe there are problems at work, or a lack of work. All of these things cause people to be on edge and their normal level of patience is reduced. If you think about their needs, you might be able to understand the situation that parents find themselves in, and cope better.

C

Today I will try to show care and respect for my family.

Year 10:1

A

Honour your father and mother (which is the first commandment with a promise) that it may be well with you, and that you may live long on the earth.

EPHESIANS 6:2-3

B

Honour means to respect. Sometimes this might not be easy; nobody is perfect and so knowing our parents pretty well we can easily spot their faults (as they can see ours). However, there must be some form of order in a family for it to work, so if we start to show respect by listening to our parents and asking them to listen to us, then our whole family situation could run more smoothly.

We learn a lot of things at school but we are not taught how to be parents. Our parents have not had this teaching either. They have picked up a few hints from their own parents, but the value of that depends on how wise their parents were. Parenting is an extremely important role, yet we tend to pick it up as we go along. Go easy on your parents if they have made some mistakes along the way. One day you may be a parent yourself.

C

Today I will show respect and try to understand my parents.

Year 10:2

A

Each of you shall return to his own property, and each of you shall return to his family.

LEVITICUS 25:10

B

When this was written to the Hebrews, family and property were tied together. Family meant everyone related to you, aunts, uncles, cousins, grandparents etc. Their family groups were massive in number.

In this country family groups were a lot closer until recent years. A speaker on TV explained how her grandparents, aunts and uncles all lived in the same village. She did not dare get into trouble because someone would see her.

It might seem a loss of freedom, but only now do we realize that it gave greater freedom. There were few worries about 'strangers', since there were plenty of family members to keep an eye on you.

Today many of us belong to the modern family i.e. parents and children, usually far away from grandparents, aunts, uncles and cousins. Jobs, training, career structures have caused a lot of people to move from their family area. It seemed the smart thing to do. Now some people are reconsidering this. The extended family can enrich and support our lives.

C

Today I will make an effort to keep in touch with my extended family.

Year 10:3

A

However tough and hard and independent you may be, there are moments when you have to have help.

LORD TEBBIT

B

We choose our friends but not our families, perhaps that is why we sometimes have to work at our relationships within the family. Sometimes the problem is that we are too similar in character to our parents and being too alike, we clash. At other times we are too opposite in character and have expectations that cannot be fulfilled.

However, over the years we need to build up relationships with the different members of our family. By overcoming problems and antagonism we make our family links stronger, then when we need help or advice we do not have far to look. We will have a group ready to stand by us and support us.

C

Today I will appreciate my family.

Year 11:1

A

I really like my family, I'm glad that I'm not in any other one.

NINA DAVISON, AGED 12

B

Family can mean brothers and sisters who fight with us, parents who annoy us and relations who patronize us. But most of all it means 'belonging'. It is being part of a group that is special to us and to whom we are unique.

Throughout life we learn, grow and change, this applies to all members of the family not just the children. Because we are not static there will be times when we are in conflict with other members of the family. Just as cars on the road get too close and bump into one another, so in families there will be times of friction when we get in the way of each other. This is all part of belonging and being on the road together.

C.

I am glad that I belong to a special group.

Year 11:2

A

We never know the love of our parents for us till we have become parents.

HENRY WARD BEECHAM, IN *THE DECADES BOOK OF BIRTHDAYS*

B

Teenage years are so often the time that children fall out with their parents. The parents know the child so well, they also know the pitfalls in life and they want to protect their offspring. The relationship between the parent and child can develop into twenty questions – Where are you going? – Who with? – When will you be in? etc.

The teenager does not see it as protection but gross interference with their life. The difficulty arises because the parent has loved and cared for the child for so many years, and they have no button to switch off suddenly. In fact do we really want our parents to switch off?

When we have children of our own it is easier to understand the feelings that our parents have for us.

C

I will try to appreciate the feelings of those who care for me.

Year 11:3

A

When I was a boy of fourteen, my father was so ignorant I could hardly stand to have him around. But when I got to be twenty-one, I was astonished at how much he had learned in seven years.

MARK TWAIN

B

Mark Twain's quote is rather tongue in cheek. He knew full well that his father had not learned a great deal more in the seven years, it was rather that Mark Twain had matured and understood his father so much better.

A study of a group of people every seven years of their life showed that usually from 14–21 they rebelled against all their parents stood for. However, by the time they were 28, they were, of their own volition, living the life their parents originally wanted for them.

We might not all attain that but it does show that, like Mark Twain, we can come to a point when we will understand our parents, and get beyond the parent/child relationship, to one of mutual respect and friendship.

C

Today I will look for the wisdom in the members of my family.

13 INTERCULTURAL HARMONY

Year 7:1

A

'You comin' out, Boxer?' his friends asked. 'There's a patrol of Brits movin' down the street. We got a few stones to bounce off their skulls.'

Boxer and his gang were ordinary boys living in a tough, working-class area of Belfast, in sunless red-brick streets, with few green playing fields. Games of cops and robbers had been replaced by live war-games – stoning the British troops on patrol in the area. It was a fairly safe game as the army couldn't hit back provided the boys stuck to stones and nothing worse.

Boxer, a leading spirit, usually enjoyed the glamour of the games as much as his friends. But now he stood silent.

'What's the matter?' they asked. 'Gettin' scared?'

'No – but if I stone the Brits, I shan't be allowed back at Corrymeela.' One week of glorious holiday at Corrymeela had had its effect on Boxer.

MARY BATCHELOR'S EVERYDAY BOOK

B

Corrymeela is a Christian community in Northern Ireland dedicated to the work of peace and reconciliation. Both Protestants and Roman Catholics are involved, and while there are branches in Belfast and elsewhere, the centre itself is a beautiful house on the Antrim coast. It provides a holiday for children and adults away from bombs and fighting, where they can learn to live with those they once thought enemies.

MARY BATCHELOR'S EVERYDAY BOOK

C

Today I will let go of my 'offensive thoughts' and choose peace and harmony instead.

Year 7:2

A

We are always wrong when we do not respect the personalities of other people. We want for ourselves, the right and the opportunity to be our best. We must also want for all others the right and opportunity to be their best. It is in this way that we ought to love others.

ADAPTED FROM HERBERT LEGGATE, *ON THE WAY*

B

The human race is a huge mixture of personalities. Sometimes we can pass judgement and be critical of people we do not know at all. For example, a person who looks successful or speaks well; we can think: 'I don't like that person, she seems too posh and stuck up.' In fact, everybody needs acceptance and respect.

C

I will accept and respect the people I meet today.

Year 7:3

A

Remember the story of the great big enormous turnip? It grew so large that the man who planted the seed could not pull up the turnip that grew. So he called his wife but together they couldn't do it. They had extra help from the boy ... and the dog ... and the cat ... and the mouse. As the mouse added his strength the turnip came up and the mouse said, 'I did it!'

But did the mouse do it? It was the combined effort of everyone that made it possible. It was too much for any of them to do alone. So we find in so many things that we just cannot succeed on our own. We have to work together with other people. It is not the goal-scorer who wins a hockey match but the team working together that enabled the person to score. No individual can make a school into a good school; it is dependent upon everyone working to that end.

ADAPTED FROM ROWLAND PURTON, *ASSEMBLIES*

B

Whether in the tutor group, school, village, town, city, country or world; there is a need for people to work together in order to achieve peace, fulfilment and harmony.

But in reality some people are not treated fairly: opportunities are sometimes only open to certain people; resources may not be shared out properly and some people are taken advantage of by others.

Respecting the rights of others, regardless of racial origin, colour, religion or sex is an important value to uphold.

C

Today I will look for opportunities of working together with others in order to bring harmony to my world.

Year 8:1

A

A young, white man who was blind from birth fell in love with a black woman. All went well until a friend told him that the woman was black. At that minute he lost interest in her. Too bad! He had been 'seeing' her very well. It was his friend who was blind.

ADAPTED FROM ANTHONY DE MELLO, *THE HEART OF THE ENLIGHTENED*

B

Sometimes people react not to reality, but to ideas in their heads. They don't see what is there, but what they've been trained to see.

All too frequently, we can see people not as they are, but as we think they should be like. Instead of meeting the real person, we deal with an image in our heads. But where do these images come from?

ADAPTED FROM ANTHONY DE MELLO, *THE HEART OF THE ENLIGHTENED*

C

I will make an effort to see clearly today.

Year 8:2

A

Be tolerant with one another and forgiving, if any of you has cause for complaint: you must forgive as the Lord forgave you. Finally, to bind everything together and complete the whole, there must be love. Let Christ's peace be arbiter in your decisions, the peace to which you were called as members of a single body. Always be thankful. Let the gospel of Christ dwell among you in all its richness; teach and instruct one another with all the wisdom it gives you. With psalms and hymns and spiritual songs, sing from the heart in gratitude to God.

COLOSSIANS 3:13–16

B

St Paul gave this advice on the right kind of attitude to life.

On 10 October 1977, it was announced that the 1976 Nobel Prize for Peace had been awarded to two women who thought of themselves as ordinary people doing what they ought to do.

One day in August 1976 a terrorist getaway car hit and killed three children aged eight, two and six weeks. People everywhere were shocked. The aunt of the three children, Mairead (Maree'ad) Corrigan and Betty Williams, herself a mother of four children, decided they would do something. They formed the Ulster Peace Movement.

In spite of threats from terrorists they demanded peace. They were ill-treated and abused but became even more determined. They spoke at rallies and they organized marches. Soon they had thousands of followers.

When the award was announced, Mairead said, 'Nobel was the man who invented dynamite. We hope to change things without dynamite. We haven't brought peace to Northern Ireland yet – but if we've managed to save just one life I'm extremely happy.'

ROWLAND PURTON, *ASSEMBLIES*

C

I am determined to see people and situations differently. I can see peace and love instead of fear and hate.

Year 8:3

A

I sought my soul, my soul I could not see;
I sought my God, but God eluded me;
I sought my neighbour – and I found all three.

ADAPTED FROM *AN ANTHOLOGY OF HOPE*

B

It was Easter Day and the people of Buenos Aires in Argentina went to the cathedral expecting the usual Easter message. But Bishop Benavente preached mainly about peace. To many people it came as a surprise because everyone was talking about war – war with their neighbouring country, Chile, over some lakes and land high in the Andes mountains on the border between the two countries.

Many people disagreed with the bishop but some thought he was right. One who was pleased to hear what the bishop had said was

Bishop Java of Chile. Of course, it was wrong and un-Christian to fight about such things. And so he travelled up and down his country also calling for peace.

As more and more people took notice of the two bishops, the governments too decided to talk and they invited King Edward VII of Britain to sort out their problem, which he did. They agreed that this would be the best way to sort out future problems.

Now in one of his sermons, Bishop Benavente had said, 'I should like to see Christ standing between the two peoples, guiding and leading them.' A woman named Angela de Costa remembered that and raised the money to build a huge statue of Jesus Christ and set it up on one of the mountain peaks. On 13 March 1904, the people of both countries gathered for the unveiling ceremony and heard the prayer 'that these mountains may crumble into dust before the peoples of Argentina and Chile break the peace which, at the feet of Christ, they have given their word to keep.'

And so the statue, 'The Christ of the Andes', stands today as a symbol of peace and a reminder of those who worked many years ago to keep the peace.

ROWLAND PURTON, *ASSEMBLIES*

C

Today I will look for peaceful ways to settle my differences with others.

Year 9:1

A

Harmony exists in difference no less than in likeness.

MARGARET FULLER, IN *EACH DAY A NEW BEGINNING* (29 JULY)

B

Harmony exists everywhere. Our personal attitudes bring the disharmony to a situation. An attitude of love can bless all situations and all people.

The opposite is true. We all desire harmony in our relation-ships. And we will find it, if we want it.

How we feel, today, about this person or that situation, reflects how we feel about ourselves. We can see people and situations differently by changing our minds about what we want to see. We will observe harmony, then, even in the mid-dle of what appears to be an unfriendly situation.

ADAPTED FROM *EACH DAY A NEW BEGINNING* (29 JULY)

C

Harmony is everywhere. I will celebrate it today.

EACH DAY A NEW BEGINNING (29 JULY)

Year 9:2

A

What is he?
– A man of course.
Yes, but what does he do?
– He lives and is a man.
Oh quite! But he must work. He must have a job of some sort.
– Why?
Because obviously he's not one of the leisured classes.
– I don't know. He has lots of leisure. And he makes quite beautiful chairs
There you are then. He's a cabinet maker.
– No, no!
But you said so.
– What did I say?
That he made chairs and was a joiner and carpenter.
– I said he made chairs, but I did not say he was a carpenter.
All right then, he's just an amateur.
– Perhaps. Would you say a thrush was a professional flautist or just an amateur?

I'd say it was just a bird.
– And I say he is just a man.
All right! You always did quibble.

D.H. LAWRENCE

B

It is very easy to put people into boxes and treat them as types rather than seeing them as individuals. It is very easy to tie a label on people: black, white, Asian, AIDS victim, teacher or student – and judge them not by what they are within themselves, but by what they do or what they look like. Instead all people should be treated with respect, regardless of racial origin, colour, religion or sex and the use of offensive words should be avoided.

C

I can see people differently by changing my mind about what I want to see. Today I am responsible for what I see.

ADAPTED FROM *LOVE IS LETTING GO OF FEAR*

Year 9:3

A

A great many people think they are thinking when they are merely rearranging their prejudices.

WILLIAM JAMES, IN *DAYS OF HEALING, DAYS OF JOY* (20 MAY)

B

We may have destructive prejudices – not only against people of other colours or faiths, but also against ourselves. We could imagine that we know all about the characteristics and qualities of other people and ourselves. Like all prejudices, these 'certainties' are based on ignorance and lack of reflection.

Real thinking challenges ignorance and preconceived

opinions. 'Who says?' and 'What's the basis of that idea?' are questions that thinkers ask. 'I just know' and 'That's what they always told me' are answers thinkers won't accept.

Under thoughtful examination, the evidence we've held against others and ourselves often proves to be 99 per cent hearsay – other people and I are not who my prejudices say we are.

ADAPTED FROM *DAYS OF HEALING, DAYS OF JOY* (MAY 20)

C

Today I will challenge any negative judgements I make about other people or myself.

Year 10:1

A

Christian teaching:	*Treat others as you would like them to treat you.*
Buddhist teaching:	*I will act towards others exactly as I would act towards myself.*
Hindu teaching:	*This is the sun of duty: Do naught to others which, if done to thee, could cause thee pain.*
Jewish teaching:	*What is harmful to yourself do not to your fellow men.*
Muslim teaching:	*None of you 'truly' believe, until he wishes for his brothers what he wishes for himself.*

JOE JENKINS, *INTRODUCING MORAL ISSUES*

B

Although the main religions of the world have developed at different times and in different places, they have this in common: they all teach that we should treat others as we ourselves would like to be treated.

If we all lived by this code of conduct, then the world could be a much happier place.

ADAPTED FROM *INTRODUCING MORAL ISSUES*

C

Today I will try to treat others as I would like to be treated.

ADAPTED FROM *INTRODUCING MORAL ISSUES*

Year 10:2

A

As much as you can, Camera, see people as human and as individuals first who have been socialised into their cultural claims. As a young boy, I was well aware that whites judged me not as an individual but according to what they believed about blacks in general. You must not do the same to others.

ARTHUR ASHE, FROM A LETTER TO HIS DAUGHTER, CAMERA, *DAYS OF GRACE*

B

'Differences' do not mean 'problems'. Schools are places where young people from a wide range of backgrounds come together each day for the purpose of learning. One of the most important aspects of education is learning to live in harmony with others, irrespective of their sex, race, religion or accent.

C

Today I will look to what unites rather than divides me from others.

Year 10:3

A

Reality is what we take to be true.

What we take to be true is what we believe.
What we believe is based upon what we see.
What we see depends upon what we look for.
What we look for depends upon what we think.
What we think depends upon what we see.
What we see determines what we believe.
What we take to be true is our reality.

ADAPTED FROM GARY ZUKAV, *NEW METHODS IN RE TEACHING*

B

It is very easy for us to be blinkered, believing that our picture of reality is so obvious that it is the only possible view. It doesn't always occur to us that what we see is our interpretation of the world around us.

Our experiences and images of other people are affected and influenced by what we have learned from others: parents, teachers, friends, the media. It is easy to make assumptions about people of the opposite sex, or of another ethnic group, culture or religion.

Developing a sympathetic understanding of other people's cultures, religions and life-stances; that is being able to see or imagine ourselves in the other person's place is very important.

ADAPTED FROM *NEW METHODS IN RE TEACHING – AN EXPERIENTIAL APPROACH*

C

Today I will try to understand other people.

Year 11:1

A

During my lifetime I have dedicated my life to this struggle of the African people. I have fought against white domination, and I have fought against black domination. I have cherished the ideal of a democratic and free society in which all persons live together in harmony with equal opportunities. It is an ideal which I hope to live for, and to see realized. But my Lord, if needs be, it is an ideal for which I am prepared to die.

NELSON MANDELA, THE RIVONIA TRIAL, OCTOBER 1963

B

Nelson Mandela spent ten thousand days in prison. On 11 February 1990, he was released from Pollsmoor Prison just outside Cape Town. There was intense media attention on the event. An estimated billion viewers watched his release on television.

By 1994, he had made the incredible journey from prisoner to president. Such a transition would have unsettled many, but not Nelson Mandela. His inner strength, wisdom and vision helped him to withstand the colossal adjustments to his life. At an age when many people are well into retirement, Nelson Mandela toured the world, sharing his vision of peace through negotiation, love and forgiveness. All the world now watches as the drama unfolds in South Africa. Before our very eyes, we are witnessing his dream of intercultural harmony becoming a reality.

C

I will consider the ideal of living in a democratic and free society in which all persons live together in harmony with equal opportunities.

Year 11:2

A

The development of a kind heart (a feeling of closeness for all human beings) does not involve the religiosity we normally associate with conventional religious practice. It is not only for people who believe in religion, but is for everyone regardless of race, religion or political affiliation. It is for anyone who considers himself or herself, above all, a member of the human family and who sees things from a larger and longer perspective.

THE DALAI LAMA, IN *A HUMAN APPROACH TO WORLD PEACE*

B

Tensin Gyatso is the religious and political leader of Tibet. He is better known as The Dalai Lama. He has lived in exile since 1959, due to the Chinese occupation of his country.

The Dalai Lama travels to many countries, meeting their leaders and giving lectures on world peace. His message is simple and from the heart. He talks about the need for compassion and tolerance of others. He doesn't see 'foreigners', he sees people – members of the human family.

He knows that peace and harmony will come about when enough people have 'a good heart'.

C

Today I will endeavour to be compassionate and tolerant towards others.

Year 11:3

A

I am the same as any other human being … I am the child, the sinner, the saint, the one who hopes and the one who despairs, the one who can feel joy and the one who can feel sadness. I discover that only the thought concepts, the customs, the surface are different, and that the human substance is the same.

ERICH FROMM, *BEYOND THE CHAINS OF ILLUSION*

B

Fear is stopping us from seeing strangers as neighbours. If we can let go of fear and love our neighbours as ourselves, then there is real hope for humankind. The place to begin is to accept and love ourselves.

When we love ourselves, we can give up the need to control others; to feel more powerful than others; to win, over others; to feel more superior than others; to feel that our way is the right and only way'.

In order for intercultural harmony and peace to become a reality, we need to transcend our fear of different cultures, customs and beliefs.

C

I will endeavour to accept and respect other ways of life.

14 CHRISTMAS

Year 7:1

A

And the angel said unto them, Fear not: for behold I bring you good tidings of great joy.

LUKE 2:10

B

Several hundred years before Jesus was born, the Jewish prophets began to explain to the rest of the people that God was going to send someone special, a new leader, who would be like their great King David. This is what they said:

'For to us a child is born
To us a son is given
And the government will be upon his shoulders
And he will be called
Wonderful Counsellor,
Mighty God,
Everlasting Father,
The Prince of Peace.' (Isaiah 9:6–7)

Christmas is a time when we all would long for peace, in ourselves, in our family, in our country and in the world.

C

Today I will try to live at peace with all I meet.

Year 7:2

A

Glory to God in the highest, and on earth peace to men.

LUKE 2:14

B

If you ever visit the Imperial War Museum, you will see as you enter the World War I section, a collection of letters and diaries. They all recount a very unusual Christmas. Both sides of the war were fighting in the trenches. If anyone was brave enough to lift their head above the trenches they would be shot. This had gone on for months and now Christmas had arrived. Then the sound of carols was heard. The German soldiers were singing, the Allies joined in. The men eventually trusted each other, came out of the trenches, played football together, chatted and shared photographs.

The power of the peace of Christmas was greater than the power of war.

C

Let us look for opportunities to be peacemakers today.

Year 7:3

A

You shall find the babe wrapped in swaddling clothes and lying in a manger.

LUKE 2:12

B

Suppose Jesus had been born in modern times. How might the story have gone? This is the beginning of one boy's version:

'The lights splashed off the neon lighting on to the puddles in the street. The double-decker bus jerked and two muffled figures swung off shoulder to shoulder and made their way to the park gates. Mary, one of the couple, groaned, "Never mind, Mary," said Josh, "we'll find some place."

They saw ahead, through the growing darkness of the wind-swept, mid-winter afternoon, a small summer-house and went in. Inside there was that typical disgusting smell, and the cold concrete floor was covered with litter. Josh took off his camel-coloured duffle coat and spread it over Mary, who had lain down on the carved-up green park seat. Then he sat down beside her and tried to comfort her, but in the dark it was difficult to sound cheerful, and he fell silent.'

Sometimes the tinsel, the presents and the food block out the dirt and poverty of the first Christmas.

C

Today I will be aware of the needs of others.

Year 8:1

A

But when did I see you hungry and feed you...

MATTHEW 25:37

B

There is a story of a fourth wise man who brought a sapphire, a ruby and a pearl to give to the new baby king. As he went to meet his companions he was delayed as he stopped to help a dying man. This meant that he had to sell the sapphire to buy food for him.

He reached Bethlehem too late, Mary, Joseph and the child had gone to Egypt to avoid Herod. As Herod's soldiers killed all boys of two and under, the wise man gave the ruby to bribe the soldiers to not kill a child.

He searched for years for the baby that was born to be king. On one occasion he gave a father his last remaining gift, the pearl to stop his daughter being sold into slavery.

The years passed by, and Jesus was on the cross when at last he found him. But he had no gift to give but Jesus had already received his gifts. 'In as much as you did it for the least of my brothers and sisters you did it for me.'

C
Let me be willing to give when help is needed.

Year 8:2

A
Still the night, holy the night!
Sleeps the world; hid from sight,
Mary and Joseph in stable bare
Watch o'er the Child beloved and fair,
Sleeping in heavenly rest!

JOSEPH MOHR

B
The well-known Christmas story tells how Mary laid her son in a manger, because there was no room for them in the inn. Today many people who live on the streets must feel that there is no room for them either.

Throughout the year, people all over the country have been organising a special Christmas Cracker. It is not a gaudily decorated cardboard tube filled with worthless gifts, but a year-long effort of fund raising so that people who live on the streets can have a decent Christmas dinner and a warm bed for the night.

C
May I be selfless this Christmas.

Year 8:3

A

Christmas isn't Christmas till it happens in your heart.
Somewhere deep inside you is where Christmas really starts.

CAROL OWENS

B

Christmas was a time when the collection boxes in church were opened and the money given to the poor. In Warwickshire it was the custom for the farmers to give flour to the poor to make their Christmas bread.

Times have changed but there are still plenty of people in need of help. Christmas is a time of gifts and giving. We do not have to look far to find Christmas cards that are sold in aid of a charity, stockings or collecting boxes in shops. We can show our thankfulness for all we have by giving to others.

ADAPTED FROM ROWLAND PURTON, *ASSEMBLIES*

C

Let us be thankful today for all the good things that we have.

Year 9:1

A

They brought out their gifts of gold, frankincense and myrrh and presented them to him.

MATTHEW 2:11

B

Strange gifts to give a baby! The wise men came from a land far away to worship Jesus and present their gifts. Each gift had a significance of its own.

One man thought that the child would be a king and gave

gold as a fitting gift. The second saw the child as a great priest and gave frankincense, a symbol of praise. The third gave myrrh, a perfume used on the dying or dead. He saw that the child, when a man, would sacrifice his life.

Here, at the beginning of Jesus' life, his role in the Christian faith as King, Priest and sacrifice is revealed.

C

May I be willing to give wisely this Christmas.

Year 9:2

A

See Him lying on a bed of straw;
a draughty stable with an open door;
Mary cradling the babe she bore –
the Prince of glory is His name.

MICHAEL PERRY, IN *MISSION PRAISE*

B

A place of birth is a significant thing. Children can be born in palaces, stately homes, caravans, refugee camps, hospitals or houses. Our place of birth can make a statement about us. So what is the significance for Christians of their Lord being born in a humble stable? It tells them that although he is their Lord he can be approached by anyone, whoever they are, whatever their background. The shepherds and the wise men had equal access to the stable.

C

May I become more approachable.

Year 9:3

A

When they saw the child with his mother Mary, they knelt down and worshipped him.

MATTHEW 2:11

B

Instead of asking you what you are getting for Christmas, I am asking you to consider what you are giving this Christmas, because real giving always means something more than the gift.

One Christmas Santa Claus brought me a toy engine. I took it with me to the convent and played with it while mother and the old nuns discussed old times. But it was a young nun who brought us in to see the crib. When I saw the Holy Child in the manger I was very distressed because, little as I had, he had nothing at all. For me it was fresh proof of the incompetence of Santa Claus. I asked the young nun politely if the Holy Child didn't like toys, and she replied composedly enough: 'Oh, he does, but his mother is too poor to afford them.'

That settled it. My mother was poor too, but at Christmas she at least managed to buy me something, even if it was only a box of crayons. I distinctly remember getting into the crib and putting the engine between his outstretched arms. I probably showed him how to wind it as well, because a small baby like that would not be clever enough to know. I remember too the tearful feeling of reckless generosity with which I left him there in the nightly darkness of the chapel, clutching my toy engine to his chest.

FRANK O'CONNOR, IN *GET TOGETHER*

C

May our lives be a gift to those around us.

Year 10:1

A

There was the true light which, coming into the world, enlightens everyone.

JOHN 1:9

B

For many people Christmas begins when the term ends and the holidays start.

Christians prepare themselves for Christmas during Advent. This starts on the fourth Sunday before Christmas Day. Advent means 'arrival'. Most churches have a wreath with five candles attached to it. Each Sunday one of the candles is lit until Christmas Day when all five are alight together.

Sometimes there are candle-lit services, where everybody carries a candle and their flickering light is the only light in the church. This is all to symbolize Jesus Christ being born as the light, to shine in the darkness caused by the world's greed, oppression, suffering and pain. Sometimes it does not seem possible that the birth of a baby could have such an impact, but 2000 years later the candle flame of love flickers on, always ready to ignite new lights.

C

Today I will look for the light in the world.

Year 10:2

A

The light shines in the darkness, but the darkness has not overcome it.

JOHN 1:5

B

There is nothing to suggest that Jesus was born on 25

December. It was not possible to find out the exact date, so a date was chosen which was already a time of celebration.

We do know that Jesus was born in Bethlehem, probably in wintertime, during the reign of the Roman Emperor Augustus. Herod was King of Judaea and was suffering failing health; the last thing he wanted was a new 'King of the Jews'. He knew where to find the child because the scriptures had foretold that it would be in Bethlehem. He planned to kill the child but was too late and in a rage killed 200 innocent children. He tried to put out the 'light' but he failed.

It is difficult to make a room completely dark. Even if all the windows are blacked out and the door shut, the light manages to creep in through the slightest crack. And if we do manage to black out a room it takes only a small candle flame to dispel the darkness, because light can always overcome darkness, but darkness can never overcome light.

C

May I see the light in the darkness.

Year 10:3

A

Joy to the world! The Lord has come,
Let earth receive her King.
Let every heart prepare Him room,
And heaven and nature sing.

ISAAC WATTS

B

For many people Christmas means presents, holidays, lots of food. But it has not always been like this. When the Puritans ruled Britain they disapproved of all the jollity. Consequently in 1652 an Act of Parliament was passed that cancelled

Christmas. It had to be treated as a normal day, there was to be no special food, no church attendance and work went on as usual.

During a lesson on Christmas, two groups of teenagers discussed their feelings about the subject. One group still felt all the excitement of Christmas and loved the atmosphere. They loved the surprise of the presents, they did not care if they cost a lot or not.

The other group was cynical; the magic had gone, there were no surprises any more. This group had cancelled Christmas themselves.

C

Today I will think of what I can do to make Christmas special to those around me.

Year 11:1

A

Even though by New Year's Eve the starving might have died;
Even though the lonely may have thoughts of suicide;
Even though from want, or war, a million children hide;
Self-indulgence, gluttony, can both be justified –
It's Christmas!

Even though society's engaged in senseless wars;
Even though communities are slaughtered without cause;
Even though humanity's ignoring humane laws;
Think of crackers, cakes and custard, cards and Santa Claus –
It's Christmas!

Even though I don't believe in greed or selfishness;
Even though I hate to see my fellow in distress;
Even though I normally might think my world a mess;
As usual, these next few days, I'll think a little less –

It's Christmas!
GORDON BAILEY, *PLASTIC WORLD*

B

This hard-hitting poem about Christmas makes us aware that although Christmas is a time of celebration, for many people it highlights their loneliness, suffering and need.

The first Christmas highlighted the similar issues of poverty, oppression and greed. Perhaps to be truly in the spirit of Christmas we should address these issues.

C

I will remember others at Christmas.

Year 11:2

A

If Jesus was born today
it would be in a downtown motel
marked by a helicopter's flashing bulb.
A traffic warden, working late,
would be the first upon the scene.
Later, at the expense of a TV network,
an eminent sociologist,
the host of a chat show
and a controversial actor
would arrive with their good wishes
– the whole occasion to be filmed as part of the
'Is this the Son of God?' one-hour special.
Childhood would be a blur of photographs
and speculation
dwindling by His late teens into
'Where is He Now?' features in Sunday magazines.

STEVE TURNER, *UP TO DATE*

B

The stark reality of the Christmas story has been glamorized into a chocolate box scene. There was no room at the inn, but the rough draughty stable has been turned into a cosy thatched cottage. The smelly animals are made pristine clean, with warm comforting faces. The unusual location even fooled the wise men who went to the palace looking for the King. But being born in the most humble of circumstances means that no one can say to Jesus, you don't understand what I have been through.

C

I will look beyond the tinsel to the true meaning of Christmas.

Year 11:3

A

A Time for Peace
Christmas is a time for peace.
Peace in the world,
peace in the nation,
peace in the home,
peace in our hearts.
We all long for peace.
The first Christmas brought
a message of peace
for the whole world.

NAVAL AND MILITARY BIBLE SOCIETY

B

What a stroke of genius to use a baby as a symbol of peace. The political activist looked for a military commander, the priesthood looked for a religious leader, the wise men looked for a royal king. What they were given was a baby with a very ordinary background. Who can take offence at a baby? It has no power to hurt, it depends upon others totally for its survival, it is capable only of loving and being loved. Surely this is the most powerful symbol of all.

C

This Christmas I will seek to behave in a more loving and peaceful way.

15 Living in the Moment

Year 7:1

A

When I am anxious it is because I am living in the future.
When I am depressed it is because I am living in the past.

JIMMY R, IN *DAYS OF HEALING, DAYS OF JOY* (16 NOVEMBER)

B

The following words of advice were given by the *Independent* newspaper to students about to take examinations.

'After the exam avoid the post-mortem syndrome. There is nothing you can do to improve the marks on the paper you have just taken. Instead, concentrate on the next exam. There is something you can do to influence the marks on that.'

Sometimes we can apply this advice to other situations in life. We can spend a lot of time thinking, talking and worrying about mistakes we have made, when the time is passed and there is nothing that we can do about them. The past is over. This instant is the only time there is. Surely then, it is better if we put our energy into what we are doing now, where we will still have the opportunity to give of our best.

C

I will let go of the past by learning from it.

Year 7:2

A

The future is made of the same stuff as the present.

SIMONE WEIL, IN *EACH DAY A NEW BEGINNING* (18 SEPTEMBER)

B

Tomorrow I will be better, tomorrow I will do my work, tomorrow I will start my diet, tomorrow I will get myself organized. Everything is going to happen tomorrow, that is until tomorrow becomes today.

Nothing is – but now. When we spend our time thinking about what was, or what may be, we are cutting off the present – the now.

The only reality is the present, because it is only in the present that we can contribute to life, to our life and to the lives of those around us. The present holds all we need to fulfil our lives.

C

I will let go of the past and the future. My only reality is here, now.

Year 7:3

A

So do not worry about tomorrow; it will have enough worries of its own. There is no need to add to the troubles each day brings.

MATTHEW 6:34

B

It is easy to hang on to yesterday's problems. Or perhaps we try to see too far ahead. Each day brings along new experiences, and each day we are given the strength to deal with those experiences. As we deal with each experience so we grow without even realizing it. We need not worry about the future. It will offer us whatever it will, but it cannot do so until we have experienced these 24 hours before us.

C

Today I will enjoy each moment.

Year 8:1

A

Hey, try to open up your heart
To beauty; go to the woods someday
And weave a wreath of memory there.
Then if the tears obscure your way
You'll know how wonderful it is
To be alive.

ANONYMOUS, 1941, IN *I NEVER SAW ANOTHER BUTTERFLY*

B

This is the third verse of a poem called 'Birdsong'. Each verse celebrates some aspect of beauty in the world. It was written by a child in a place called Terezin, which is 60 kilometres from Prague. In 1941 when this poem was written, Terezin was a holding camp for Jews. They were kept there before being moved on again to the extermination camps. They stayed at Terezin between three months and two years. Fifteen thousand children passed through Terezin but only one hundred returned.

The children saw all the evil things that happened at Terezin, the hard labour, the queues for food, the beatings and the executions – but they saw beyond that, they saw the beauty in the world around them and they rejoiced in being alive.

C

I will enjoy every moment of my day.

Year 8:2

A

Terezin is full of beauty.
It's in your eyes now clear
And through the street the tramp
Of many marching feet I hear.

In the ghetto at Terezin
It looks that way to me
Is a square kilometre of earth
Cut off from the world that's free.

MIROSLAV KOSEK, IN *I NEVER SAW ANOTHER BUTTERFLY*

B

If you visit an art gallery, you will probably be amazed at how the artist has captured a moment, or a quality of texture on canvas. Some of the paintings are so alive that you feel as if you could reach out and touch the object on the canvas.

Artists and poets have a great gift for taking a moment in time, or a scene and capturing it for us all to enjoy.

C

Today I will appreciate the beauty around me.

Year 8:3

A

What is this life if, full of care,
We have no time to stand and stare

FROM WILLIAM HENRY DAVIES, 'LEISURE'

B

At times our lives seem only concerned with 'what happens next'. When is the next lesson, what will we be doing next, what time is lunch, what have we got this afternoon etc? Slowly we wish our life away, obsessed with the next thing. By doing this we are missing out on the 'now', we are not making the most of the present.

When the leaves on the trees turn to their beautiful autumnal colours it is no good thinking, 'I will look at them next week', because by the next week they could be on the ground, dirty and dishevelled. We need to make the most of each day as it happens and experience it fully, drink in all the sights and sounds around us.

C

Today I will take time to stand and stare.

Year 9:1

A

Can any of you live a bit longer by worrying about it.

MATTHEW 6:27

B

In an old black and white film Groucho Marx said that there was no such thing as a problem. His reasoning was that if there is something bothering you, either it can be changed so that it doesn't bother you or it stays. In which case it isn't a problem but a fact which has to be accepted.

Maybe when we change the things that we can, and come to terms with the things that we can't change, we will then free ourselves to enjoy each moment for itself.

C

Today I will look at the problems in my life with new insight.

Year 9:2

A

Give me a mind that is not bored,
That does not whimper, whine, or sigh;
Don't let me worry overmuch
About the fussy thing called I.
Give me a sense of humour, Lord,
Give me the grace to see a joke,
To get some happiness from life
And pass it on to other folk.

PART OF A PRAYER FOUND IN CHESTER CATHEDRAL

B

Some people worry their life away, it becomes a habit. They worry that certain things will not happen, that other things will happen, and when everything turns out all right they are looking for the next obstacle on the horizon to start worrying about. They cannot actually enjoy life as there is too much to worry about.

In contrast we occasionally meet people who are overflowing with joy and happiness. Nothing seems to phase them. They always seem interested in other people and their happiness is infectious. Are their problems different or less than others? No. What is different is their attitude to life, making the most of each day and sharing it with others.

C

Today I will try to pass some happiness on to those around me.

Year 9:3

A

This is why I tell you not to be worried about the food and drink you

need in order to stay alive, or about clothes for your body. After all, isn't
life worth more than food? And isn't the body worth more than clothes?

MATTHEW 6:25

B

We live in a consumer society and every day we are bombarded
with advertisements on the TV showing us the latest products.
They usually imply that the product will not only make us
look good but also make us popular with those around us. It is
easy to get drawn into the race to acquire the latest trendy
clothes or gadgets.

Our perspective can become distorted. Like the small child
who ignores a present to play with the wrapping paper, we get
caught up with the peripheral things of life and miss the enjoyment of simply being alive.

C

Today I will be content with my possessions.

Year 10:1

A

Lost, yesterday, somewhere between sunrise and sunset,
two golden hours, each set with sixty diamond minutes.
No reward is offered, for they are gone for ever.

HORACE MANN, IN *DICTIONARY OF QUOTATIONS AND*
PROVERBS

B

Time is precious. Once it has gone we cannot retrieve it. Nor
can we collect it together to save it for a more appropriate
occasion. Like the sands in an hour glass, time slips easily by
and just as the sands cannot be pushed back up to the top of
the glass, so time cannot be reversed to start again.

We can feel trapped in time if we don't make the most of each precious moment.

C

Today I will value each hour.

Year 10:2

A

Yesterday will not be called again.

16TH-CENTURY PROVERB, IN *DICTIONARY OF QUOTATIONS AND PROVERBS*

B

Sometimes this can be a happy thought because we have had such a bad day that we are glad that it will never be called again. If we have had such a day it is good to let go of it, and not to torment ourselves by going over the details in our thoughts.

However, it may be that the writer was not thinking of this, but reminding the reader that each day offers its own opportunity. Life can be full of regrets, wishing that we had done something, or said something. We can find peace by letting go of the past.

C

I will make the most of today.

Year 10:3

A

I expect to pass through this world but once. Any good thing therefore that I can do, or any kindness that I can show to any fellow-creature, let me do it now, let me not defer or neglect it for I shall not pass this way again.

ATTRIBUTED TO STEPHEN GRELLET, IN *DICTIONARY OF QUOTATIONS AND PROVERBS*

B

'As a small child I remember seeing this prayer in a picture frame, standing on my mother's dressing table. I didn't fully understand all the words but I knew that it meant that I should try to help people now, because it may be my only opportunity.' (J.A.H.)

Sometimes life is such a rush, there is so much to do that we don't have time for people. There is a book called 'People matter more than things'. Perhaps today we could be aware of those around us and really experience being with them.

C

Today I will be aware of those around me.

Year 11:1

A

All my possessions for a moment of time.

LAST WORDS OF ELIZABETH I, IN *DICTIONARY OF QUOTATIONS AND PROVERBS*

B

Time is a great leveller. We do not get extra time because we are rich and less if we are poor. Nor do we get more time if we pass a certain exam and less if we fail. No, we all get the same 24 hours each day.

These poignant last words of Elizabeth I show that even though she was a powerful queen, and had a lot of wealth, there was nothing that she could do to buy an extra moment of time. Time is a gift and each day we are all given equal amounts. If we recognize it as a precious gift and value each moment we will enjoy life to the full.

C

I will not waste time today.

Year 11:2

A

Never boast about tomorrow. You don't know what will happen between now and then.

PROVERBS 27:1

B

We always think that tomorrow has more hours in it than today. We are always going to get more things done tomorrow than we ever achieve today. In fact the hours in tomorrow must be elastic because it does not matter how much we have to do, it is all going to fit into 'Tomorrow'.

Of course, we know that this is not true. Each day has only 24 hours and each hour contains just 60 minutes. None of us knows what tomorrow will bring, that is why it is important to enjoy today, and to make the most of every second.

C

I will not put off till tomorrow what I can do today.

Year 11:3

A

Young people, enjoy your youth. Be happy while you are still young.

ECCLESIASTES 11:9

B

The media often give us an image of young people having the time of their lives. They go to raves, discos, parties. They spend their money on clothes, magazines and fast food. Most of the time they are with their friends having a laugh and don't appear to have a care in the world. But very often this image of young people is only a thin veneer.

Many young people feel lonely, isolated and misunderstood. They feel pressurized into doing well at school, and sorting out a decent future. Sometimes they feel that they are treated like children when they need independence, and made to grow up when they still feel like children. Even friendship can be a pressure, trying to live up to our friend's expectations.

But it does not have to be like this. You have reached an age where you can begin to analyse your life and its problems. Once you have worked out a problem, action can be taken to put it right, one day at a time.

It is a time to take charge of your life rather than letting your life take charge of you.

C

I will take a positive attitude to things that happen to me today.

16 SILENCE

Year 7:1

A

If you stand very still in the heart of a wood
You will hear many wonderful things
The snap of a twig, the wind in the trees
The whirr of invisible wings

If you stand very still in the turmoil of life
And you wait for the voice from within
You'll be led down the quiet ways of wisdom and peace
In a mad world of chaos and din

If you stand very still and you hold to your faith
You will get all the help that you ask
You will draw from the silence the things that you need
Hope and courage and strength for your task

B

As much as our physical body needs water in order to live, we need
silence in order to have a rich emotional and spiritual life.

SUE PATTON THOELE, *THE WOMAN'S BOOK OF COURAGE*

C

Today I will appreciate the sound of silence.

Year 7:2

A

It is as important to develop your silence power as it is your word power.

ADAPTED FROM *TOUCHSTONES* (4 SEPTEMBER)

B

We give ourselves a present when we allow ourselves to have a few private moments of silence. But it is very difficult to become still and quiet especially since we are so used to noise and action.

We can quiet our inner selves by concentrating on relaxing our muscles, thinking about a short reading, or praying. The power we can get from silence is not produced by us; it comes to us.

ADAPTED FROM *TOUCHSTONES* (4 SEPTEMBER)

C

Today I will make time for silence and enjoy the power it gives in my life.

ADAPTED FROM *TOUCHSTONES* (4 SEPTEMBER)

Year 7:3

A

When we reflect, we bend back to see where we have been so we can know where to go next.

EARNIE LARSEN, IN *DAYS OF HEALING, DAYS OF JOY*
(21 AUGUST)

B

Reflection can bring insight: 'I never thought of it that way before!'. These insights bring opportunities into our lives to help us see life and its possibilities in a new way. We need to make time to stop, be still and reflect upon our experiences. Then they will have meaning and value for us.

ADAPTED FROM *DAYS OF HEALING, DAYS OF JOY* (21 AUGUST)

C

Today I will take time to reflect upon my experiences and give myself time to look at the opportunities that I find.

Year 8:1

A

We go alone into an empty room and turn on the TV or radio; so the emptiness, the silence, is filled.

JOHN PEPPER, *HOW TO BE HAPPY*

B

Always wanting to be surrounded by noise and sounds can be entertaining, a habit or maybe an escape. Tuning in to music, watching TV or constantly playing computer games, could be a sign that we're avoiding being quiet and alone with our thoughts.

Sometimes it needs courage to stop and listen to our thoughts and to face up to what is in our heart, but people who do this realize that it's a way to growth and becoming strong inside.

C

Through silence I can become strong.

Year 8:2

A

God is the friend of silence.

188

We need to find God and He cannot be found in noise and restlessness. See how nature, the trees, the flowers, the grass grow in perfect silence – see the stars, the moon and the sun, how they move in silence. The more we receive in silent prayer, the more we can give in our active life.

MOTHER TERESA, *PRAYER SEEKING THE HEART OF GOD*

B

Silence can feel strange and even frightening if you're not used to it, but for people who regularly build quiet spaces into their days, silence becomes a friend – a source of strength, inspiration and renewal.

C

I will use times of quiet and silence in order to recharge my batteries.

Year 8:3

A

We shall have to repent in this generation, not so much for the evil deeds of the wicked people, but for the appalling silence of the good people.

MARTIN LUTHER KING

B

Everybody in school has a part to play in creating and shaping a happy and secure environment in the classroom. We all share the responsibility to ensure that bullying doesn't happen. We have the responsibility to tell if it does happen.

Sometimes it's difficult to speak up for yourself, let alone other people. However, if we don't speak out for ourselves and others, then the school could become an insecure and less happy place, affecting everyone.

It takes courage to speak out and uphold what is fair and just. Keeping quiet, though, changes nothing and can even be taken as silent support – so, be courageous.

C

I have the courage to speak up when I or others are treated unfairly.

Year 9:1

A

As much as our physical body needs water in order to live, we need silence in order to have a rich emotional and spiritual life.

SUE PATTON THOELE, *THE WOMAN'S BOOK OF COURAGE*

B

It is the natural order of things, that as well as enjoying busy, active, noisy lives, we must also experience restful times of solitude and silence. Just as night follows day, our periods of activity must give way to times of rest. Just as the plants bud, flower and fruit; they also withdraw for the period of winter to prepare themselves for the following spring.

When we take time to be in silence, we have the opportunity to withdraw from the rush of our everyday lives and replenish ourselves.

In the silence we are able to look at our emotions more clearly and develop greater self-awareness. With this comes the flowering of our spiritual life.

C

I will use silence to replenish myself.

Year 9:2

A

*Everything has its wonders
even darkness and silence.
I learn that*

whatever state
I may be in
therein
to be
content.

HELEN KELLER, IN *BAG OF JEWELS*

B

We can be frightened by a lack of noise. Generally speaking, we are not used to silence, and the emptiness and 'nothingness' can evoke feelings of insecurity and fear within us.

Helen Keller was deaf and blind from the age of nineteen months. She had no choice but to accept, embrace and appreciate the wonder of her dark, silent world, if she was to find any peace and contentment.

In the darkness and stillness we may feel afraid and alone, but we too can find comfort and tranquillity, if we allow ourselves to be fascinated by the silence.

C

I will appreciate darkness and silence.

Year 9:3

A

Because lives focused on outward activity rather than inner contemplation seem more socially acceptable, it takes courage to have the self-discipline to pause each day in the oasis of silence. However, it is important that we persevere – for in quiet solitude, listening only to the sounds of ourselves, we can begin to hear the whispers and urgings of our guidance.

Only in the oasis of silence can we drink deeply from our inner cup of wisdom.

SUE PATTON THOELE, *THE WOMAN'S BOOK OF COURAGE*

B

Sometimes less is more. We can often gain a great deal more from doing less – less rushing around, socialising, watching television, computer games and listening to music, for example, give us more time for ourselves.

If we encourage ourselves to sit for a period of silence each day and listen, we can get more in touch with our thoughts, emotions and needs, as well as our inner wisdom – and this will help us in all we do.

C

Silence unlocks the door to our wisdom.

Year 10:1

A

The Lord is my pace-setter, I shall not rush,
He makes me stop and rest for quiet intervals,
He provides me with images of stillness, which restore my serenity.
He leads me in the ways of efficiency; through calmness of mind,
And his guidance is peace.
Even though I have a great many things to accomplish each day
I will not fret for his presence is here.
His timelessness, his all-importance will keep me in balance.
He prepares refreshment and renewal in the midst of my activity
By anointing my mind with his oils of tranquillity,
My cup of joyous energy overflows.
Surely harmony and effectiveness shall be the fruits of my hours
For I shall walk in the pace of my Lord, and dwell in his house for
ever.

TOKI MIYASHINA, A JAPANESE WOMAN

B

Each day doesn't have to be busy, full of action, all rush and speed. Ticking off achievements, becoming more efficient and doing lots of activities need to be balanced with periods of quiet, empty spaces and stillness. Silent reflection on who we are, what we want from life and a vision of where we are going, can give our lives direction, meaning and a sense of being alive.

C

Today I will make time to stop, rest and be quiet.

Year 10:2

A

It is when we are quiet, when the mind is still, free from its insistent chatter, when anxiety drops away that we can hear the blackbird break the silence with a melody we have never heard before, that we receive in our hearts the exquisite colour and form of every particular flower that blooms.

BOB KNIGHT, *JOYFUL JOURNEY*

B

Allowing silence to happen can open up a whole new world of sounds and experiences. Stopping what we are doing; listening to sounds around us; being still; seems simple, but requires concentration and effort.

Walking in a wood, sitting by the sea or simply being in the countryside are opportunities for being still, listening and opening up to the sounds of nature. Sounds which can so easily be blocked out as background noise – and lost – can be found through silence.

C

Today I will spend a few moments listening to the sounds of nature.

Year 10:3

A

You discover in the silence that you are loved and that you are lovable.
It is the discovery that everyone must make in their lives if they are going
to become fully themselves, fully human.

JOHN MAIN, *THE JOY OF BEING*

B

The act of loving increases our aliveness, heals us, expands us
and allows us to give ourselves unconditionally to others.
To love is to bring light into the world – it is heaven on earth.
Love is our true nature – it is what we are.
To receive love from others is a priceless gift; to love others
leads to inner peace.

C

Today I will give out loving thoughts.

Year 11:1

A

Muddy water becomes clear when still
and reflects the moon at night distinctly.

ANTHONY DE MELLO, *WELLSPRINGS*

B

So still the mind. Stop the thinking process.
Thoughts cannot be stopped directly.
The way to do it is to give the mind
something to focus on …

Become aware of the difference
between the incoming and the outgoing breath:
the difference in duration,

in temperature,
in the smoothness or roughness of the flow.

Make no reflections or consideration.
Just be aware and watch,
the way you watch a river flow
or the motion of the sea
or the passage of a bird across the sky.

Looking at one's breath
can be as fascinating
as looking at a river.
It can still the mind,
and so give rise
to wisdom,
silence,
and a sense of the divine.

ANTHONY DE MELLO, *WELLSPRINGS*

C

I will be silent and still, letting my thoughts settle; so that I can see clearly.

Year 11:2

A

I imagine that I walk into a desert place.
I spend some time exploring the surroundings,
then settle down to contemplate my life.

I see how frequently I rush outside myself
– to people, occupations, places, things –
in search of strength and peace and meaning,
forgetting that the source of all
is here within my heart.
It is here that I must search.

ANTHONY DE MELLO, *WELLSPRINGS*

B

Each person carries thoughts
that have the power to bring instant peace.
I search for mine.

I also search for the thoughts
that help me face life's challenges
with fortitude and courage.

What are the thoughts that make me warm and gentle,
that exorcise the hate and anger in my heart?
What thoughts put meaning in my life?
produce contentment?
give me joy?
propel me into service?

ANTHONY DE MELLO, *WELLSPRINGS*

C

I will find strength, peace and meaning within silence.

Year 11:3

A

I imagine I retire to a lonely place
to give myself the gift of solitude,
for solitude is a time when I see things as they are.

ANTHONY DE MELLO, *WELLSPRINGS*

B

What are the little things in life
that lack of solitude has magnified unduly?

What are the really big things
that I find too little time for?

Solitude is the time to make decisions.

What decisions do I need to make
or reconsider
at this juncture of my life?…

My life will not bear fruit
unless I learn the art of lying fallow,
the art of 'wasting' time creatively.

ANTHONY DE MELLO, *WELLSPRINGS*

C

I will use silence to give me direction in my life.

17 COMMUNICATION

 Year 7:1

A

*I know you believe you understand what you
think I said, but I'm not sure you realize that what
you heard is not what I meant.*

SKILLS FOR ADOLESCENCE

B

One of the ways you can show appreciation to others is
through good listening. Good listening is a skill to be learned
and practised. Having a couple of ears which are in good working order, doesn't make a person a good listener.

There are three keys to good listening:
* the first key is focusing total attention on the speaker
* the second key is showing acceptance for the other person's
  ideas
* the third key is asking questions to draw the speaker out.

Good listening is a hard thing to do.

What things could you do to improve your listening skills
and be a better listener?

ADAPTED FROM SKILLS FOR ADOLESCENCE

C

Today is a good day to begin the process of learning to listen.

Year 7:2

A

If we were supposed to talk more than we listen,
we would have two mouths and one ear.

MARK TWAIN

B

Communication is the lifeblood of a relationship. But the obstacles to real communication are many. Much can be achieved if, in the first place, we talk less and listen more.

When Calvin Coolidge was President of the United States, he saw dozens of people each day. Most had complaints of one kind or another.

One day a visiting governor told the President that he did not understand how he was able to meet so many people in the space of a few hours.

'Why, you are finished with all your visitors by dinnertime,' said the governor, 'while I am often in my office till midnight.'

'Yes,' said Coolidge. 'That's because you talk.'

ADAPTED FROM *THE HEART OF THE ENLIGHTENED*

C

Today I will try to listen more than I talk.

Year 7:3

A

Communication leads to community – that is, to understanding, intimacy, and mutual valuing.

ROLLO MAY, IN *TOUCHSTONES* (18 JANUARY)

B

Have you ever thought: 'If I tell my friends certain things about myself or say honestly how I feel about something, I'll be rejected or put down.' This can be a real fear for a lot of people, but by lowering our barriers and letting others know us better and sharing our feelings, we can be liked more and our friendships can become stronger and deeper.

Should we be totally open with others all the time? Definitely not! We can choose to keep certain feelings to ourselves, but it is important to be honest. For example, it's OK for a person to say to a friend, 'Oh, I'm really upset about a quarrel I had at home, but I don't want to talk about it.' However, saying, 'Nothing is the matter', when something is clearly wrong, is a phoney response and just sends mixed messages, which confuses the person listening.

So it is not appropriate to be totally open about all our feelings with everyone at all times. We have to decide for ourselves when, where, to whom and how much of our inner world it is appropriate to share.

ADAPTED FROM *TOUCHSTONES* (18 JANUARY)

C

Today, I will honestly express my feelings and ideas so others can know me better.

Year 8:1

A

Your deep feelings are even closer to the truth about you than your thoughts – and can be more accessible than you may realize. Inject into your everyday conversation the phrase 'I feel…' and say whatever it is that you're feeling. Communication theorists call these 'I messages' to distinguish them from 'You messages'.

No one knows the truth. But at least what you feel is 'your truth'. It may sound silly … but it works.

TOM RUSK AND RANDY READ, *I WANT TO CHANGE BUT I DON'T KNOW HOW*

B

Becoming aware of and describing our feelings help us to understand ourselves.

The more we expand our vocabulary of 'feeling' words, then the more accurate we become in pin-pointing how we're feeling.

When we know how we're feeling, then we can start to understand ourselves and communicate our feelings to others accurately.

C

I will get in touch with how *I* feel.

Year 8:2

A

The arrow that has left the bow never returns.

PERSIAN PROVERB, IN *PROVERBS FROM AROUND THE WORLD*

B

'The Quakers, those masters of silent prayer, have a useful little trio of questions which we might well get into the habit of thinking about before uttering any doubtful words:

1. Is it true?
2. Is it kind?
3. Is it necessary?'

(*The Friendship Book of Francis Gay 1988*, 5 April)

Gossiping is not real communication. True communication happens when people speak to each other from their hearts.

How many times have we betrayed a confidence in order to gain attention; or put someone down in order to build ourselves up; or helped spread a rumour?

Once spoken, words cannot be retrieved.

C

I will pause to think before I speak.

Year 8:3

A

Can you imagine a family in which no one speaks? Father never speaks to the children and they never speak to him? Everyone would agree that there would be something very wrong. But are they as ready to believe that something is wrong when God's children never speak to their heavenly Father? Prayer is a conversation with God.

A conversation, of course, is always two-way. We would consider someone very bad-mannered if he kept on talking and did not allow us to say a word. Yet how often are prayers like that? We do all the talking and no listening.

ROWLAND PURTON, *ASSEMBLIES*

B

There is a huge difference between saying prayers and praying. John Main, in the book *The Joy of Being* writes: 'The wonderful beauty of prayer is that the opening of our heart is as natural as the opening of a flower. To let a flower open and bloom it is only necessary to let it be, so if we simply *are*, if we become and remain still and silent, our heart cannot but be open, the Spirit cannot but pour through into our whole being. It is this we have been created for.'

C

When I speak, I must also remember to listen with my heart.

Year 9:1

A

In the house

of Mr and Mrs Spouse
he and she
would watch teevee
and never a word
between them spoken
until the day
the set was broken.

Then 'How do you do?'
said he to she,
'I don't believe
that we've met yet.
Spouse is my name.
What's yours?' he asked.

'Why, mine's the same!'
said she to he,
'Do you suppose that we could be –?'

But the set came suddenly right about,
and so they never did find out.

EVE MERRIAM, *THE KINGFISHER BOOK OF CHILDREN'S POETRY*

B

Wonderful though the television is, it can stop us communicating with others. If we are always watching television, when we could be talking with our friends and family, our relationships can suffer, because we stop sharing things together.

Sometimes we can know more about what's going on in the lives of 'soap' characters than we do about the lives of people in our own families.

Television watching can be a source of information, inspiration and relaxation, but so can the people around us.

The television is only 'one-way conversation', whereas by taking time to chat and swap ideas with others, the conversation is two-way.

C

I will talk with people rather than just watching TV.

Year 9:2

A

Listen to yourself. Are there any particular phrases which you wish you didn't use? Do you end your statements with a question as though you want someone's approval or confirmation? Do you apologise before you say what you think?

CLAIRE WALMSLEY, *ASSERTIVENESS – THE RIGHT TO BE YOU*

B

The phrases that we use and the ways that we speak are an important part of communication. When a neighbour or friend says: 'How are you?', do you give an automatic response like, 'Fine' or 'Very well, thank you', instead of saying how you really feel? Do you say, 'This is an interesting book, isn't it?', instead of saying: 'I find this book interesting'. Have you said in the past, 'Oh, I'm sorry the present isn't much, I hope it's all right', instead of, 'Here's a present for you'. We all have a need to understand and be understood. The more direct and assertive we are when we talk with each other, the easier it is to get across how we feel and appreciate what each other has to say.

C

Today I will speak directly, honestly and kindly.

Year 9:3

A

People invent words all the time; that's one of the marvels of the English language, which is so quick to embrace new words and concepts. If you look through a current dictionary you'll discover the contributions of many foreign languages, and especially from all kinds of special-interest groups.

For example, people in the surfing culture have created words like 'tubular' and 'rad' to translate their 'totally awesome' experience of the waves to their day-to-day lives.

ANTHONY ROBBINS, *AWAKEN THE GIANT WITHIN*

B

Language is a living thing! It is ever growing and developing to express and accommodate the shifts and changes in the way we view and experience life on this Earth. Now that newspapers and televisions are an everyday part of many people's lives, we have access to greater information about world events.

Whatever the language spoken, we all share and understand: joy, when a child's life is saved; sadness, when we see millions of starving people; horror, when we learn of war atrocities; and laughter, when we are happy or amused.

Our shared experiences communicate a common human experience and language, uniting us as a human race.

C

Today I will enjoy language and all it helps me share with people.

Year 10:1

A

Teach us to listen Lord...
To one another with enjoyment and especially:
To the diffident with encouragement,
To the sad with understanding,
To the repetitive with patience,
To the happy, joyfully,
To the aggressive, calmly;
But to the gossip – never.

CLEMENCY GREATORIX, *THE FRIENDSHIP BOOK OF FRANCIS GAY 1988* (15 APRIL)

B

Good communication isn't just about talking, but about really listening and being able to respond appropriately.

Gossip, by its very nature, is at best second-hand information. What value can this be to us or others?

Although you might say, 'But I would never spread rumours or gossip', just by listening to stories about others, you are taking an active part in the gossip process.

C

Today I will choose not to listen to gossip.

Year 10:2

A

I may be able to speak the languages of men and even of angels, but if I have no love, my speech is no more than a noisy gong or a clanging bell.

CORINTHIANS 13:1

B

The power of words can be electrifying. Words can bring about huge changes in people.

Words can touch or pierce a heart; they can make you laugh or cry. Words can inspire or oppress people.

The same words can be used and yet they can communicate different messages. It's not only what you say, it's how you say it. Our ears are used for hearing but our eyes help us to listen.

C

Today I will speak from my heart.

Year 10:3

A

Jim comes in from school and I say, 'Had a good day?' and he says, 'All right.' Then I say, 'What did you do?' and he says, 'Nothing.' Then he disappears into his room. Getting conversation out of him is like pulling teeth.

RUTH, AGED 48, IN *ADOLESCENCE (THE SURVIVAL GUIDE FOR PARENTS AND TEENAGERS)*

B

Does this sound familiar?

If the people in your life start to sound like a broken record, then maybe it's time for you to start asking them how their day has been and so open up channels of communication.

Conversations are a two-way process. They are not only about asking the right questions, but also about listening and responding. It takes time and practice to develop communication skills, but good relationships are built up on these.

C

Today I'll have a two-way conversation with someone.

Year 11:1

A

Set some time aside each day specifically to practise not making other people wrong. Instead of attacking when you find yourself in disagreement, try saying something like 'Tell me more – that's a point of view I've never considered before'.

DR WAYNE W. DYER, *YOU'LL SEE IT WHEN YOU BELIEVE IT*

B

Our gut reaction, when we disagree with the opinions of others, is often to attack back with our own thoughts and points of view – we defend our position.

By letting go of the need to be 'right' and have 'all of the answers', we can create a space in ourselves to listen to others and thereby communicate more freely and openly.

C

I will be more open to the viewpoints of others.

Year 11:2

A

For years I was so afraid of rejection that I swallowed my opinions, ideas, and resentments in order to avoid upsetting anyone. As I began to have the courage to be myself, I spoke out more often.

SUE PATTON THOELE, *THE WOMAN'S BOOK OF COURAGE*

B

It can be liberating to be able to say how we really think and feel. Part of having the courage to be ourselves is about valuing and appreciating who we are. As our feelings of self-love grow and develop, we find that it becomes easier to express our thoughts and feelings, with less fear of being rejected by others. We can communicate in a more honest and open way, because we love ourselves and believe in ourselves.

C

I will have the confidence to speak out more often.

Year 11:3

A

Wisdom is not in words;
Wisdom is meaning within words.

KAHLIL GIBRAN, *THE WISDOM OF KAHLIL GIBRAN*

B

We can read books, go to talks and study literature, but still be none the wiser. It is not enough to listen to words, we need to really feel and experience what they mean.

Just because we all use the latest buzz words, it doesn't mean that we are wise or that we truly communicate. For one person, 'I love you' can mean, 'I'm fond of you', while to another, it could mean, 'I'd give my life for you'. So the words 'I love you' may need more explaining in order to get the true meaning of our message across.

C

I will listen to the meaning within words.

18 LAUGHTER/HUMOUR

Year 7:1

A

A chicken and a pig were walking out into the countryside when they came upon a poor family living in awful conditions, no food and little prospect of work of any kind.

'Do you realise,' said the chicken, 'that between us we could keep this poor family in eggs and bacon for several weeks.'

'Just a moment,' said the pig, 'for you that would be a generous act of charity but for me it would be total commitment.'

B

Humorous stories can often contain a lot of truth and can allow hard questions to be asked. For example the story touches on how easy it is to volunteer others.

There is a further message about the importance of listening to our hearts, before we get swept along with the enthusiasm of others. Before realizing it, we could be in a situation in which we aren't in control, a situation which is over our heads.

C

Today I will listen to my heart and be thoughtful about what I promise.

Year 7:2

A

'Oh! come on – it's only a joke!'

B

The way we laugh, what we laugh at, and when we laugh can say a lot about the kind of people we are.

Having a sense of humour is a very positive thing. Sharing a joke with others can bring people together. Laughing with people can bring happiness and closeness, as well as relieving a lot of stress.

Laughing at others, however, can be both hurtful, harmful and divisive and can cause a lot of pain and sadness.

C

Today I will use humour in a positive way.

Year 7:3

A

A rabbi confessed to nightly noshes. He had fixed a lock to his fridge, and told his wife to hide the key. Did it work? No, he kept a secret reserve of smoked salmon in his study.

A vicar added that the only diet which worked with him was the Seafood Diet. We looked up hopefully – how much was allowed? He gave a grim laugh, 'I see food, then I eat it'.

RABBI LIONEL BLUE, *BLUE HORIZONS*

B

'When you wake up in the morning, Pooh,' said Piglet at last, 'what's the first thing you say to yourself?'

'What's for breakfast?' said Pooh. 'What do you say, Piglet?'

'I say, I wonder what's going to happen exciting today?' said Piglet. Pooh nodded thoughtfully.

'It's the same thing,' he said.

BENJAMIN HOFF, *THE TAO OF POOH*

There are many jokes and humorous stories to be told around the subject of food. Food, after all, is a very important part of our lives. Not only does it provide energy and help to maintain our bodies, it is also a source of pleasure and delight. But whether we are short, tall, fat or thin, there are times when food just doesn't seem to satisfy us – no matter how much we eat, we can feel empty inside.

Rabbi Lionel Blue says that: 'In times of stress, a big black hole opens up inside us, but however much food we shovel into it, we never feel full.' Sometimes, 'it isn't our bellies that need nourishment. It's our minds and souls that are starved. That's why we feel so hungry.' (*Blue Horizons*)

C

As well as feeding my body, I will feed my mind, emotions and spiritual life.

Year 8:1

A

Travelling on a crowded InterCity train, I overhead a male passenger reporting the theft of his mobile telephone to the ticket inspector. I suggested he could dial his number from the train's pay phone and wait for the tell-tale ring.

He thought this was a good idea and recruited volunteers to listen in the eight coaches. He duly dialled himself and the missing telephone rang – down the side of his own seat.

GARY SAPSFORD, *THE READER'S DIGEST*

B

On losing the phone, the man jumped to the conclusion that it had been stolen rather than lost. Once our mind is set on an idea like that, it becomes closed to other possibilities and, like the man on the train, we can look rather foolish. The saving grace in a situation like this is the ability to learn about and to laugh at ourselves and see the funny side of it.

C

The answer to a problem is often right under your nose.

Year 8:2

A

What goes ha! ha! bump! bump!?
A person laughing her or his head off!

B

Whether that joke is amusing or not depends on your sense of humour. Clearly, laughing so much until your head drops off is not a healthy thing to do. However laughter can play a very important role in our lives. Laughter eases tension and helps the body to release held-in emotions. Laughter is a form of medicine.

The next time that you feel sad, or you feel crushed by the problems around you, try a little laughter.

When we can rise above our situations and predicaments our burden becomes lighter; we feel freer rather than being overwhelmed by life.

C

Today I will allow laughter to flow through me.

Year 8:3

A

'How I wish I could be really wealthy,' said Nasrudin to his cronies in the teahouse, 'like, say, Kara Mustafa the great lord, who has every-thing.'

'How strange that you should say that,' said the potter, 'because in my shop a few minutes ago Mustafa himself was saying how much he wished that he were a poor and simple man.'

'But that is only because he is rich already!' said Nasrudin; 'he has the wish and also knows the method of becoming poor. I only have the desire to be rich!'

IDRIES SHAH, *CARAVAN OF DREAMS*

B

Kara Mustafa is a rich man who wishes to be poor. Clearly he has a problem, but also he has the solution to his problem. All he has to do is give his money and possessions away.

Mustafa probably finds it very painful to let go of his wealth. He might wish to be poor, but does he really *want* to be poor? Mustafa seems unwilling to act – he is fearful. He may be a rich and powerful man, but he is powerless in becoming poor. Yet in a funny way he is already poor – he is poor in heart and spirit. He is not able to do what he wants to do.

C

Today I will act on something that I want to do, rather than wait or wish for it to happen.

Year 9:1

A

In a recent poll conducted by Entertainment Weekly *magazine, they found that 82 per cent of the people who go to movies want to laugh, 7 per cent want to cry, and 3 per cent want to scream. This gives you an idea how we value the sensations of laughter over so many other things.*

ANTHONY ROBBINS, *AWAKEN THE GIANT WITHIN*

B

Laughter and humour can be two of our best allies – making

us feel good about ourselves; building confidence; releasing energy and giving us the feeling of a love of life.

It's human nature to enjoy a good laugh – not only does it relax us, but it also fortifies us on our life's journey. When we laugh and choose to see the humorous side of life, we feel stronger and more capable.

Both laughter and humour can act as an antidote to fear, giving us a sense of courage and a feeling of expansion. Try having a good laugh before going in to see the dentist and feel your fear diminish and your spirits lift.

C

I will watch a film to make me laugh.

Year 9:2

A

Why not find someone who laughs and mirror them? Have some fun. Say, 'Will you do me a favour? You've got a great laugh. Let me try and duplicate it. Coach me.' I guarantee you'll crack each other up in the process! Breathe the way they breathe; take on their posture and body movements; use the same facial expressions; make the same sounds. You'll feel stupid when you start, but after a while you'll get into it, and you'll both be laughing hysterically because you both look silly ... As you do this again and again, you'll find it very easy to laugh and you'll certainly have fun.

ANTHONY ROBBINS, *AWAKEN THE GIANT WITHIN*

B

If we are in the habit of frequently being serious, unsmiling and grim, then when it is time to laugh, we may find it difficult. Babies have the ability to laugh merrily and also spontaneously. If we have forgotten how to do this, we need a little work and practice until we can laugh naturally again.

C

I will practise laughing.

Year 9:3

A

It takes courage to laugh, to have a sense of humour. Why? Because when something is really funny it is a reflection of our own foibles and weaknesses, those things about ourselves which make us cringe. To have a good sense of humour, we must be able to not take ourselves too seriously – to be able to laugh with, not at, ourselves as we stumble and stagger through the comedy of life.

SUE PATTON THOELE, *THE WOMAN'S BOOK OF COURAGE*

B

We can laugh with ourselves and develop our sense of humour, when we know things about ourselves. We can know things about ourselves when we use our courage to look honestly and truthfully at how we really are.

Instead of rejecting our weaknesses and less attractive qualities, we can learn to laugh with ourselves and see the humorous side. We need to love ourselves even when we behave in ridiculous ways; it is then more likely that our confidence and self-love will develop.

C

When I see those things about myself that make me cringe, I will have the courage to laugh with myself.

Year 10:1

A

Norman Cousins was suffering from a painful and disabling condition in his muscles and had difficulty in walking. His doctors predicted a long and crippling disease, possibly resulting in death. After intensive hospital treatment he decided to leave hospital, book into a hotel and try a therapy of vitamin C and laughter. He hired a number of comedy films including the Marx Brothers and laughed all day. Over a period of time, his symptoms abated and his disease resolved itself. His laughter provided a cure in a situation where medicine had failed.

DR BRIAN ROET, *ALL IN THE MIND? – THINK YOURSELF BETTER*

B

Every month in the *Reader's Digest* there is a section called 'Laughter, the Best Medicine', which is a collection of jokes and humorous stories. In one sense, medicine did not fail in this story, because laughter was used as a very effective medicine.

Had Norman Cousins experienced a miracle? Well, certainly the recovery was miraculous. However, the beneficial effect of laughter on the human organism has been known for a long time.

The well-known proverb could be re-written so that it reads 'A laugh a day keeps the doctor away'.

C

Today I will look for appropriate opportunities to have a good laugh.

Year 10:2

A

A woman, who had just died, arrived at the gates of heaven. St Peter welcomed her and invited her on a tour of heaven, which she gladly accepted, for she was very curious to see what it was like. She was amazed to find that heaven was made of many huge circular buildings and the circular outside walls of these buildings were so high as to disappear out of view. Gigantic notices were pasted all around the walls containing the same message: 'Sshh! Quiet Please!'

After a while, the woman turned to St Peter and said, 'Excuse me St Peter, but what's inside each of the buildings.'

'People,' replied St Peter.

'Are they happy?' asked the woman.

'Oh yes!' answered St Peter.

'But who are the people in each of these buildings?' she persisted.

Smiling, St Peter said, 'Each building contains a different religious group.'

'I still don't understand why they're so happy,' commented the woman, with a bewildered expression on her face.

'Well, you see,' answered St Peter, 'they think they're the only ones here!'

A STORY TOLD BY BOB KNIGHT

B

Who knows what heaven is really like? In this story the people in each of the circular buildings are under the illusion that they, and only they, have arrived in heaven – they are the exclusive residents of heaven.

An exclusive view of the world which cherishes ideas such as: 'I have all the answers', 'I've arrived – there's no need to journey' closes the mind down and builds mental barriers. On the other hand attitudes of tolerance, respect for other people's ways of life and retaining a sense of humour in all things dissolve and break down barriers which divide people.

C

Today I will reflect on the mental barriers I put up which stop me from being close to people.

Year 10:3

A

Everybody lies in a circle on the floor. Each person lies with his or her head on the belly of someone else. The first person goes, 'Ha.' The second, 'Ha – ha.' The third, 'Ha – ha – ha.' And so on, around the group. Usually shrieks of resounding laughter ensue, and the effect heightens as people laugh at the laughter.

HOWARD LEWIS AND HAROLD STREITFELD, *GROWTH GAMES*

B

This is a game I've played many times and it always results in uncontrollable fits of infectious laughter. The laughter flows from person to person; followed by tears of joy. That game then becomes special for the group of people playing it – a shared experience – a moment to remember and look back on; a time of closeness and fun.

Games which are fun for everybody and which produce laughter, draw people together.

C

I will be more adventurous and take part in fun games when the opportunities arise.

Year 11:1

A

When laughter falls, like a cascade of stars, we are delighted.

S.E-W.

B

Let us bring joy into each corner of our lives. Let our laughter flow freely, shining light into even the saddest heart. Humour may not make our sorrows and unhappiness go away, but they will be easier to bear.

A sense of humour can be especially valuable at times of stress and crisis. It can give us the opportunity to look at seemingly hopeless situations from a different angle.

C

I will remember today that retaining a sense of humour can transform how I feel about my situation.

Year 11:2

A

Angels fly because they take themselves lightly.

ALAN WATTS, IN *LIVING MAGICALLY – A NEW VISION OF REALITY*

B

When we focus on our 'failings' and 'defects', and become very serious about the parts of us that fall short of the way we would like to be, we become serious and down-hearted.

By accepting and loving ourselves, and not taking ourselves too seriously, we can rise above feeling bad about the way we are.

Treating ourselves harshly stunts our growth and development, however when we are loving and kind to ourselves, our personality flourishes. By laughing at ourselves and being gentle with ourselves, we can take ourselves lightly.

C

Today I will take myself lightly.

Year 11:3

A

The clouds above us join and separate,
The breeze in the courtyard leaves and returns.
Life is like that, so why not relax?
Who can stop us from celebrating?

LU YU, IN BENJAMIN HOFF, *THE TAO OF POOH*

B

If we are endeavouring to create a 'Heaven on Earth', then it is natural to make our world a place of joy.

We will all have times of suffering in our lives, but we also have the capacity to experience great happiness.

By focusing on the beauty, wonder, delight and peace in our lives, we can embrace each day with a glad heart – and when we feel light-hearted, it is so much easier to make the world a place of love and laughter.

C

I will make my world one of love and laughter.

19 A POSITIVE APPROACH TO LIFE

Year 7:1

A

Two frogs fell into a can of cream,
Or so I've heard it told:
The sides of the can were shiny and steep,
The cream was deep and cold.

'Oh, what's the use?' croaked Number 1,
'Tis fate; no help's around.
Goodbye, my friends! Goodbye, sad world!'
And, weeping still, he drowned.

But Number 2, of sterner stuff,
Dog-paddled in surprise,
The while he wiped his creamy face
And dried his creamy eyes.

'I'll swim awhile, at least,' he said,
Or so I've heard he said:
'It really wouldn't help the world
If one more frog were dead.'

An hour or two he kicked and swam,
Not once he stopped to mutter;
But kicked and kicked and swam and kicked,
then hopped out, via butter!

T.C. HAMLET, IN *FROGS IN CREAM*

B

So often when we look at all the things that we have ahead of us, like assignments, projects and exams, we can feel like giving up. But if we take one thing at a time; working step-by-step, then we can find life more manageable and positive.

C

Today I will take one thing at a time in bite-size pieces.

Year 7:2

A

A few months ago I met a young girl who had been in a serious car accident. Before the accident she was popular and had lots of friends. She was a positive person. She knew exactly what she wanted in life. But then everything changed. Since the accident, she has become a different person. She has given up. She says, 'There's nothing to live for.'

Meeting this girl reminded me of another young girl I'd met several years ago. She too had been in a bad accident, one that changed her life by creating lasting medical problems. But there was something very different about this other girl – a sparkle, a warm smile, an attitude of confidence. After her accident she started a group to help other people who have been injured in accidents.

What was different about the second girl? She had turned her 'scars into stars'. She knew she couldn't control what had happened to her. But she could control how she would choose to live the rest of her life – in anger or in love.

RICK LITTLE, *CHANGES – BECOMING THE BEST YOU CAN*

B

You can develop a positive attitude by recognizing that there will be both good and bad in your life and then deciding to emphasize the good. When you do this, the good in your life increases. Why is this true?

Because goodness attracts goodness. In a similar way, people with a positive attitude attract others to them.

CHANGES – BECOMING THE BEST YOU CAN

C

Today I will take some quiet moments to notice the good things coming my way.

Year 7:3

A

For as he thinks within himself, so he is.

PROVERBS 23:7

B

What we think about, we talk about. And what we talk about, we bring about.

Suppose that each of us had a recorder taping our thoughts for a whole day. What would we hear when we played the tape. Would our thoughts be negative, discouraging and put ourselves down? Or would our thoughts be positive, appreciative, and hopeful about ourselves and our world?

Positive thoughts bring positive things. When we think in terms of the positiveness of life, we see the positive, talk the positive, and positivity comes to be part of our lives.

C

I will examine the quality of my thoughts each day.

Year 8:1

A

Believe you can achieve what you want and expect the best. Above all, don't limit yourself.

M.W.

B

Tell yourself that you can do it, and you probably will. Before Roger Bannister became the first person to run a mile in less than four minutes in 1954, everyone said that it was physically impossible for that limit to be broken – humans simply could not run that fast. But Bannister didn't set limits on himself – he did his best, and his best broke the 'impossible' limit. When others found out it could be done, they did it too – because they now believed it was possible.

DR PAT PALMER AND MELISSA ALBERTI FROEHNER, *TEEN ESTEEM*

C

Today I will look beyond my limits.

Year 8:2

A

Two things cannot be in one place.

Where you tend a rose, my lad,
A thistle cannot grow.

FRANCES HODGSON BURNETT, *THE SECRET GARDEN*

B

In the book *The Secret Garden*, a boy called Colin found himself thinking about his fears, ill-health and hatred of people. He didn't know he had the power to get well and break free of the wheelchair that confined him. The more he reflected on these thoughts, the gloomier he became.

'When new, beautiful thoughts began to push out the old, hideous ones, life began to come back to him, his blood ran healthily through his veins, and strength poured into him like a flood. His scientific experiment was quite practical and simple

225

and there was nothing weird about it at all. Much more surprising things can happen to anyone who, when a disagreeable or discouraged thought comes into his mind, just has the sense to remember in time and push it out by putting in an agreeable, determinedly courageous one. Two things cannot be in one place.

Where you tend a rose, my lad,
A thistle cannot grow.' (*The Secret Garden*)

C

Today I will 'push out' all my disagreeable thoughts with agreeable ones.

Year 8:3

A

Your most important job in life is to be yourself. Believe it or not, no one expects you to be anyone else. You are already wonderful and magnificent. So why not relax and be you? Inside you is a marvellous person with skills, talents, gifts, warmth, love and caring – yes, and your share of human faults. There may be some things you'd like to change about yourself. Well, funny as it sounds, the first step toward becoming the person you want to be is to accept the person you are!

DR PAT PALMER AND MELISSA ALBERTI FROEHNER, *TEEN ESTEEM*

B

A positive way to approach life is to accept and love yourself as you are right now. With this attitude of self-acceptance, great happiness is possible.

C

Today I will relax and be me.

Year 9:1

A

I have not the shadow of a doubt that any man or woman can achieve what I have, if he or she would make the same effort and cultivate the same hope and faith.

MAHATMA GANDHI

B

Gandhi was an inspiration to all who knew him, and to this day his life still has a positive influence on people.

Gandhi's inner strength came from deeply held spiritual beliefs. His empowering beliefs affected everything he did and allowed him to act courageously even when faced with death.

Gandhi's life was guided by his values – the values of love and tolerance for others, non-violence and a detachment from material things. He committed his life to doing what he felt was right and just.

C

Today I will adopt a positive approach to life.

Year 9:2

A

Human beings can alter their lives by altering their attitudes of mind.

WILLIAM JAMES, IN *THE POWER OF POSITIVE THINKING*

B

Our thoughts affect our attitudes and how we feel about ourselves. If we have negative thoughts about ourselves we may be sad. If our thoughts are positive, we are more likely to be cheerful.

Every time we criticize, blame, put down or judge ourselves, we can simply replace those thoughts with fresh, positive and energizing ones.

Positive thoughts can alter our lives.

C

An example of a powerful positive thought is: 'I am lovable and valuable.'

Year 9:3

A

Do not hold mental pictures of difficulties and failures, but lift your mind above them and visualise powers and achievements.

NORMAN VINCENT PEALE, *THE POWER OF POSITIVE THINKING*

B

We can choose how we look at situations. Our perceptions depend on our point of view. When we see a half-filled glass of water, we have a choice to see it negatively and consider it 'half-empty' or positively and see it as 'half-full'. We can hold negative pictures in our minds which pull us down or positive pictures which lift us up.

We can choose.

C

Today I will choose my point of view.

Year 10:1

A

Our deepest fear is not that we are inadequate. Our deepest fear is that we are powerful beyond measure. It is our light, not our darkness, that most frightens us. We ask ourselves: 'Who am I to be brilliant, gorgeous, talented, fabulous?' Actually, who are you not to be? You are a child of God.

NELSON MANDELA

B

As children of God, we are all seeds of brilliance. Everybody can awaken and release the power that's locked inside. Maybe the fear of handling the responsibility of becoming who or what we can become, holds us back?

Be courageous, face the fear, and enjoy being brilliant, gorgeous, talented and fabulous.

C

Today I will embrace my power and potential.

Year 10:2

A

Your playing small doesn't serve the world. There's nothing enlightened about shrinking so that other people won't feel insecure around you. We are all meant to shine, as children do.

NELSON MANDELA

B

We are all special and unique. Inside each of us is our own particular brilliance and creative power that can blossom. By watching little children we can learn how to reach our potential. They have the ability to be unselfconscious and natural – expressing who they are in all they do.

Even if those around us feel uncomfortable because we shine, as Nelson Mandela says, 'Your playing small doesn't serve the world.'

C

Today I will not shrink from being great.

Year 10:3

A

We were born to make manifest the glory of God that is within us. It's not just in some of us; it's in everyone. And as we let our own light shine, we unconsciously give other people permission to do the same. As we're liberated from our own fear, our presence automatically liberates others.

NELSON MANDELA

B

When we accept ourselves, wonderful possibilities open up.

When we are in touch with the light within, we can let our greatness flow and shine out. Becoming a beacon of light, illuminates and sets others free to follow their path. When we are true to ourselves and stop pretending to be something we're not – other people can do the same.

C

Today I will allow my light to shine.

Year 11:1

A

You must feed your mind even as you feed your body, and to make your mind healthy, you must feed it nourishing, wholesome thoughts.

NORMAN VINCENT PEALE, *THE POWER OF POSITIVE THINKING*

B

Over the next twenty-four hours, every time we catch ourselves thinking or speaking in a negative way, let's stop and replace these thoughts with positive ones. Positive thinking needs daily practice. Negative thoughts like: 'These exams are too difficult for me'; 'I'm hopeless at revision'; 'I'm bound to fail'; 'There's nothing I can do, so I might as well give up', only serve to drain us of energy, fill us with tension and fear, and make the future look bleak.

Thoughts like: 'I'll work as hard as I can and do my best in these exams'; 'I'm getting better at revision'; 'There's a lot I can do and I'm going to keep on trying', empower us and give us the freedom to take charge of our lives.

By simply changing 'I can't' to 'I can', we are able to build our confidence and achieve our potential.

C

Today I will feed my mind with healthy and nourishing thoughts.

Year 11:2

A

Why put yourself in a position to feel miserable when it's so easy to feel great?

SUSAN JEFFERS, *FEEL THE FEAR AND DO IT ANYWAY*

B

We were challenged to speak positively for twenty-four hours. If we now continue this practice for one week, then we will discover that what we meant by 'realistic' a week ago was actually pessimistic, but what we now mean by 'realistic' is something entirely different; it is the dawning of the positive outlook. When most people say they are being 'realistic' they delude themselves; they are simply being negative.

ADAPTED FROM NORMAN VINCENT PEALE, *THE POWER OF POSITIVE THINKING*

C

As we think, so shall we be.

Year 11:3

A

A famous trapeze artiste was instructing his students how to perform on the high trapeze bar. Finally, having given full explanations and in-struction in this skill, he told them to demonstrate their ability.

One student, looking up at the insecure perch from which he must perform, was suddenly filled with fear. He froze completely. He had a terrifying vision of himself falling to the ground. He couldn't move a muscle, so deep was his fright. 'I can't do it! I can't do it!' he gasped.

The instructor put his arm around the boy's shoulder and said: 'Son, you can do it, and I will tell you how.' Then he made a statement which is of inestimable importance. It is one of the wisest remarks I have ever heard. He said: 'Throw your heart over the bar and your body will follow.'

NORMAN VINCENT PEALE, *THE POWER OF POSITIVE THINKING*

B

'Heart is the symbol of creative activity. Fire the heart with where you want to go and what you want to be. Get it so deeply fixed in your unconscious that you will not take no for an answer, then your entire personality will follow where your heart leads. "Throw your heart over the bar" means to throw your faith over your difficulty.' (*The Power of Positive Thinking*)

In other words let your faith and courage lead you, not your limitations.

C

Everything is possible for the person who has faith.

MARK 9:23

20 HEALING

Year 7:1

A

We used to believe that illness was something over which we had absolutely no control. If we were sick or injured there was no choice but to put our fate in the hands of doctors. With research, medical experts now know that a patient is much more in control of her healing than was previously believed. Our attitudes, beliefs, and emotions all affect how we heal.

SUE PATTON THOELE, *THE WOMAN'S BOOK OF COURAGE*

B

Some years ago there was a popular belief that with enough scientific research and development, illness and disease in the West could be conquered by using medical drugs – 'a pill for every ill'. Even after millions and millions of pounds have been spent on AIDS research, scientists are only a little closer to finding a cure for that disease. In fact, scientists still do not fully understand what causes AIDS.

There is a lot we can do for ourselves against illness and disease. Our emotions, thoughts and our spiritual outlook on life all play an important part in our physical health. Often the message of illness is to be quieter and spend some time just being in contact with our inner self. Illness often forces us to relax, let go of all our busyness and 'efforting' and drop into a deep stillness where we can receive the nourishing energy that we need.

'Preventative medicine' is always the best. For example,

replacing negative and 'sickening' thoughts with pictures of ourselves in good health can be a natural form of healing.

ADAPTED FROM *CREATIVE VISUALISATION*

C

Today I will often tell myself that I am healthy and full of energy.

Year 7:2

A

Love cures people. Both the ones who give it, and the ones who receive it.

KARL MENNINGER, IN *DAYS OF HEALING, DAYS OF JOY*
(16 APRIL)

B

We can achieve many things in life, but the history of human experience tells us that, without love, all other rewards are hollow.

The more we are able to share in positive and loving relationships, the more healthy and at ease we become, for relationships heal when they are loving, reliable, committed and loyal.

In order to feel love, we have to give it away. We will know love when we give love. Under this law, when we give our love away to others we gain, and what we give, we immediately receive.

ADAPTED FROM *DAYS OF HEALING, DAYS OF JOY* (16 APRIL)
AND *LOVE IS LETTING GO OF FEAR*

C

Today I will think about the healing power of love.

Year 7:3

A

There are many things you can do for yourself, without using drugs. Laughing and having fun can bring about big changes in your physical and mental well-being.

PAT PALMER AND CATHERINE PONDER

B

Nature heals: a walk through tall grass, climbing a tree or looking after plants can help us get in touch with ourselves. Beauty heals: music, a poem, a novel, or a picture can move us and teach us about life. Silence heals: this might be a meditation, prayer or a quiet relaxation which can bring us inner peace. Physical activity heals; so make time for a favourite sport. Perhaps the biggest healer is laughter. Laughter recharges our whole body. Choosing to see the bright side of life, laughing at our mistakes, lessens pain. Laughter encourages wellness. Bringing laughter to others can heal them as well.

We all want health and happiness in ourselves and others, and we can find it by creating it. The best prescription for whatever ails us may well be a good laugh.

ADAPTED FROM *TOUCHSTONES* (12 APRIL) AND *EACH DAY A NEW BEGINNING* (10 JANUARY)

C

Today I will look on the bright side of life!

Year 8:1

A

When I was a child the best healing ointment for any scratch, bruise or hurt feeling was for mum to 'kiss it better'!

M.W.

B

Having faith and confidence in the remedy helps the healing process, but when it's applied with love, then that makes all the difference.

C

The great healer is love.

Year 8:2

A

Nature heals – a flower; a walk through the woods; a gentle breeze on the face; the sound of a wave as it breaks on to shingle – uplift, inspire and transform the body, mind and heart.

M.W.

B

We can become so trapped in our daily activities that nature simply becomes background. It's possible to go for a walk, be surrounded by nature, and yet neither see it, hear it or experience it.

Being still and silent and becoming aware of the natural surroundings can be a fulfilling experience. To be at one with nature can flood our whole being with love and a sense of wonder. Nature heals.

C

Today I will take a moment to notice nature.

Year 8:3

A

Most of us will know someone whom we are not getting along with particularly well, where there are unspoken resentments, hurts that have not healed yet.

JOHN PEPPER, *HOW TO BE HAPPY*

B

Mental bruises that are obtained from hurtful comments or from falling out with friends can sometimes take a long time to heal.

If we are to blame for the hurt, then a sincere 'sorry' is often the best medicine. Sometimes apologies aren't accepted and are inadequate to relieve the pain that's been caused.

The only thing to do then is to wait and try saying 'sorry' again at a later date.

Time can be a great healer.

ADAPTED FROM *HOW TO BE HAPPY*

C

I will look for the right time to use the healing word – sorry.

Year 9:1

A

As an experiment, assume a position that is depressed and down. Hang your head and let your tummy sag out. Check your feelings. Do they match your posture? Now... sit, or better yet, stand up tall – stretch to your full height. Hold your head up proudly and look up. How does that feel?

SUE PATTON THOELE, *THE WOMAN'S BOOK OF COURAGE*

B

The thoughts and feelings that we focus on can have a healing or depressing effect on our bodies. Likewise, the manner in which we hold our body can affect our thoughts, feelings and outlook on life.

When we are unwell and feel out of balance, by simply changing our posture, we can feel uplifted.

C

Whenever I remember, I will help myself feel uplifted by straightening up!

Year 9:2

A

Forgiveness is the key to happiness.

GERALD G. JAMPOLSKY, *LOVE IS LETTING GO OF FEAR*

B

A woman lost her only daughter to a violent criminal act. For the next eighteen years the woman was consumed by the desire for revenge … For eighteen years the mother was unable to function in a satisfying way … she sought help for her unhappiness from a variety of sources. It was ultimately the act of forgiveness that freed her. When she visited and forgave her daughter's murderer, still on death row eighteen years later, she described it as a spiritual experience of love for herself, her daughter, and the murderer.

TOLD TO DR WAYNE W. DYER BY EARL NIGHTINGALE, IN *YOU'LL SEE IT WHEN YOU BELIEVE IT*

C

Today I will allow forgiveness to heal past hurts.

Year 9:3

A

In these twenty years of work amongst the people, I have come more and more to realize that it is being unwanted that is the worst disease that any human being can ever experience. Nowadays we have found medicine for leprosy and lepers can be cured … For all kinds of diseases there are medicines and cures. But for being unwanted, except there are willing hands to serve and there's a loving heart to love, I don't think this terrible disease can ever be cured.

MOTHER TERESA

B

The feeling of being unwanted, rejected by society can leave an open wound that never heals. In Britain today there are many groups of people who feel ignored and discarded and carry a look of despair in their eyes – the homeless, the lonely, the hungry, the isolated elderly, the poor and the forgotten.

All of these people are our neighbours, they are unique people who deserve to be valued and cared for. Perhaps one day, the people who have enough will view it as a privilege to show compassion and kindness to their neighbours in need.

By serving and giving to others we share in the healing process because by our loving actions we too are healed.

C

Today I will give to those who are ignored and discarded.

Year 10:1

A

Open my eyes to the beauty that shines within all who walk the earth. Keep me from imagined hurts, from seeing foes where only friends are to be found. And give me insight into my own heart, that I may uproot all that weakens me. Help me to be patient when others misunderstand me, open to the thoughts of those who are near me, and quick to forgive all who wound me ...

ANONYMOUS (JEWISH), IN *PRAYERS FOR PEACE*

B

The power of forgiveness and love can soothe the hurts of arguments and unkind actions. They heal the very centre of our being, creating an inner peace.

Learning to heal our relationships with others is not easy, but is necessary if we want to experience real joy.

C

I will use forgiveness and love to heal past hurts.

Year 10:2

A

Every time we laugh when we are hurt, or smile when we feel angry, it is like burying an unripe fruit inside us. Instead of ripening into an edible delight, the emotion begins to rot and decay, and eventually its poison spreads throughout our body.

GILL EDWARDS, *LIVING MAGICALLY – A NEW VISION OF REALITY*

B

Emotions move and flow through us. They are to be experienced and felt but not grasped and held. Emotions which are locked up inside us can be painful.

Sitting on our feelings uses up a lot of energy and leaves us exhausted. Facing our emotions, accepting them and releasing them can lead to inner peace and wholeness.

C

I will stop fighting and fleeing from my emotions, but instead, accept and flow with them.

Year 10:3

A

Do we not know from the gospels that simply to touch God is endless health? 'If I but touch the hem of his garment I shall be healed': so said the woman who came to Jesus.

THE EPISTLE OF PRIVY COUNSEL, *THE DART OF LONGING LOVE*

B

A common theme of religions around the world is that people are in need of healing – healing of their fears and all kinds of wounds. Giving time and attention to our spiritual life can help us to understand ourselves. Turning to our spiritual life can create the conditions for healing and strength. A child-like trust in a power greater than ourselves can be all that is needed for the healing process to begin. When we believe that we can be brought back to good health, we possess a powerful gift.

C
God's love is my strength.

Year 11:1

A
No matter how old or mature we are, there are times when we need to be nurtured as if we were a child.

SUE PATTON THOELE, *THE WOMAN'S BOOK OF COURAGE*

B
Rather than responding to our feelings of need by acting tough and bottling our feelings up, we can respond to the need of our 'inner child' with loving care and attention. We can talk to ourselves in a kind and nurturing way or share our feelings with a friend – asking for a hug if we require one.

By listening to and getting to know the part of ourselves that is needy, we are in a better position to ask for comfort when we require it, and get our needs met.

C
I will be aware of the times when I need to be nurtured.

Year 11:2

A
It's OK to cry!

LYDIA, AGED 4

B

Our culture doesn't generally encourage us to cry, which is a great pity as shedding tears can be an important part of healing ourselves. We need to adopt the belief that 'it's OK to cry' and give ourselves encouragement and permission to do so, because crying can be of great benefit to us.

We can release blocked emotions and thoughts like grief, anger, sadness and frustration. When we cry, we may feel engulfed by pain at the time, but this eventually gives way to a feeling of peace and calm – we feel healed by our tears.

It is not a weakness to weep, but a strength, for it takes courage to face our feelings and let them flow through us.

Crying doesn't only happen when we are low, for we can also cry with laughter, joy and relief.

C

I will cry when I need to.

Year 11:3

A

Our breath is the most precious substance in our lives, and yet we totally take for granted when we exhale that our next breath will be there. If we did not take another breath, we would not last three minutes.

LOUISE L. HAY, *YOU CAN HEAL YOUR LIFE*

B

The air that we breathe helps to maintain us. Without food we could live for weeks, without water we could stay alive for days, but without air we would only last a few minutes.

The way in which we breathe can affect our emotions and health in general. When we feel anxious; deep, slow, calm breathing can help to soothe away tension and fear. This is a good way to reduce our stress levels. When we are tense or tired, spending a few minutes breathing steadily and deeply can help us to feel energized and ready to tackle life again.

In his book *Unlimited Power*, Anthony Robbins claims that taking ten deep breaths three times a day can bring about dramatic improvement in our level of health.

It can also be helpful to check regularly throughout the day the way that we are breathing. Are we taking small shallow breathes, or are we making full use of our lungs and sometimes expanding them to their full capacity?

C

I will appreciate each life – giving breath.

21 LOVE IN HUMAN RELATIONSHIPS

Year 7:1

A

A hug.
Feels good
Dispels loneliness
Overcomes fears
Builds self-esteem
Slows down ageing, huggers stay younger longer,
Eases tension
Fights insomnia
Keeps arm and shoulder muscles in condition
Is ecologically sound, does not upset the environment,
Is democratic, anyone is eligible for a hug,
Is portable,
Affirms physical being,
Is energy efficient, saves heat
Makes impossible days possible,
Makes happier days happier.
A hug makes you feel good all day.

KATHLEEN KEATING, *THE TINY BOOK OF HUGS*

B

A hug can be embarrassing! We like to keep our distance, and often the only physical contact we have is when we hit or slap somebody. It is not always a nasty 'hit' but often the only way we can touch someone. In Junior School the boys often 'hit' the girls they really like. It's a case of 'Ouch! he hit me – he really must love me!'

In American films fathers and sons often give one another a hug, or families and friends have a 'group hug', but as yet it has not crossed the Atlantic. 'Good job too,' some will say, but a hug is a lot more reassuring and far less painful than a hit.

C

Today I will start by giving myself a hug.

Year 7:2

A

Let's stop loving things and using people, and start using things and loving people.

B

When someone we love goes away it is not the size of their house or the make of their car that we remember, but what they said to us, how they listened to us, how much they showed they cared for us. Those are the important things when dealing with one another.

Real love is a selfless love. It expects nothing in return. We should not go searching for this love, because we only find it by giving it away!

C

Today I will act in a loving way to others.

Year 7:3

A

Love is patient and kind; love is not jealous or boastful; it is not arrogant or rude. Love does not insist on its own way; it is not irritable or resentful, it does not rejoice at wrong, but rejoices in the right. Love bears all things, believes all things, hopes all things, endures all things. Love never ends.

1 CORINTHIANS 13:4–8

B

You made me understand myself,
When I thought I never would,
You made me see myself,
For what I really am,
I accept myself now,
More easily than before,
I see myself in a different way,
You showed me what no person,
Had ever shown me before,
You made me understand,
Nobody's perfect, not even me.
You made me realize that
People can love and care
Without hurting someone.
I now know it does not
Matter what anyone says
Because you showed me
You love me.

A. THOMSON

C

I will take a moment today with a friend who needs my love.

Year 8:1

A

Love is patient and kind; it is not jealous or conceited or proud.

1 CORINTHIANS 13:4

B

The love mentioned here is not a sentimental love, it is deeper than any emotional love. It is a sacrificial love, which flows out to other people, expecting nothing in return.

Love is patient. It is easy to be impatient with people and situations, wanting what we want and wanting it now – but that is not love.

Love is kind; this is having a generous spirit, or being big-hearted.

Love is not jealous; so often love is associated with a 'you belong to me' attitude, but that is not love. When we love we are not jealous of people, but glad when others do well.

Loving is not about acting in a conceited or proud way, but rather acting with humility.

These are high ideals, but then, don't we want the best for ourselves and those around us?

C

I will be patient with those around me today.

Year 8:2

A

Let no one ever come to you without going away better and happier.
Let there be kindness in your face, kindness in your eyes.

MOTHER TERESA

B

The patience, kindness and humble spirit that we associate with being truly loving can be seen in Mother Teresa of Calcutta. She is a nun who went to India to teach Geography. When she saw the poor and sick on the streets of Calcutta she decided to leave the security of the convent and to retrain as a nurse, to work amongst the sick and dying.

She had to beg for medicines and for a room to treat patients. She took in the dying, the lepers and the unwanted children.

It can be easy in modern-day life to get used to seeing people on the streets. If we have a generous, kind heart we would find it impossible to pass by without helping.

C

I will be kind to those I meet today.

Year 8:3

A

What these people need even more than food and shelter is to be wanted. They understand that even if they only have a few hours left to live, they are loved.

MOTHER TERESA

B

Mother Teresa could be the president of her charity, sitting in a fine office away from the poor and dying. She could live in the finest house and wear the finest clothes, and we could all say, she deserves it.

She has spent fifty years helping the poor; now she is an old lady, well past the retirement age; she deserves some comfort. But this is not the case. She is spending her remaining years caring for the sick and dying. Telling them by her life, and by her words, that they are loved.

C

I will care for those I meet today.

Year 9:1

A

Love does not demand its own way. It is not irritable or touchy. It does not hold grudges and will hardly even notice when others do it wrong.

1 CORINTHIANS 13:5

B

They say that we can judge how loving we are by taking out the word 'love' from the quote and inserting the word 'I'. So we get, 'I do not demand my own way. I am not irritable or touchy. I do not hold grudges.'

We often feel justified in holding a grudge, we feel that we would be letting the person 'off the hook', if we forgave them. It is only natural to keep a mental record when somebody has wronged us. But with love we can be a supernatural people. The famous Indian leader, Gandhi, said, 'An eye for an eye and soon the whole world will be blind.'

How different life would be if we returned hate with love.

C

Today I will not hold on to grudges.

Year 9:2

A

There is nothing that love cannot face; there is no limit to its faith, its hope, and its endurance. Love will never come to an end.

1 CORINTHIANS 13:1,8

B

As one can imagine, after the war there was a lot of hatred between people and between the nations. There was a lot of hurt and a lot of forgiveness was needed.

Corrie Ten Boom was a Dutch woman who had suffered in Ravensbruck Concentration Camp because she and her family had hidden Jews from the Nazis. Her father died in prison and her sister in the camp. Yet after the war Corrie travelled to Germany to speak about God's forgiveness.

At a church in Munich she recognised a former prison camp guard. She vividly remembered all the horror, anguish and humiliation she suffered the last time she saw him. He did not recognise her, but conscious of the part he played in the war he approached her and asked her forgiveness. She did not want to shake his hand, she just felt a coldness as she stood there. Eventually, she mechanically put out her hand and they shook hands. Only then did she feel the love of God flow through her to him.

ADAPTED FROM HANS POLEY, *RETURN TO THE HIDING PLACE*

C

There is nothing that I cannot face if I have love.

Year 9:3

A

When you look at someone with eyes of love, you see a reality different from that of someone who looks at the same person without love, with hatred or even just with indifference.

DESMOND TUTU, IN *PRAYERS FOR PEACE*

B

If anyone had the right to look at people with hatred, or indifference, surely Desmond Tutu had that right. As a black South African, he suffered many injustices. Even though he was an educated man he was not entitled to vote because of the colour of his skin. When he was appointed Archbishop of Cape Town and head of the Anglican Church in South Africa, many whites within the church turned their backs on him. He did not return hate for hate, indifference for indifference. He looked at his oppressors with the eyes of love.

C

I will see people with the eyes of love.

Year 10:1

A

Love never gives up; and its faith, hope, and patience never fail.

1 CORINTHIANS 13:7

B

It is easy to give up on people. When someone breaks a promise or lets us down it's natural to think, 'That's it, I'm having nothing more to do with them.'

It can get very tiring and very exasperating when we try to help a friend in trouble and a week later they do the same thing again. The common reaction is 'why bother?' But love is about helping our friends again, and again and again. It is sticking by our friends and never giving up on them.

C

I will stand by my friends.

Year 10:2

A

Love is not getting, but giving. It is sacrifice. And sacrifice is glorious.

JOANNA FIELD, *EACH DAY A NEW BEGINNING* (12 MARCH)

B

David Wilkerson was a minister of a small church in a small village in America. When he read of a murder trial involving some gang members in New York, he felt compelled to try to do something. He went to New York to attend their trial, but was kicked out of the court. This did not deter him, he did not give up. Eventually he met some gang members. He was threatened with flick-knives, slapped on the face and spat on, but he did not give up.

The result of his patience and endurance with the gangs in New York resulted in many members giving up the gangs, the killings and the drugs. Teen Challenge Centres have been set up where thousands of addicts have been given support to get off drugs. Some of the gang leaders who first threatened his life are now Christians and doing the same work as he did when he first went to New York.

C

I will not give up with people.

Year 10:3

A

He was still a long way from home when his father saw him; his heart was filled with pity, and he ran, threw his arms round his son, and kissed him.

LUKE 15:20

B

This passage is part of a story about a young man. He felt unable to wait for his father to die to inherit his portion of the property, so he asked his father for his share immediately. The father granted his son's wish, but within a few days the son had sold his property to get some cash. Now he had some money he went to a country far away to spend, spend, spend.

Eventually the money ran out, and destitute, he realized that he would be better off working for his father. His father must have been feeling quite hurt, not only had the son sold the family property but he had moved far away, rejecting the family. However, the father did not reject the son. Arms outstretched, he welcomed his son back into his home.

Love never rejects; love never gives up.

C

Today I will try and find love for those I could reject.

Year 11:1

A

Love cures people. Both the ones who give it, and the ones who receive it.

KARL MENNINGER, *DAYS OF HEALING, DAYS OF JOY* (16 APRIL)

B

There are three words for *love* in the Greek New Testament; one is 'eros' – romantic love; another is 'philos' – love between friends. The third word is 'agape' – this is more than romance or friendship. This is understanding and goodwill to all people.

Dr Martin Luther King said, 'This is what Jesus meant when he said, "Love your enemies". And I'm happy that he didn't say, "Like your enemies", because there are some people that I find it very difficult to like. Liking is an affectionate emotion, and I can't like anyone who would bomb my home. I can't like anyone who would exploit me. I can't like anyone who would trample over me with injustices. I can't like them. But Jesus reminds us that love is greater than liking. Love is understanding, creative, redemptive goodwill towards all people.' ('A Christmas Sermon', in *The Trumpet of Conscience*)

C

I will try to love those that I cannot like.

Year 11:2

A

Love can be its own reward.

ARNOLD LOBEL, IN *TOUCHSTONES* (18 FEBRUARY)

B

About seven million children live on the streets of Brazil's cities. Sometimes their parents cannot take care of them because they are too poor or sick, or problems in the home force the children to run away. They live by finding food in rubbish bins and by stealing. Many get involved with drugs which help them to forget the awful existence they are living. As a result, many also get AIDS.

Some Brazilian Christians try to help these children by providing a safe place for them to stay, giving them food and clothing and eventually, if they can, a family.

Some of the street children they helped originally are now adults, have changed lives and are now helping street children themselves.

Not only are they returning the love given to them, but passing it on to others.

C

Today I will be thankful for all the loving things that happen to me.

Year 11:3

A

To love is to open our hearts to people
to listen to them,
to appreciate them
and see in them their own unique value,
to wish deeply that they may live and grow.
To love is to give our lives for one another.
It is to forgive,
and to be compassionate.

J. VANIER, IN *MANY THOUGHTS*

B

Love is active, not passive. It is no good passing by someone in need and thinking, 'I love you', because our actions have shown that inside we do not care.

In Portsmouth, there is an organization called the Isaiah 58 Trust. It is run by a young woman who gave up a good career to help the homeless. She organizes daily meals, clothing and accommodation in the winter. She has no personal money so she also has to spend time persuading people to give of their time and their money. When the homeless sit down for a meal she makes sure that they are treated with dignity – no queuing. She then takes time to listen to them, to appreciate them and see in them their own unique value.

C

I will try to see people from the inside out – and not from the outside in.

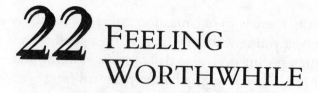

22 FEELING WORTHWHILE

Year 7:1

A

My Declaration of Self-esteem:

I am me. In all the world there is no one else exactly like me. There are persons who have some parts like me, but no one adds up exactly like me. Therefore, everything that comes out of me is uniquely mine because I alone chose it.

VIRGINIA SATIR, *EACH DAY A NEW BEGINNING* (13 NOVEMBER)

B

The miracle of birth. A Jewish viewpoint:

'The days of Biblical miracles are long past. The sea does not divide for us, and the blast of the shofar does not shatter the walls of a city. But the greatest miracle occurs a thousand times every day. The miracle of birth.

Birth is a double miracle for Jews. First is the miracle of life itself, the creation of a new human being. Second, although this miracle has occurred billions of times in the past, each birth brings forth a totally new, totally different individual.

The Talmud teaches: "Man stamps many coins from the same mould, and every coin is exactly the same. But God has stamped many people from the same mould, yet not one is like his fellow man. Therefore, one must say, 'For my sake was the world created' ".' (Harry Gersh)

We are all different, unique, a 'one-off'. Nobody thinks like us, nobody feels the same way we do. Consequently the life we lead will be distinct from the life anyone else will lead. It is quite an exciting prospect.

Fortunately there are signposts and guides to help us throughout the journey of life, but we need to choose which steps to take. Yes, it is an exciting prospect!

C

Today I will be aware of who I am, and what is special about me.

Year 7:2

A

Love your neighbour as you love yourself.

MATTHEW 22:39

B

We understand about loving our neighbour, helping those in need, but we lose sight of the second half of the saying, 'as you love yourself'. It can be difficult to love ourselves, possibly because we know ourselves too well, or because we are not the sort of person that we want to be.

We need to learn to accept and then to love ourselves. We can feel inadequate, dull and unattractive when we look in the mirror in the morning, but we need to like the person that we see staring back at us. It does not mean being proud or boastful, it just means accepting ourselves as we accept those around us. The more we accept ourselves the more we can appreciate those around us. Other people will not be a threat to us, because we already see ourselves as loveable and worthwhile.

C

Today I will accept myself and those around me.

Year 7:3

A

Myself.
I have to live with myself, and so
I want to be fit for myself to know:
I want to be able as days go by
Always to look myself straight in the eye.
I don't want to stand with the setting sun
And hate myself for the things I've done.

EDGAR A. GUEST, IN *POEMS FOR ASSEMBLIES*

B

When we see a fall of snow it is easy to forget that it is made up of millions of individual snowflakes. Each flake is unique, with its own pattern and its own beauty. Yet, when all these snowflakes merge together and they lose their individuality, they combine to form a different type of beauty.

We are all unique, we are all different and we all have our own gifts to offer to the rest of humanity. We might not think that we have anything to offer others, but because we are all special we all have something to share.

If we have never thought about this before perhaps now is the time to consider what our special gift is.

C

Today I will think about what is special about me.

Year 8:1

A

We must first accept ourselves, and learn to love ourselves, if we are to do anything meaningful with our lives.

JAN THOMPSON, *MANY THOUGHTS*

B

It is easy to judge yourself by making comparisons. I am not as tall, strong, slim, beautiful or intelligent as the next person. But then nobody is! There will always be someone who has that edge on us, but it does not matter. We are all a part of creation and each one of us is different.

We must be glad of the difference. We can do nothing if we dislike ourselves. We will feel that all we do will fail because we are worthless.

We need to love ourselves, to accept ourselves, just as we are and celebrate being a unique individual.

C

Today I will be glad that I am me.

Year 8:2

A

As long as I live
I shall always be
Myself and no other
Just me.
Like a tree
Willow, Elder, Aspen, Thorn
or Cypress forlorn.
Like a flower for its hour,
Primrose or Pink
or a Violet sunned by the sun
and with dewdrops wet
Always Just Me;
Till the day comes on
When I leave this body
It's all then done
And the spirit within it, is gone.

'ME' BY ZOE McFADYEN, AGED 11

B

Zoe was an amazing girl. I say 'was', because she died at the age of 12. She knew that she was dying, but she never gave in to her illness or to self-pity. Whatever obstacles arose to hinder her living a normal life, she found ways to overcome them.

She would not let her family give her extra protection, nor would she let them treat her any differently because of her illness. Zoe believed in herself and accepted herself for who she was, and her indomitable spirit was an inspiration to those around her.

C

I will accept myself for being me.

Year 8:3

A

Promise yourself to be so strong that nothing can disturb your peace of mind.

CHRISTIAN D. LARSON

B

To be strong we need 'to look at the sunny side of everything'. To think only of the best, to work only for the best and expect only the best. To be just as enthusiastic about the success of others as you are about your own. To forget the mistakes of the past and press on to the greater achievements of the future.

To give so much time to the improvement of yourself that you have no time to criticize others.

To be too large for worry, too noble for anger, too strong for fear and too happy to permit the presence of trouble.

ADAPTED FROM CHRISTIAN D. LARSON

C

I will expect only the best today.

Year 9:1

A

Take away love and our earth is a tomb.

ROBERT BROWNING, IN *DAYS OF HEALING, DAYS OF JOY*
(29 FEBRUARY)

B

Love is important to us all, but we need to love ourselves before we can give or accept the love of others.

When we cannot love ourselves, we show it by our behaviour. For example, we pick on the faults in other people that we most dislike in ourselves; when we feel powerless we might try to exert power over others, or when we feel guilty we may try to make others feel guilty. When we learn to accept ourselves – then we can accept others.

C

Today I will learn to love myself.

Year 9:2

A

You don't have to be alone to be lonely … but that's when you feel it the most!

JEAN C. GRIGOR, *GROW TO LOVE*

B

Being alone is not loneliness, in fact, being alone can be an enriching experience. Loneliness is being unable to share with others, being unable to relate to others and feeling that there is nobody to relate to.

Sometimes our feelings of self-worth have taken a nose dive. For some reason or another we do not value ourselves, and therefore we cannot accept that other people value us.

We all have a worthwhile contribution to make to the world around us. When we see how special we are, and value ourselves we feel worthwhile and able to relate to others.

C

I will value myself and share with others today.

Year 9:3

A

Looking through his tears he saw her as she bent low in order to look into his eyes. 'I never prayed for you to be born crippled,' she said, 'I wanted you to be full of life, able to run and jump and talk like Yvonne. But you are you, you are Joseph not Yvonne. Listen here, Joseph, you can see, you can hear, you can think, you can understand everything you hear, you like your food, you like nice clothes, you are loved by me and Dad. We love you just as your are.'

CHRISTOPHER NOLAN, IN *MANY THOUGHTS*

B

Christopher Nolan suffered brain damage at birth and consequently he cannot speak; he cannot hear well and he cannot move himself. However, with the aid of modern technology, he is able to type. He wrote a book called *Under the Eye of the Clock* which won the Whitbread Book of the Year prize. It is basically his story, although he writes as if it is about someone else.

His mother's speech just quoted burnt in his mind. He was only three years old but he realized that he was valued just as he was.

It is often hard to accept ourselves, just as we are, when the media flood us with pictures of beautiful people. We could buy the same clothes and copy the same hair style, but often what looks great on the stars, looks ridiculous on us.

Yet look at the power of accepting ourselves as we are. Christopher Nolan could have been left on the rubbish dump of life, but he realized that he was of worth and became an acclaimed author.

C

I will love myself, just as I am.

Year 10:1

A

I'm sorry that I feel I must express this point of view:
Society's professed concern is a sham!
For I'm judged quite completely on the basis of 'IQ',
Instead of on the basis of 'I am'.

GORDON BAILEY, *PLASTIC WORLD*

B

I was invited to a meal with some new friends. As we chatted and got to know one another better, the husband admitted that he had been dreading my visit. He explained that sooner or later the question would be asked 'What do you do?' He would then feel embarrassed, as he had no employment.

It is so easy to judge people by the kind of job they do or by what exams they have passed, or by what they are studying, or by their positions of responsibility in the school or community or by the awards they've received. This man was a kind, caring and helpful person, but because he was unemployed he didn't feel good enough.

We sometimes need to stop thinking about *what* we are and need to concentrate on *who* we are.

C

Today I will consider the qualities that make me the person I am.

Year 10:2

A

Be a friend to thyself, and others will befriend thee.

DICTIONARY OF QUOTATIONS AND PROVERBS

B

When we suffer from low self-esteem we do not really like ourselves. And when we do not like ourselves we cannot accept that other people might like us, so we tend not to join in, in case we are rejected. This 'holding back' is then misinterpreted by those around us. They think that we do not want to join in, so they keep their distance. This reinforces the idea that we are not liked and our self-esteem plunges even lower. It is a vicious circle – a self-fulfilling prophecy.

So how do we break out of this vicious circle? We start by loving ourselves. We need to see ourselves as unique individuals, people of value. We need to develop our sense of personal worth. The starting point is self-acceptance – when we can accept ourselves, we will find acceptance from those around us.

C

Today I will befriend and accept myself.

Year 10:3

A

I'm not ready to die, I've got too much to do ...

PAUL BARNEY, AS REPORTED IN *TODAY*, 30 SEPTEMBER 1994

B

Most people were shocked when they woke up one morning at the end of September 1994 to hear of the sinking of the ferry

Estonia. Over 900 people drowned as the boat rapidly sank on its journey between Estonia and Sweden. Many communities in those two countries lost somebody that they loved.

Those who survived also suffered great trauma. Apart from the shock there was the big question 'Why me?'

We sometimes do not put a great value on our life, and take if for granted. It is only when we are in danger of losing our life do we realize its value. Paul Barney was one of the survivors. In the awful dark cold water where he watched people die, he decided that his life was too precious to give up. Let's value our life as a gift and make the most of it.

C

Today I will celebrate being alive.

Year 11:1

A

Who is the person sitting next to you? ...

The person nearest you is a unique world of experience. Within him is constantly going on a premiere of experiences that no person has ever had, or ever will have. He is unique cluster of memories of the past and expectations of the future. He has some things he can do well. There are some things he can do better than anybody else in the whole world. He is the only person in the whole world in direct touch with how he feels, sees, experiences.

ROSS SNYDER, *INSCAPE*

B

If this is true of the person sitting next to you, then it is also true of you. You are unique, nobody else is like you, you are special.

It follows that if we are all different, then we all have something different to contribute to life, we are all needed.

When we take on board our 'specialness', we can value ourselves for who we are, not what we could be, would be or should be. We can accept who we are right at this moment.

C

Today I will appreciate who I am.

Year 11:2

A

The crazy mirrors at the fair give us a distorted view of ourselves. The situations we encounter also get distorted when we have no self-worth.

J.A.H.

B

In a large office abroad, several people worked together. One of them was a quiet, polite English lady, close to retirement. Each day she arrived, worked and went home. Everyone in the office was much younger, and only working abroad for a limited time. She had worked there since she was a young woman and her friends had long since returned home.

One day a message was left on her desk, and her name had been mis-spelt. It suggested that she was a 'mis-fit' not a Miss Fitt. Everyone sat embarrassed as she exploded with anger. After investigation it was discovered that the messenger had made a genuine mistake, no insult was intended.

When we lose our feelings of self-worth we can become over-sensitive and see insults where they are not meant. When we feel secure in our own worth we will not take offence when it is not intended.

C

Today I will try to let my feelings of being worthwhile, guide my actions.

266

Year 11:3

A

I'm an old woman now and nature is cruel,
Tis her jest to make old age look like a fool.
The body it crumbles, grace and vigour depart,
There is a stone where I once had a heart.
But inside this old carcass a young girl still dwells,
And now again my bittered heart swells.
I remember the joys, I remember the pain
And I'm loving and living life over again.
I think of the years, all too few, gone too fast
And accept the stark fact that nothing can last.
So open your eyes, nurse, open and see
Not a crabbed old woman,
Look closer – see me!

FROM *ACORN NEWS*, JUNE/JULY 1994

B

This is part of a longer poem written by an old woman who
died in a geriatric ward in a hospital near Dundee.

This old lady recognized that on the outside she was an 'old
carcass'. She also remembers the happy life she has experienced, filled with family and friends. Outside she is a 'crabbed
old woman', but inside she is still the same young woman that
she always has been. She is crying out to be recognized for who
she is, not for what she looks like.

We all need to be recognized for who we are.

C

Today I will look for the inner person.

23 FRIENDSHIP

Year 7:1

A

Recipe for Friendship
INGREDIENTS
3 tablespoons of friendship
2 tablespoons of love
a sprinkle of trust-dust
4oz of bright smiles
2oz of sharing
sprinkle of laughter
6 teaspoons of comfort

METHOD
Mix together the 3 tablespoons of friendship and 2 tablespoons of love. Add 4oz of bright smiles and 2oz of sharing. Then a sprinkle of trust-dust followed by teaspoons of comfort. Then sprinkle with laughter and put in the oven for 20 minutes on 190. Ready when bubbling with love and friendship.

SONYA MURTON

B

Friends are people who we can laugh with, share with and turn to when we feel sad. But every friendship needs 'a sprinkle of trust-dust', because without trust we would not be able to share, and when we cannot share, our friendship cannot deepen. Once we learn to trust our friends, the sharing, the laughter and smiles will follow.

C

Today I will appreciate my friends.

Year 7:2

A

The greatest pleasure of life is love
The greatest treasure, contentment
The greatest possession, health
The greatest ease is sleep
The greatest medicine is a true friend.

SIR WILLIAM TEMPLE

B

Some of the happiest people are those who have true friends. Friends who are only out for what they can get are easy to find; but those who are loyal are worth their weight in gold. It has been said that 'a friend is someone who knows a lot about you and loves you just the same'.

Friendships make us feel good about ourselves, and help us cope with the 'ups and downs' of life; so we should appreciate our friends and be thankful for their friendship.

C

Today I will be thankful for my true friends.

Year 7:3

A

Don't walk in front of me,
I may not follow.
Don't walk behind me,
I may not lead.

Walk beside me,
And just be my friend.

ANONYMOUS, IN *A BOOK OF FRIENDS AND FRIENDSHIP*

B

Friends are people who we are content just 'to be' with. There is no need to talk, laugh or joke. The relationship is so complete that you can walk together in silence, for words are unnecessary.

Friends accept our moods. Friends know when to speak and when to be silent. Friends are always there when we need them.

C

Today I will accept people for what they are, not for what I want them to be.

Year 8:1

A

A faithful friend is the medicine of life.

ECCLESIASTICUS, IN *A BOOK OF FRIENDS AND FRIENDSHIP*

B

Recent medical studies show that people who own a cat or a dog live longer. Apparently the action of stroking an animal is calming and lowers the pulse rate while tensions and stresses fall away.

Those of us who are able to have a dog or a cat know that they offer a lot of love and friendship as well. They never judge us, they are not concerned with our progress or our possessions. They just accept us for who we are.

Jerome K. Jerome said that when things go wrong a dog will look at you with his big brown eyes, as if to say 'Well, you've always got me, you know. We'll go through the world together, and always stand by each other, won't we?' (in *A Book of Friends and Friendship*).

C

I am thankful for friendships.

Year 8:2

A

I always feel better when I've been with my friend.

CHARLOTTE Y, *DAYS OF HEALING, DAYS OF JOY* (6 DECEMBER)

B

Sometimes the most unlikely people become friends. There is no set formula for this interaction. Maybe a word said, or a common experience, and something clicks into place.

Having friends makes us feel good about ourselves. A friend, by being a friend, is saying that they like us. This does not mean that they approve of all we do and say, but it does mean that they see beyond these things and like us, as a person.

This friendship can bring out the best in us, and gives us the freedom to be ourselves.

C

I will appreciate my friends.

Year 8:3

A

Friendships multiply joys and divide griefs.

DICTIONARY OF QUOTATIONS AND PROVERBS

B

I have a friend who loved to tour around Scotland with her

husband. They didn't plan a route, they just took what looked like the most interesting road. They stopped to admire the grand scenery whenever they felt like it. Unfortunately her husband died suddenly. She returned to Scotland another year for a holiday, but it was not the same. She could choose whatever road she wanted, stop whenever she wanted, but there was no joy when there was no friend to share the experience.

Friendships give more meaning to our lives. The experiences shared among friends are special. It is no accident that we have been drawn here together. What we have will help one another.

C

Today I will strengthen my friendships.

Year 9:1

A

Treat your friends as you do your pictures, and place them in their best light.

JENNIE JEROME CHURCHILL, IN *EACH DAY A NEW BEGINNING* (6 APRIL)

B

When a friendship develops and we grow comfortable with our friends it is easy to take them for granted. We can expect them to accept the odd and annoying things that we do, but in return we might expect perfection from them.

It is easy to make friends the butt of our jokes, and think that it does not matter because we are friends, yet how often we get hurt by jokes directed at us.

Friendship is good, it makes us feel special. If we want the best for our friends then how we treat them will reflect this – being positive towards them, building them up, showing our appreciation of them and encouraging them – will be a natural outflow of our friendship.

C

I will appreciate my friends.

Year 9:2

A

Speak well of your friends, of your enemy say nothing.
DICTIONARY OF QUOTATIONS AND PROVERBS

B

Generally speaking, friendship is a good thing. It gives us companionship, it helps our self-esteem and it encourages us to share with others. There is a negative side though, when we use our friendship to make others feel excluded.

We see this usually in small children when they first discover this new relationship called 'friendship'. Other children then are classed as 'my friend' or 'not my friend'. Many a youngster has run from the playground crying because they have not been allowed to join in a game, because 'You are not my friend'. Childish, yes, but it happens all the way through life, even into adulthood. We find people use the excuse of 'friendship' to exclude others. We can sometimes even try to make our friends break friends with those we do not like.

If friendship is to be good, it must be good for all. If we value our friends, we must give them the freedom to choose other friends. If the friendship is true and real, we have nothing to fear.

C

I will value my friends.

Year 9:3

A

Faithful are the wounds of a friend.

PROVERBS 27:6

B

It is strange to think of a friend wounding us, but a few hurtful words from a friend are more painful than a hundred wounding words from a stranger. If something like this happens to us we need to understand what is going on. Is the person really a friend? Did they mean to hurt us or are they trying to tell us something about ourselves that they think will be of help?

Sometimes we can feel hurt because a friend has spoken a truth that we don't want to accept. That friend can help us make changes and heal wounds.

C

I am thankful for my faithful friends.

Year 10:1

A

The only reward of virtue is virtue; the only way to have a friend is to be one.

RALPH WALDO EMERSON, *DICTIONARY OF QUOTATIONS AND PROVERBS*

B

A little girl starting at her first infant school came home crying because she had no friends. The mother asked her teacher for help. The teacher suggested that at playtimes the little girl might stop hiding behind the wall, then maybe somebody would notice her and befriend her. The problem was soon solved.

When we are teenagers it can be harder to make friends. We have lost the openness of childhood, the easy trust of other people. There is a fear of rejection, of being put down.

To get friends, we need to be friendly. We need to care about other people, take time and an interest in other people. There is a fear of rejection, of being put down.

To get friends, we need to be friendly. We need to care about other people, take time and an interest in other people. The friendships will develop without us realizing it.

C

I will be friendly to others.

Year 10:2

A

Friendship is a sheltering tree.

SAMUEL TAYLOR COLERIDGE, *DAYS OF HEALING, DAYS OF JOY* (1 JUNE)

B

Some people think that they do not want or need friends. Maybe they have been hurt in the past by friends and think that it is better to keep oneself to oneself. However, there are many good things about friendship. First, you can share with a friend: sadness, happiness, hopes, fears and dreams.

Secondly, if everything is getting too much for us, a friend can listen and give us wise advice. It sometimes takes a friend's insight to help us see our problems and discuss them with us.

And thirdly, a friend is someone who we can just be with and enjoy their company.

C

I realize that I need friends.

Year 10:3

A

Even though I can't solve your problems, I will be there
as your sounding board whenever you need me.

SANDRA K. LAMBERSON, *EACH DAY A NEW BEGINNING* (10 APRIL)

B

When we are small most of our problems can be solved by a cuddle, or a few words, or some cream to heal a wound.

As we grow, so do the problems and we soon learn that they cannot be solved as easily as when we were young.

Even though we cannot solve one another's problems, it does help to share them, to talk about them and to look for ways of resolving them. That's what friendship is about. It is being interested in what our friends have to say without looking for gossip and giving attention to others, forgetting ourselves.

C

I will listen to my friends.

Year 11:1

A

A friend is never known till needed.

14TH-CENTURY PROVERB, IN *DICTIONARY OF QUOTATIONS AND PROVERBS*

B

We all have 'ups and downs' in our life, and it is often in the 'downs' that we discover who our real friends are. It is really good when someone we have considered our friend is there for us when things go wrong, it reinforces our belief in human nature. But it can also be upsetting when those we thought cared do not really show an interest in our problem, and give out all the signals that they are switching off to our troubles.

When those we know are not there for us, we can be pleasantly surprised to find someone we hardly know will care for us and support us through the difficult times.

It is on these occasions that we begin to understand what true friendship is about.

C
I am thankful for friendship.

Year 11:2

A

A friend's frown is better than a fool's smile.

DICTIONARY OF QUOTATIONS AND PROVERBS

B
It is very hard to accept criticism, even if it is considered to be 'constructive'. However, knowing that we could all improve the sort of person we are, criticism is important. And who would advise us better than a friend? Friends can point out things about us that we never really notice, and because they are our friends we know that they only want the best for us.

A friend will tell us if we have cabbage caught in our teeth. A friend will also point out the more important issues, such as whether we are being fair to others, whether we are being honest with ourselves and whether we have life in perspective.

Do we want a friend like a nodding dog, always smiling and approving of all we do, or do we want a friend who tells the truth?

C
Today I will learn from my friends.

Year 11:3

A

Friendship, 'the wine of life', should, like a well-stocked cellar, be thus continually renewed.

JAMES BOSWELL (1740–95), IN *A BOOK OF FRIENDS AND FRIENDSHIP*

B

As we travel through life we will lose some of our friends. This happens a lot today when so many people move around the country because of the work situation. Also, when we leave school, we often go in different directions to our friends and it is difficult to maintain the contact.

Some people will always be our friends and even though we do not meet them often, when we meet it will be as if there has been no absence.

If we continually look for new friends, although it takes some effort, it brings a worthwhile reward.

C

Today I will be open to new friendship.

24 HUMAN RIGHTS AND RESPONSIBILITIES

Year 7:1

A

Each pupil is an individual with the right to attend school and receive a good quality education. At the same time there is an expectation that each individual will contribute to and conform to the simple operational rules of the site. This individual responsibility includes consideration and respect for teachers and all who work in the school, and includes visitors and fellow pupils.

As part of the system of values which underpins the ethos of Bohunt School the following code of conduct has been prepared.

There is an expectation that each individual will follow basic good standards of behaviour in regard to politeness and manners. For example, in queuing, receiving a marked book, listening to the comments or contribution of another.

FROM *BOHUNT CODE OF CONDUCT*

B

The Bohunt Code of Conduct contains the ground rules for Bohunt School. It is the responsibility of all pupils to keep to them, because they provide discipline, direction, comfort and safety for everyone there.

Everyone, and that means everyone, has a responsibility for making their school a happy and safe place to be in.

C

Today I will remember that what I do has an effect on the atmosphere in my school.

Year 7:2

A

This we know:
All things are connected,
like the blood that unites one family.
Whatever befalls the earth, befalls all the sons of the earth.
Man did not weave the web of life,
he is merely a strand in it.
Whatever he does to the web, he does to himself.
This we know.

CHIEF SEATTLE, DWAMISH INDIAN (1855)

B

These words were part of a letter written by Chief Seattle to the President of the United States of America. They were written in about 1855 in response to an offer from the United States government to buy an area of Indian tribal land. The letter begins:

'The President in Washington sends word that he wishes to buy our land. But how can buy or sell the sky? The land? The idea is strange to us. If you do not own the freshness of the air and the sparkle of the water, how can you buy them?'

The letter ends:

'We love this earth as a newborn loves its mother's heart-beat. So if we sell you our land, love it as we have loved it. Care for it as we have card for it. Hold in your mind the memory of the land as it is when you receive it. Preserve the land for all children and love it, as God loves us all.

'As we are part of the land, you too are part of the land. This earth is precious to us. It is also precious to you. One thing we know: there is only one God. No man, be he Red Man or White Man, can be apart. We are brothers after all.'

Can we learn from this wisdom today?

C

Today I will remember that we are all part of the Earth and responsible for its well-being.

Year 7:3

A

This is a story about four people
named Everybody, Somebody,
Anybody, and Nobody.
There was an important job to
be done and Everybody was sure
that Somebody would do it.
Anybody could have done it,
but Nobody did it.
Somebody got angry about that
because it was Everybody's job.
Everybody thought Anybody could
do it, but Nobody realized
that Everybody wouldn't do it.
It ended up that Everybody
blamed Somebody
when Nobody
did what Anybody
could have done.

B

Everybody has rights. Everybody has the right to be treated well, to be physically safe and to have their property respected. We all have the right to believe and say what we like. But there can be no rights without responsibilities. If we expect our own rights to be respected we must uphold the rights of others. The claiming of rights is a two-way process. As we grow older, we can shape our world as our rights and responsibilities increase at home, at school in the community.

Sometimes rights can compete and conflict, for example: everybody wants freedom of movement but somebody will complain if it's across *their* private land.

Achieving a balance between people's rights and responsibilities – so that it is fair for all – needs everybody's co-operation and support.

C

Today I will remember that: 'Nobody is an island, separated from others; everybody is a piece of the continent, a part of the whole.'

Year 8:1

A

All human beings are born free and equal in dignity and rights. They are endowed with reason and conscience and should act towards one another in a spirit of brotherhood.

THE UNIVERSAL DECLARATION OF HUMAN RIGHTS – ARTICLE 1

B

Everybody is not the same; everybody is different – a unique individual, but human rights should be the same for everybody.

In school, we all work very hard to behave in ways which are kind, co-operative and respectful. Schools operate best when there is mutual respect between pupils, between school staff and between school staff and pupils.

In society, people, regardless of their status, power, colour, religion, culture, sex, age, abilities or special needs, should be treated fairly and properly as equal fellow human beings. This is our human responsibility.

C

I will treat people fairly and with respect.

Year 8:2

A

All are equal before the law and are entitled without any discrimination to equal protection of the law.

THE UNIVERSAL DECLARATION OF HUMAN RIGHTS – ARTICLE 7

B

The law is the same for everybody. Laws must not deal with people differently because of culture, religion, ethnic group or ways of life.

The laws of the land should treat all people the same and protect people from the kinds of discrimination which rob people of their rights.

Apartheid in South Africa, which was based on discrimination by skin colour and imposed by law, will be judged by history as a major crime of the twentieth century. For many years, South African law stated that white and black people must live in separate areas, travel in different buses, work in different places and learn in different schools. Black people, who formed the majority of the population, were not allowed to vote in elections. Marriage between whites and 'non-whites' was illegal.

Tragically and alarmingly, the government and many of the white people in South Africa believed that keeping apart people of different races and colours was the right thing to do. Race was at the centre of the discrimination and fear was the driving force.

Like all the people in the world, the people of South Africa belong to one race – the human race.

C

Every member of school is of equal value.

Year 8:3

A

If civilization is to survive, we must cultivate the science of human relationships – the ability of all people of all kinds to live together in the same world, at peace.

ELEANOR ROOSEVELT

B

Eleanor Roosevelt, an American woman who devoted a lot of her life to just causes and peace, was a major influence in the shaping of the thirty-point document called 'The Universal Declaration of Human Rights'. This outlines the basic human rights of every human being in the world and the responsibilities of nations.

A declaration is a collection of words. The words need to be acted upon – put into practice. For peace and harmony to be established on earth, we need to become more skilled at communicating; more committed to forgiving and letting go of past injustices; and to have the strength to love. These are the basic requirements.

C

Do for others just what you want them to do for you.

LUKE 6:31

Year 9:1

A

I have the right to speak out
I have the right to be heard
I have the right to be treated as a person,
not just as a daughter/wife/son/grandad.

CLAIRE WALMSLEY, *ASSERTIVENESS – THE RIGHT TO BE YOU*

B

We all have the right to be treated with respect and treated as an individual. We also have the responsibility to treat others in the same way.

It is easy to take others for granted – especially those we live with and love or the people that we see each day. We have the capacity to show respect to everyone that we meet – whether it's our brothers or sisters; parents or neighbours; lunchtime supervisors or classmates, or the assistant in the sweetshop. They all have the right to speak, be heard and be treated as individuals.

Developing respect for ourselves goes hand in hand with valuing the rights of others.

C

I will exercise my rights to speak and be heard and show the same respect to others.

Year 9:2

A

The Hunt

A bugle sounds,
The sound of dogs are in the distance,
I'm off,
The hunt begins.

Up hill and down dale,
Through fields and woods,
Over hedge and under fence,
They're getting closer,
Where will I go?

Into the wood,
Through the bracken,

Over a log,
Down into the den,
Will they find me?

The hunters are getting closer,
The dogs are here,
They're digging me out,
The end is near.

MARK GIBSON, AGED 12, *GO GREEN*

B

Do animals have rights? Over the centuries people have often treated animals in a way that suggests that they thought animals hadn't got rights. In the Bible it says, 'Be fruitful and multiply, and fill the earth and subdue it; and have dominion over the fish of the sea and over the birds of the air and over every living thing that moves upon the earth' (Genesis: 1:28).

However, to 'have dominion' does not mean that we should hunt animals for sport, imprison them in zoos, make them do stupid tricks for us in circuses, use them for medical experiments, torture them and so on. It means that we should be responsible in the way we treat animals.

JOE JENKINS, *INTRODUCING MORAL ISSUES*

C

I will consider what my responsibilities are towards animals.

Year 9:3

A

It often happens that I wake at night and begin to think about a serious problem and decide I must tell the Pope about it. Then I wake up completely and remember that I am the Pope.

POPE JOHN XXIII, IN YOU *CAN'T AFFORD THE LUXURY OF A NEGATIVE THOUGHT*

B

When we have responsibilities in our lives it can be alarming to realize that there is no one else to pass the problems on to. Sometimes we need to face up to our duties and obligations and say 'the buck stops here'.

We may have responsibilities in the home, like keeping our room tidy or putting the dustbin out. It may be our job to walk the dog or feed the rabbit and guinea pig regularly.

Also, in school we have certain responsibilities. For example, meeting homework deadlines or helping to keep the school site tidy.

If we all carry out our responsibilities, life will run smoothly for everyone.

C

I will take pride in carrying out my responsibilities.

Year 10:1

A

When the officer enquired whether after the war people would not ask what happened to the millions of Jews, Eichmann replied: 'A hundred dead is a catastrophe. A million dead is a statistic.'

A WITNESS AT THE NUREMBURG WAR CRIMES TRIALS

B

The murder of millions of Jews by Adolf Hitler's Nazis was a brutal, horrific and evil act. Adolf Eichmann's job was to round up and send all Jews to their deaths in the gas chambers. The Nazi killers planned to hunt down and totally exterminate all Jews. The Jews were stripped of their rights; were regarded as numbers not people, and so killing millions of Jewish people became a statistical problem to be solved efficiently, effectively and clinically. How is it possible for people to be so cruel to each other? How can this possibly be allowed to happen?

Nowadays, we are bombarded with information and news as it happens worldwide. Large scale atrocities, wars and disasters across the world are graphically described in both words and pictures. Do we see people suffering and identify with their plight or do we just hear a statistic?

C

What response can I make?

Year 10:2

A

Everyone has the right to recognition everywhere as a person before the law.

THE UNIVERSAL DECLARATION OF HUMAN RIGHTS – ARTICLE 6.

B

'The Declaration of Human Rights' was born out of the horrors of World War II and, in particular, the killing of millions of Jews.

Article 6 states that people should be regarded as persons and not things. From 1935 onwards, newspapers and propaganda notices in Germany portrayed Jews as evil and corrupt. The media referred to individual Jewish people as 'a Jew' or 'the Jew'. Names weren't used.

The words we use to describe people are important. Any words which make others into 'types' instead of individuals can be dangerous and are offensive.

C

Calling people by their names and name-calling are two very different activities. One is respectful, whilst the other is abusive.

Year 10:3

A

On almost any day you can open your newspaper and read about repression around the world. People imprisoned for their beliefs or religion in countries like South Korea or Peru. People tortured in China, Pakistan or Turkey. Thousands waiting to die on the death rows of the USA, Jamaica and Japan. But what can I do about it? I am only one person, I cannot make a difference.

TAKEN FROM AMNESTY INTERNATIONAL, *SUGGESTED ASSEMBLY*, 1994

B

In 1961, a lawyer called Peter Benenson read a newspaper article about two students who were having a drink in a cafe in Lisbon, Portugal. At one point during their conversation they raised their glasses and toasted 'liberty'. For this simple act they were arrested and imprisoned.

What could Peter do about it? He was only one person and was not even in the country it had happened in. He finally came up with the idea of writing a newspaper article to tell the world that these students were not alone but were just two cases amongst thousands of what he was to term 'prisoners of conscience'.

The newspaper article was published in *The Observer* and called on people to begin working impartially and peacefully for the release of thousands of men and women and children imprisoned throughout the world for their political or religious beliefs. The article and subsequent response led to the birth of Amnesty International – the largest human rights organization in the world.

You can make a difference. You can write a letter. You can join Amnesty International. You can spread the word to others about human rights.

ADAPTED FROM AMNESTY INTERNATIONAL *SUGGESTED ASSEMBLY*

C

I will remind myself that one person can make a difference.

Year 11:1

A

Love yourself. I love my Dad, Mum and my brother and sister – and myself. That's very important. You always have to remember yourself. You can care for other people but you must never forget yourself.

FRANCESCA, AGED 7

B

It is our right, as a human, and our responsibility to love and take care of ourselves, as far as we are able. We are then in a good position to attend to the needs of others. We cannot help people if we work so hard that we end up in a state of collapse. Living in balance involves striving to love ourselves, as well as all of those around us.

C

I will remember the importance of loving myself, as well as others.

Year 11:2

A

We have heard with our own ears the cry of the poor. We have seen with our own eyes our society being driven in a direction that contradicts the Gospel.

CHURCH ACTION ON POVERTY, *RICH WORLD, POOR WORLD*

B

Jesus spent a lot of time with the poor and 'outcasts' of society. His stories were about feeding the hungry, welcoming the stranger and comforting the sick and needy. Jesus taught that the significance of a person's life was measured by the compassion shown towards the poor and those in need.

A declaration by Church Action on Poverty makes a very searching and important statement: 'It cannot be right to learn from experience that market forces favour the rich and dispossess the poor and yet do nothing about it.'

How we treat the poor and needy says something about the values which underpin our society.

C

Where I see an injustice, I have a responsibility to act.

Year 11:3

A

We all have the right to express our thoughts and opinions, although others may not like them. While it can be difficult for us, we need to give ourselves permission to speak out from our hearts.

SUE PATTON THOELE, *THE WOMAN'S BOOK OF COURAGE*

B

Our opinions and views are as valid and important as those of the next person. Others may be better at expressing themselves, but this alone doesn't mean that what they have to say is of greater value. We may feel uncomfortable to say what we feel because of what others might think of us. Nevertheless, it is our right to communicate the way we think and feel. When this seems difficult we need to encourage ourselves to stand up for our rights.

C

I will have the courage to express my thoughts and opinions.

---

25 EASTER

Year 7:1

A

The next day the large crowd that had come to the Passover Festival heard that Jesus was coming to Jerusalem. So they took branches of palm trees and went out to meet him, shouting, 'Praise God! God bless him who comes in the name of the Lord! God bless the King of Israel!' Jesus found a donkey and rode on it, just as the scripture says, 'Do not be afraid, city of Zion! Here comes your king, riding on a young donkey.'

JOHN 12:12–15

B

It has been said that, 'What cannot be said must be shown' (Wittgenstein). And a common phrase says, 'Actions speak louder than words'.

The people of Israel at the time of Jesus wanted a great military leader to get rid of the Romans who ruled them. A fine white horse would have been more appropriate than a donkey. Jesus had been trying to tell his disciples that he was bringing in a different sort of kingdom, not one to overthrow the oppressors, because there would always be the oppressed and those who would oppress. His kingdom was to be a spiritual kingdom that would affect all lives down through the ages.

Entering the gates of Jerusalem on a donkey showed the people what he meant far more than any words could. The Romans were not worried about a man on a humble donkey, but then they did not know the ancient prophesy that told of Israel's king riding on an ass.

There were many people in Israel who understood the symbolism of this event. Some joined in, while others planned to get rid of Jesus.

C

Today let me show what I believe in my actions.

Year 7:2

A

Pilate said to the people, 'Here is your king!' They shouted back, 'Kill him! Kill him! Crucify him!' So they took charge of Jesus. He went out, carrying his cross, and came to 'The Place of the Skull', as it is called. There they crucified him; and they also crucified two other men, one on each side, with Jesus between them.

JOHN 19:14–18

B

Crucifixion is a particularly painful form of execution, where the victim slowly suffocates to death while their body is suffering the pain and agony of the nails. We would expect the victim to be concerned only with their suffering at this time and we would expect them to cry out in pain. But the words we hear from Jesus are, 'Forgive them, Father! They don't know what they are doing.' He was asking God to forgive the people causing his suffering.

It is not an easy thing to forgive someone who has hurt or upset us. Often we hold grudges for years remembering the hurt. Jesus was remarkable in that he was forgiving. For everybody this is an example to follow.

C

Today I will free myself from the grudges that I hold.

Year 7:3

A

Very early on Sunday morning the women went to the tomb, carrying the spices they had prepared. They found the stone rolled away from the entrance to the tomb, so they went in; but they did not find the body of the Lord Jesus. They stood there puzzled about this, when suddenly two men in bright shining clothes stood by them. Full of fear, the women bowed down to the ground, as the men said to them, 'Why are you looking among the dead for one who is alive? He is not here; he has been raised.'

LUKE 24:1–6

B

For a lot of Christians, Easter is the most important part of the year. They remember that not only did their Saviour suffer and die for them, but that he overcame death.

People who have been the first to find new routes across uncharted lands have been a source of inspiration and help to those who followed them. The futuristic space series *Star Trek* claims to send the spaceship through space: 'the final frontier'. But surely the final frontier is death? For Christians, Jesus has crossed that barrier and come back so others can follow.

The early Christians were so convinced of the truth of Jesus' coming back from death that they suffered much persecution rather than give up their faith.

For Christians, the Easter story means that they see death and life in a new way.

C

Today I will try to look at life in a new way.

294

Year 8:1

A

You know that after two days the Passover is coming, and the son of Man is to be delivered up for crucifixion.

MATTHEW 26:2

B

Passover is a Jewish festival that is still celebrated every year. It recalls the time that the Jews were freed from slavery 3000 years ago. As they celebrate this event with a special meal, Jewish people retell the story of how God sent ten plagues on the Egyptians to encourage the Pharaoh to release the people. The last plague was the death of the first-born in each household. The Jewish people ate a meal of roast lamb on that first Passover, and put its blood on the door posts so that God would pass over their houses and leave their first-born untouched.

Jesus not only knew that he was going to die, but when he was going to die.

Passover and Easter are linked together. For Jews, Passover remembers the time they were given life and freedom, for Christians Easter means new life and spiritual freedom.

C

Today I will value the freedom which lives in my heart.

Year 8:2

A

And while they were eating, Jesus took some bread, and after a blessing, He broke it and gave it to the disciples, and said 'Take, eat; this is my body'.

MATTHEW 26:26

B

The bread that was broken was symbolic of the agony that was to happen to the body of Jesus on the cross.

Just as Jews remember the great event of their past in Passover, so Christians remember the death of Jesus when they share bread and wine in communion. It is like a living picture, there are no photographs for people to say 'Look what happened at the cross', but there is a symbolic meal to say, 'This is what happened'.

There are times when we all go through some sadness and feel broken – but there is always hope of new and better things emerging from the despair.

C

Today I will accept the bad times in the knowledge that the good times will follow.

Year 8:3

A

And they departed quickly from the tomb with fear and great joy.
MATTHEW 28:8

B

This is the account of the women who visited the tomb of Jesus. They were frightened because they had received a shock, the body of Jesus was missing. They were also full of 'great joy' because they had been told that Jesus had risen from the dead. They were probably too excited to understand fully what was happening, but they had been given some hope. All the despair and defeat of Good Friday was over, something unexpected had happened. Life suddenly looked very different.

There are often times in life when we think that nothing good will come out of a situation, but we should always have hope.

C

Where there is despair I will look for hope.

Year 9:1

A

And as they were reclining at table and eating, Jesus said, 'Truly I say to you that one of you will betray me – one who is eating with me.'

MARK 14:8

B

To betray is to give information to the enemy. In the incident quoted above, the person doing the betraying was a friend, in fact a constant companion for three years.

Nothing hurts more than when someone we have trusted and shared with, turns on us. We would expect those that we do not get on with to turn on us, but it is really painful when this is done by a friend.

Judas who was one of Jesus' friends, betrayed him to the authorities and as a result Jesus was captured and crucified.

In the reading, Jesus states the betrayal as a fact, and does not retaliate or seek to persuade Judas to change. Maybe we could tell our friends more about how we feel when they behave in ways which hurt us and celebrate our loyal friends.

C

I will appreciate those friends who stick by me.

Year 9:2

A

And Peter kept saying insistently, 'Even if I have to die with you, I will not deny you.'

MARK 14:31

B

There is a song that says, 'When the going gets tough, the tough get going', but this really depends on the toughness of the situation.

Most of us have witnessed or have been a part of a situation where members of a group turn on one individual. This is when we expect our friends to support us, but they are often frightened that they too will be turned upon, so they keep quiet, or even deny being our friend.

In this reading, we see Peter, a friend of Jesus, who says that he is willing to die for him. But he does not keep his word and when Jesus is arrested he says that he does not know him. It is not the end of the friendship though as Jesus recognizes the weakness of Peter, forgives his behaviour and still accepts him as a friend.

C

I will try to be a loyal friend.

Year 9:3

A

The members of the council were amazed to see how bold Peter and John were and to learn that they were ordinary men of no education. They realized then that they had been companions of Jesus. So they called them back and told them that on no condition were they to speak or to teach in the name of Jesus. But Peter and John answered them, 'You yourselves judge which is right in God's sight – to obey you or to obey God.'

ACTS 4:13, 18, 19

B

So here we have 'wimpy' Peter who previously denied even knowing Jesus, now amazing people with his boldness. Before the crucifixion he denied knowing Jesus to a servant girl, now after the resurrection (rising from the dead), he tells the council (the leaders of the people) that he cannot stop speaking about what he has seen and heard.

The experience of Easter has turned Peter from a frightened man into a fearless preacher.

C

Today I will speak up for the things that I believe in.

Year 10:1

A

On the way they met a man named Simon, who was coming into the city from the country, and the soldiers forced him to carry Jesus' cross. (Simon was from Cyrene and was the father of Alexander and Rufus.)

MARK 15:21

B

In Roman times, when a criminal was crucified, they had to carry their cross to the place of execution. They were made to walk the longest route so more people would see it as a warning.

Simon was from Cyrene in Africa and probably resented being forced to carry the cross by the Roman soldiers. We can only speculate but probably this event changed his life. The fact that his sons are mentioned indicates that the writers of the Gospel must have known them. Simon and his sons are also mentioned at other times in the New Testament.

Simon was 'forced' to help a man on his way to a crucifixion, however he ended up willingly spreading the message of that same man. We can feel trapped into doing things that we don't want to do, but out of these situations new opportunities can arise.

C

Even in the darkest moment there is a glimmer of hope.

Year 10:2

A

When Pilate saw that it was no use to go on, but that a riot might break out, he took some water, washed his hands in front of the crowd, and said, 'I am not responsible for the death of this man! This is your doing!'

MATTHEW 27:24

B

Pilate will always be remembered for this act. We still talk of 'washing our hands' when we wish to disassociate ourselves from some action.

However much Pilate stressed that he was not responsible for the death of Jesus, he cannot abdicate his responsibility so easily. He did try four times to release Jesus, but he was the representative of the Emperor in Rome. He had the power to release him, but he was frightened that he would be reported to Rome by the local people. He had already upset the Jewish community several times and could not risk upsetting them again. So rather than risk his own neck he let the people have their way. He is remembered as a man who lacked the courage of his convictions.

C

I will try to have the courage to stand up for what I believe is right.

Year 10:3

A

They stood still, with sad faces. One of them named Cleopas, asked him, 'Are you the only visitor in Jerusalem who doesn't know the things that have been happening these last few days?'

LUKE 24:18

B

This story in the New Testament is about two people leaving

Jerusalem after the crucifixion. They are on their way to Emmaus. They are sad because their leader has been crucified and all they hoped for is lost.

Accompanying them is a stranger who does not seem to know about the crucifixion. When they tell him, he in turn explains the meaning and purpose of it all.

They realize that the stranger is Jesus back from the dead. The sadness goes, the tiredness of the journey does not matter, even though it is late they hurry back to Jerusalem to tell the other followers the good news.

Easter is transformed from sadness into joy.

C

I will explore quietly the turning points of my life.

Year 11:1

A

It was about twelve o'clock when the sun stopped shining and darkness covered the whole country until three o'clock, and the curtain hanging in the Temple was torn in two. Jesus cried out in a loud voice, 'Father! In your hands I place my spirit!' He said this and died.

LUKE 23:46

B

Nothing could have been more crushing to the disciples than the death of Jesus. He was their friend, their leader, and their teacher. They had abandoned their work to follow him, they had walked hundreds of miles across Judaea, Samaria and Galilee to spread his word. They totally believed in him as someone who was very special, the promised man of God.

Now he was dead, and all they believed in must have died with him. They must have gone over every detail in their minds, wondering how it had all gone wrong. In a couple of days their belief would be restored but until then they would be in the depths of despair.

It is good that we do not know the future but often it contains more good surprises than we ever thought possible.

C

I will let go of bad times and celebrate the good times.

Year 11:2

A

It's Friday but Sunday's a'coming.

TONY COMPOLO

B

Tony Compolo, an American sociologist and preacher, once told the story of a black Pentecostal preacher in America who used the phrase 'It's Friday but Sunday's a'coming' as his main theme for a sermon. He spoke of the despair of the disciples at the death of Christ on Good Friday – but Sunday's a'coming – and this was transformed into the joy of the resurrection. He then listed the problems and despair that everybody faces at some time in their life – but Sunday's a'coming.

The message of Easter is the message of hope.

C

Today I will concentrate on the good news that out of despair comes hope.

Year 11:3

A

They have taken my Lord away, and I do not know where they have put him!

JOHN 20:13

B

Frank Morrison who wrote the book 'Who moved the stone?' went to great lengths to disprove the resurrection of Jesus. The result was that he believed that it actually happened! He reasoned that if any of the authorities had taken the body of Jesus or had known where it was buried they would have produced it to prove the disciples wrong. In fact if it had existed there would probably be a shrine at the appropriate site.

The other option was that the disciples took the body to support the idea that Jesus had risen. If this was true, why did the disciples allow themselves to be killed for their faith, if they knew that it was based on a lie? This is definitely not logical.

For Christians, the triumph of Christ over death means that death itself is destroyed, death has no power to hurt and need not be feared. There is a life beyond.

C

For Christians, resurrection is a living experience.

26 Nature

Year 7:1

A

The beauty of nature can be seen in a flower or a furry animal.

The power of nature is in a lightning bolt, a gigantic wave or a hurricane.

ADAPTED FROM *TOUCHSTONES* (8 JANUARY)

B

The wildness of nature is everywhere around us and can be enjoyed fully when we get in touch with it.

When was the last time you walked across fields for the pleasure that that gives? When did you stand in a wood in order to take in the beauty of nature all around you – especially the sights and sounds?

Appreciating nature around us is important because by doing so, we can come to realize that we are nature. When we open our eyes and learn to be a part of nature, it renews and lifts our spirits.

ADAPTED FROM *TOUCHSTONES* (8 JANUARY)

C

Today I will take notice of the beauty of nature which is all around me.

Year 7:2

A

To everything there is a season, and a time to every purpose under

heaven: a time to be born, and a time to die; a time to plant, and a time
to pluck up that which is planted.

ECCLESIASTES 3:1–2

B

The different cycles in nature need to be understood and appreciated. The beginnings of a cycle can sometimes go unnoticed: the signals that new growth is underway are often very small at first. When the little sprouts of growth first develop, we often don't even see them unless we search.

Time will bring vast changes, as the season of growth progresses. That is how the natural world works, and we are part of this work.

We need to apply the lessons of nature to our own lives. We need to be aware of the 'season to work'; the right time to rest and when to harvest the crop that our work has grown for us. If we work all the time, then we miss the fruits of our labour!

We can search for signs of progress in our lives. The little things we see may signal bigger changes yet to come.

C

There are many seasons in life and I will experience them all.

Year 7:3

A

Reverence concerning all life is the greatest commandment …
we take this so slightly, thoughtlessly plucking a flower,
thoughtlessly stepping on a poor insect, thoughtlessly
disregarding the suffering and lives of our fellow men and women.

ALBERT SCHWEITZER

B

Albert Schweitzer (1875–1965) was a medical missionary in

Africa and a Christian thinker. He believed that the most important thing we can have is a respect for life. He felt that all our behaviour should come from a deep understanding of the gift of life.

Albert Schweitzer believed that there was a 'terrible blindness' in our world. We cannot see that life is a wonderful, precious and mysterious gift.

ADAPTED FROM *INTRODUCING MORAL ISSUES*

C

I will try to open my eyes to the beauty around me.

Year 8:1

A

You have noticed that everything an Indian does is in a circle, and that is because the Power of the World always works in circles, and everything tries to be round ... The Sky is round, and I have heard that the earth is round like a ball, and so are all the stars. The wind, in its greatest power, whirls. Birds make their nests in circles, for theirs is the same religion as ours ... Even the seasons form a great circle in their changing, and always come back again to where they were.

BLACK ELK (1863–1950), OGLALA SIOUX HOLY MAN, IN *NATIVE AMERICAN WISDOM*

B

The North American Indians had a great knowledge of and respect for nature – their lives and survival depended upon it. We too are dependent on nature for the air we breathe and the water we drink. The sun is the driving force behind the great cycles of nature. We see this in the water cycle, where water is purified and again in the oxygen cycle where trees and other plants produce oxygen, essential for life. The recycling of water and oxygen is a continuous flow; with no beginning and no end.

By being respectful and increasing our knowledge, we too can flow with nature.

C

Today I will notice the circles and cycles in my life.

Year 8:2

A

No artist can ever reproduce even the least of Nature's surpassing creations and miracles. Besides, what profit is there in imitating Nature when she is so open and so accessible to all who see and hear? The business of art is rather to understand Nature and to reveal her meanings to those unable to understand. The mission of art is to bring out the unfamiliar from the most familiar.

KAHLIL GIBRAN, *THE WISDOM OF KAHLIL GIBRAN*

B

Nature is always changing. As we gaze at a tree, the wind can change its shape; the sun can light it up and passing clouds can alter the shading. The picture moves, changes with time and becomes 'alive'. It is as if there is some great artist at work.

C

I will watch the picture of nature change before my eyes.

Year 8:3

A

All living things look hopefully to you.
and you give them food when they need it.
You give them enough
and satisfy the needs of all.

PSALM 145:15, 16

B

In our society it is easy to gather food from overflowing supermarket shelves. We can live solely on pre-packed, boxed, individually wrapped, tinned, cartoned, processed, dried, frozen and preserved meals; losing sight of where they originated.

As we become more aware of the Earth's fragility and the importance of living in harmony and balance with nature, we realize that we cannot continually take from the Earth's resources without giving something back. When we understand this, our respect for nature can grow.

C

Today I will be thankful for all the food that nature provides.

Year 9:1

A

Tropical Rain Forests

Rain forests are being wiped out fast,
If we don't do something now they'll never last.
They're disappearing bit by bit,
Soon we'll have nothing but an ugly pit.

Is the cleared land more important than the trees,
Think about the plants and the animals needs.
Many cures and remedies,
May be found amongst the trees.

Many tribes-people have homes in the forest,
Soon their homes may be demolished.
A lot of animals have been wiped out,
Many of the others are in doubt.

This is something important to me,
So think about it, and save those trees!

REBECCA HOPKINS, AGED 13, *GO GREEN*

B

The rainforests are disappearing at a rate of about 1.5 acres each second. Unless we act urgently, they will vanish from the Earth within fifty years. The oxygen, animals and medicines which are provided by the rainforests will also be lost forever.

The rainforests are of such outstanding beauty and importance, it is vital that they are saved. Many of the rainforest countries say that they desperately need the money that chopping down the trees brings in order to pay off loans and debts.

What can be done?
What response can the world community make?
Once the rainforests have gone, everybody will lose out.

C

I will let the beauty of the rainforests inspire me to protect them.

Year 9:2

A

Do You Care?
Ask yourself this:-
Do you care about the earth?
Ask yourself – what's it worth?
What we take is not replaced,
We destroy with all our waste.
It's the price we're paying for what we do.
It's affecting me and affecting you.
Do you care?

Ask yourself this:-
Do you care about the seas?
Consider the pollution, please.
Toxic waste and oil spills,
Think of all the life it kills.
The seas are dying you know it's true.

It's affecting me and affecting you.
Do you care?

Ask yourself this:-
Do you care about the air?
Do you know there's a hole in the ozone layer?
Think about the smoke from the factories,
Vehicle fumes and CFCs.
Someone has to stop it, do you know who?
It's affecting me and affecting you.
Do you care?

Ask yourself this:-
If everyone stopped and learned to care
If everyone became environmentally aware
We could make this earth a cleaner place
With fresh air, and water for the human race.
Think about what you can do.
It matters to me, does it matter to you?
Do you care? Enough?

EBONY ELLIOTT-WILDMANE, AGED 11, *GO GREEN*

B

As a society, we are becoming more aware of the way we are polluting the Earth. We are all affected by the human-made poisons in our environment.

The poem is asking not only if we care – but also if we care enough to *act*.

C

If I care – what am I going to do?

Year 9:3

A

Look how the wild flowers grow:

they do not work or make clothes for themselves.
But I tell you that not even King Solomon
with all his wealth had clothes as beautiful as one of these flowers.

MATTHEW 6:28, 29

B

Whatever we create, can any of it really match up to the beauty, splendour and wonder found in the natural world?

Consider a simple daisy. It has a green stem, yellow centre and white petals tinged with pink. Now pluck another from the grass and compare it with the first daisy. You will find that no two are ever exactly the same. It is like this for every blade of grass, tree, snowflake and flower that you will ever see. On close inspection, each is as individual and beautiful as can be.

C

I will enjoy and appreciate the beauty and individuality of everything in the natural world.

Year 10:1

A

Soul and Nature converse together while Man stands speechless and bewildered.

KAHLIL GIBRAN, *THE WISDOM OF KAHLIL GIBRAN*

B

When the birds sing, do they call to the flowers in the fields, or are they speaking to the trees, or are they echoing the murmur of the brooks? For Man with his understanding cannot know what the bird is saying, nor what the waves whisper when they touch the beaches slowly and gently.

Man with his understanding cannot know what the rain is saying when it falls upon the leaves of the trees or when it taps at the window panes. He cannot know what the breeze is saying to the flowers in the fields.

But the Heart of Man can feel and grasp the meaning of these sounds that play upon his feelings. Eternal wisdom often speaks to him in a mysterious language; Soul and Nature converse together, while Man stands speechless and bewildered.

THE WISDOM OF KAHLIL GIBRAN

C

I will open my heart to nature.

Year 10:2

A

Nature reaches out to us with welcoming arms, and bids us enjoy her beauty; but we dread her silence and rush into the crowded cities, there to huddle like sheep fleeing from a ferocious wolf.

KAHLIL GIBRAN, *THE WISDOM OF KAHLIL GIBRAN*

B

When walking by water or by trees, stop and listen to nature, and allow the apparent silence to change to quiet and then after a while notice the sounds in the quiet and experience the peace of it all.

By tuning in to the rhythm of nature, we can become aware of the same beat in us. We are nature. The beauty and wonder of nature can be found in us. We can breathe and drink in the sights and sounds of nature, allowing it to touch us and restore our spirits.

C

I will accept the gifts of nature.

Year 10:3

A

Every time the wind blows it is singing you a song of the gods. Every

time a flower blossoms it is bringing you a message from the higher law.
Every time you hear the ocean as it beats against the shore and recedes
in musical rhythm, it is speaking to your soul – a voice from nature,
verily a voice from God.

KATHERINE TINGLEY, *THEOSOPHY: THE PATH OF THE MYSTIC*

B

Nature is full of miracles, mystery and magic. The magnitude,
splendour and beauty of nature from the tiniest particle of soil
and smallest flower to the biggest mountain and highest tree,
leave us with a sense of awe and wonder.

Getting back to nature helps us to feel rooted and centred,
yet uplifted. Taking time to pause and receive the rhythm of
nature, we can become transfixed both by the simplicity and
complexity of all that is around us. We may experience moments that are extraordinarily special and transcendental.
Monica Furlong describes such an experience in her book
Travelling In.

'The sun behind the clouds assumed a shape which fascinated me, and between one moment and the next, although
no word had been uttered, I felt myself spoken to. I was aware
of being regarded by love, of being wholly accepted, accused,
forgiven, all at once. The joy of it was the greatest I had ever
known in my life. I felt I had been born for this moment and
had marked time till it occured.'

C

I will take time to be in tune with nature.

Year 11:1

A

Our hands are a means of communication with other human beings and
they can also be a means of communication with nature. This is why,

when you open your door or window, in the morning, you should salute
the sky, the sun, the trees, lakes and stars ... the whole of nature.

OMRAAM MIKHAËL AÏVANHOV, *GOLDEN RULES FOR EVERYDAY*
LIFE

B

Saluting nature is another way of appreciating and acknowledging the beauty of the world around us. Taking time to get
close and feel part of the natural world can be a deeply moving
and satisfying experience.

Tenderly caring, with loving hands, for animals, trees,
flowers, lakes and forests can help us to understand what the
planet needs to flourish with vibrancy and health.

C

May I communicate my appreciation of nature with loving hands.

Year 11:2

A

When I look out over the world and see humanity with its unbrother-
liness and despair, if it were not for the birds and flowers, the trees and
blue overhead, I could not bear the picture: I should lose heart.

KATHERINE TINGLEY, *THEOSOPHY: THE PATH OF THE MYSTIC*

B

When we feel distressed about the way humans treat each
other, nature's beauty can heal and soothe us.

Both the gentleness and ferocious power of nature live in
balance and harmony together. We too can learn to live in
balance and harmony with ourselves and each other.

When we argue and fight with our family or friends, or
have a bad day at school, if we can make the effort to stand still
for a while; soak up nature's loveliness and grace, we will feel
calmer and renewed in spirit.

C

I will let myself be soothed by nature.

Year 11:3

A

The following passage was written by Brian Keenan, who had spent many months in a darkened cell:

There's a bowl in front of me that wasn't there before. A brown button bowl and in it some apricots, some small oranges, some nuts, cherries, a banana. The fruits, the colours, mesmerize me … I am entranced by colour. I lift an orange into the flat filthy palm of my hand and feel and smell and lick it. The colour orange, the colour, the colour, my God the colour orange …

Such wonder, such absolute wonder in such an insignificant fruit. I cannot, I will not eat this fruit. I sit in quiet joy, so complete, beyond the meaning of joy. My soul finds its own completeness in that bowl of colour. The forms of each fruit. The shape and curl and bend all so rich, so perfect. I want to bow before it, loving that blazing, roaring, orange colour.

BRIAN KEENAN, *AN EVIL CRADLING*

B

Brian Keenan was kidnapped in Beirut in 1985 by the fundamentalist Shi'ite militiamen, and was held captive for four and a half years. In his book *An Evil Cradling*, he describes the conditions in his six-foot-long and four-foot-wide cell – the same boring, tasteless food each day, the heat, the fleas and the filthy blanket. Then one day his 'eyes are almost burned' by what he sees. The sight of an ordinary fruit fills him with an overwhelming sense of wonder and awe. He notices every single detail. The colour was so wonderful that he could not destroy it by eating the orange.

It is so easy to accept the beauty of nature around us and

not even notice the shapes, shades and colours. Starved of the beauty of nature for so long, Brian Keenan appreciated every exquisite detail of the fruit. Maybe we can learn from him!

C

To really see and experience nature can uplift and fill us with a sense of joy, gratitude and love.

27 LEISURE AND RECREATION

Year 7:1

A

Music washes away from the soul the dust of everyday life.

BERTHOLD AUERBACH, IN *TOUCHSTONES* (1 NOVEMBER)

B

Music can lift our spirits. One person might like to listen to Classic FM; another one to Virgin or Radio 1; another one might play the piano or flute, and another may go to rock concerts. For each of us, music is often a different world from the one in which we live and work.

Music touches our feelings and speaks to us in a special language. It can bring us back to special times in the past, perhaps recalling a night of fun and excitement at a disco.

Music can lift our spirits and open us to deeper feelings we weren't in touch with.

Music can change our moods – make us feel happy, sad or relaxed. Music can wash away the worries of the day and refresh us.

ADAPTED FROM *TOUCHSTONES* (1 NOVEMBER)

C

Today I will make room to be refreshed and restored by the healing power of music.

Year 7:2

A

If eyes were made for seeing,
then beauty is its own excuse for being.

RALPH WALDO EMERSON, IN *DAYS OF HEALING, DAYS OF JOY*
(5 JUNE)

B

If we work so hard and are so busy that we have no time to be with friends, to laugh, to discover and revel in beauty, then we are missing out on life.

Some people love to take long walks – when was our last walk? Some love the cinema or theatre – what was the last film or play we saw? Some simply love to take pictures or practise any number of hobbies – do we have any activity that we do just for the joy of it?

There doesn't have to be a serious reason for everything we do. The gift of sight has been given us that we may see; we need no reason to look for beauty other than the fact that it exists. And it does. Beauty surrounds us in wonderful variety when we look for it in the people and the world around us – and in ourselves.

ADAPTED FROM *DAYS OF HEALING, DAYS OF JOY* (5 JUNE)

C

I will open my eyes and find beauty in what I see.

Year 7:3

A

To believe this story, you must believe that the human race can be one joyous family, working together, laughing together, achieving the impossible.

I believe it because I saw it happen. Last Sunday, in one of the most violent, trouble-stricken cities in the world, 11,532 men, women and children from 40 countries of the world, assisted by 2.5 million black, white and yellow people, Protestants and Catholics, Jews and Muslims, Buddhists and Confucians, laughed, cheered and suffered during the greatest folk festival the world has seen.

CHRIS BRASHER, WRITING IN *THE OBSERVER*, IN *THE MARATHON BOOK*

B

Chris Brasher was writing about the 1979 New York Marathon.

Running is the classically simple, democratic sport. The popular slogan of the seventies was 'Sport for All' and that is precisely what running is. To start, you need very little in the way of expensive equipment; you don't need partners, an opponent or a team; you don't even need skill. For taking up jogging as a first step to marathon running depends on just one person: You.

All runners, new or old, fast or slow, have the same decision to make again and again: that is to get changed and get out on the road or field, even though there may be more inviting things to do. And there's the little voice in your head which says: 'Let's have a rest today, it won't matter, nobody will know.'

The toughest step is always the first one – the one which takes you to the front door and beyond.

ADAPTED FROM *THE MARATHON BOOK*

C

Today I will consider taking a first step to fitness.

Year 8:1

A

Fun and pleasure are essential elements in our lives. They can be experienced on our own or usually with other people. It may also require some level of skill which will be rewarded by a sense of achievement.

DAVID WATKINS, *URBAN PERMACULTURE*

B

Many activities entail giving, receiving or both. Try making a list of the things that give you pleasure. You may be surprised at how many cost little or nothing. Give yourself a treat at least once a week.

URBAN PERMACULTURE

C

I will give myself a treat at least once a week.

Year 8:2

A

Each day, and the living of it, has to be a conscious creation in which discipline and order are relieved with some play and some pure foolishness.

MARY SARTON, IN *MEDITATIONS FOR MEN WHO DO TOO MUCH*

B

Having fun with people we feel safe with and love can revive our spirits and give us a wonderful sense of well-being. To get the most out of life, work, rest and play need to be in balance and harmony.

In their book *Staying OK*, Amy and Thomas Harris suggest that the heart is a good example of how to share out our time. They write: 'Were we to follow our hearts we would divide our twenty-four hours into three segments, working eight hours, sleeping eight hours, and using the remaining eight hours for life-renewing activities. What a revolutionary change would come over us individually, and as a society if we followed our hearts!

C

I will try to live my life in balance and harmony.

Year 8:3

A

Many of us tend to be achievement-oriented and get anxious when taking time to relax and enjoy ourselves. It seems to be okay when you're relaxing with your friends, but when on your own, you feel you should be accomplishing something ... To help myself out, I've created the concept of the holi-hour, a shortened version of the holi-day. I allow myself at least an hour each day to relax totally.

SUSAN JEFFERS, *FEEL THE FEAR AND DO IT ANYWAY*

B

Giving ourselves a special hour each day, to do something on our own which we enjoy doing, could help us relax and keep in touch with our thoughts and feelings. The relationship with ourselves is very important, but it needs time, effort and space to discover more about who we are.

Our holi-hour could be spent reading a magazine; listening to some music; allowing ourselves to sit quietly; taking a bath or walking the dog. To feel whole we need to balance leisure with work. We need to have a balance between time spent alone and time shared with others.

C

I will try to balance my life with work, rest and play.

Year 9:1

A

One way of describing a 'Backson' is someone who is always rushing around and pushing themselves to do more and more:

You see them almost everywhere you go, it seems. On practically any sunny sort of day, you can see the Backsons stampeding through the park, making all kinds of loud Breathing Noises. Perhaps you are enjoying a picnic on the grass when you suddenly look up to find that one or two of them just ran over your lunch.

The Bisy Backson is almost desperately active ... The Athletic sort of Backson – one of the many common varieties – is concerned with physical fitness, he says. But for some reason, he sees it as something that has to be pounded in from the outside, rather than built up from the inside. Therefore, he confuses exercise with work. He works when he works, works when he exercises, and, more often than not, works when he plays. Work, work, work. All work and no play makes Backson a dull boy. Kept up for long enough, it makes him dead, too.

BENJAMIN HOFF, *THE TAO OF POOH*

B

To keep ourselves fit and well, we need to take time regularly for enjoyable pastimes and to practise relaxing and letting go.

There is a world of difference between *doing* and *being*. We can still jog or swim and be active, but it needs to be with a sense of releasing ourselves through the activity. Recognizing when to let go of tension and strain, allowing our bodies and minds to relax and unwind for a while, allowing us to 'be'.

C

I will not confuse exercise with 'work'.

Year 9:2

A

Benjamin Hoff writes about an incident in the life of the Japanese emperor, Hirohito:

From early morning until late at night, practically every minute of the emperor's time is filled in with meetings, audiences, tours, inspections, and who-knows-what ...

In the middle of a particularly busy day, the emperor was driven to a meeting hall for an appointment of some kind. But when he arrived, there was no one there. The emperor walked into the middle of the great hall, stood silently for a moment, then bowed to the empty space. He turned to his assistants, a large smile on his face. 'We must schedule more appointments like this,' he told them. 'I haven't enjoyed myself so much in a long time.'

BENJAMIN HOFF, *THE TAO OF POOH*

B

What appears to be 'doing nothing', 'just being', can in fact be usefully energizing and refreshing.

It really isn't necessary to fill in every available moment with activity. If we feel the need to be busy all the time, we need to ask ourselves: why?

C

I will enjoy the 'empty' spaces in my life.

Year 9:3

A

At the Last Judgment God will ask you 'Why didn't you enjoy all the nice things I permitted you?' Well, what sort of things? Why not drape that multi-coloured towel round your middle and rhumba round the room? Bright clothes brighten your feelings. Or lie on your back and wave your feet in the air, if that's how you feel.

RABBI LIONEL BLUE, *BLUE HORIZONS*

B

A world with an amazing variety of beautiful experiences is waiting to be enjoyed by us. While it is important to be concerned about the unjust and unpleasant things on this Earth, and to do what we can to make the world a better place, we also need to have fun and enjoy ourselves.

There is a rainbow of experiences to be enjoyed – both the sunshine and the rain. The simple pleasures in life, like dancing around the room, can help us to appreciate being alive.

C

I will allow myself to enjoy the 'nice things' in life.

Year 10:1

A

If I'm feeling sad, I might crawl into bed and cry, taking time to be very loving and nurturing to myself. Or I might find someone caring to talk to who will simply listen to me until some of the feelings are released and I feel lighter. If I've been working too hard, I learn to put work aside no matter how important it seems. I take time to play, or take a hot bath, or read a novel. If someone I love wants something from me that I don't want to give, I learn to say no, firmly, yet with love. I trust that he or she will be better off than if I did it when I didn't want to. This way when I say 'yes' I really mean it.

SHAKTI GAWAIN, *REFLECTIONS IN THE LIGHT* (13 APRIL)

B

Being good to ourselves and taking good care of ourselves are all part of loving ourselves.

Through loving ourselves we can become more aware of our needs and then we can meet life with an attitude of acceptance.

C

Today I am willing to love myself and make sure my needs are met.

Year 10:2

A

The rich industrialist from the North was horrified to find the Southern fisherman lying lazily beside his boat, smoking a pipe.

'Why aren't you out fishing?' asked the rich man.

'Because I have caught enough fish for the day,' replied the fisherman.

'Why don't you catch more than you need?' asked the industrialist.

'What would I do with it?' said the fisherman.

'You could earn more money,' was the reply.

'You could use it to have a motor fixed to your boat. Then you could go into deeper waters and catch more fish. Then you would make enough to buy nylon nets. These would bring you more fish and more money. Soon you would have enough money to own two boats. Then you would be a rich man like me.'

'What would I do then?' asked the fisherman.

'Then you could sit down and enjoy life,' said the industrialist.

'What do you think I'm doing right now?' asked the contented fisherman.

FRANCIS GAY, *THE FRIENDSHIP BOOK OF FRANCIS GAY 1988*
(28 APRIL)

B

We can think of life having three dimensions: being, doing, and having. Often we attempt to live our lives backwards. We try to have more money in order to feel we can do more of what we want, so we can be happier. The way it actually works is the reverse. We must first be who we really are, then do what we feel guided to do, in order to have what we want.

SHAKTI GAWAIN, *REFLECTIONS IN THE LIGHT* (21 JANUARY)

C

Every day I will take time to sit down and enjoy life.

Year 10:3

A

There is a natural rhythm to the active and receptive energies within us. At times our energy is strong and outgoing – it is time to pursue our goals, take risks, get things accomplished. At other times, our energy is quiet and sensitive, and we need to take time to nurture ourselves, relax and just 'be' for a while.

SHAKTI GAWAIN, *REFLECTIONS IN THE LIGHT* (4 APRIL)

B

By being aware of our productive periods and channelling our energy purposefully and effectively, we can get a sense of satisfaction and peace from jobs done well.

But it takes wisdom to know when to stop and take a break. At these times it's important to switch off and do something relaxing and pleasurable. For example: go for a bike ride; feed the ducks; pursue a hobby; listen to music or simply sit around a warm, flickering fire.

Being aware and sensitive to our energy flow can help us to enjoy a satisfying and fulfilling life.

C

I will take time to relax and just 'be'.

Year 11:1

A

Develop a plan for pleasure for each and every day. Don't just randomly hope that pleasure will somehow show up; set yourself up for ecstasy. Make room for it!

ANTHONY ROBBINS, *AWAKEN THE GIANT WITHIN*

B

If we are in the habit of seeing life as a struggle or as a passage of time to be endured, we may have left little room in our lives for leisure, recreation and pleasure. To redress the balance we may need to consciously set aside time to relax and enjoy ourselves. Maybe enrolling in a class for relaxation or keep fit – or going swimming or shutting ourselves away regularly to read a favourite book.

However busy our lives seem to be, it's essential that we play as well as work.

C

I will make room for pleasure in my life.

Year 11:2

A

There appears no time for recreation; yet people who cannot find time for recreation will, sooner or later, have to find time for illness.
AMY BJORK HARRIS AND THOMAS HARRIS, *STAYING OK*

B

We can become addicted to working at an unreasonable pace. Excessively striving to achieve, compete and complete. If we overstretch ourselves, something will eventually snap – maybe an illness or accident will stop us in our tracks, forcing us to slow down and rest.

In our daily lives, we can get into the habit of eating so quickly that we don't experience or really taste the food. When we do find ourselves with free time we may feel guilty about relaxing because it doesn't appear to be productive.

This way of living can lead to a kind of 'hurry sickness' where we never seem to have enough time and have lost our ability to rest and replenish our energy. 'Hurry sickness' arises out of a lack of care for ourselves. To be well we need to build time for recreation into our busy lives.

ADAPTED FROM *STAYING OK*

C

I will plan for recreation time.

Year 11:3

A

Thoughts are free ... Ideas are our unlimited resource. They are the very substance of human culture.

PETER RUSSELL, *PASSING THOUGHTS – VOLUME 1*

B

When we are on holiday, by resting, our bodies can recover from the stresses and strains of everyday life. Just as bodies renew their vitality with rest and gentle exercise, our minds also need time to relax and be gently stimulated in a new direction. We can do this without packing a suitcase or stepping outside the front door. We just need to slow down and unwind, letting our minds have the freedom to dream for a while. We can imagine ourselves in the future, in different circumstances and in different countries. Our thoughts are only limited by our imagination.

We can develop our creativity and imagination by playing around with the ideas and thoughts that we have. This is more than just daydreaming; it is about positively directing our thoughts and ideas and seeing how far we can take them. 'Many successful writers, scientists, artists and composers admit that their best work comes through "playing around" with ideas in fantasy' (*New Methods in RE Teaching*).

C

I will use some of my leisure time to develop my imagination.

28 Human Potential and Achievement

Year 7:1

A

Everyone has a talent. What is rare is the courage to follow the talent to the dark place where it leads.

ERICA JONG, IN *EACH DAY A NEW BEGINNING* (2 MARCH)

B

'You have a real gift!' This is often a statement made to those who create a beautiful painting, perform a superb musical solo or write something really interesting. However, behind these 'gifted' people are hours of practice and dedication. There would be many failures, pictures destroyed, paper thrown in the waste basket, exams failed before the finished item is presented to the world in general.

Have I discovered what my talents are – and how much energy have I put into developing them?

C

I will appreciate what my talents are and how I use them.

Year 7:2

A

I'm a really rotten reader
the worst in all the class,
the sort of rotten reader

that makes you want to laugh.

They say that I'm dyslexic
(that's a word they've just found out)
… but when I get some plasticine
I know what that's about.

I build great magic forests
weave bushes out of string
and paint pink panderellos
and birds that really sing.

They give me diagnostic tests,
they try out reading schemes,
but none of them will ever know
the colour of my dreams.

TAKEN FROM 'COLOUR OF MY DREAMS' BY PETER DIXON

B

Sometimes we concentrate on what we cannot do rather than what we can do.

We are all different and we all have different things to contribute to the rest of humanity. Some people even take their weaknesses and turn them into strengths, like Oliver Reed and Susan Hampshire – actors who rely on words, yet they are both dyslexic!

C

Today I will view any weakness as a potential strength.

Year 7:3

A

Each of us lives each day with special gifts which are part of our being, and life is a process of discovering and developing these God-given gifts within each one of us.

JEANNE DIXON, IN *EACH DAY A NEW BEGINNING* (4 MAY)

B

Everybody has something to contribute. Maybe we are good at expressing ourselves, or maybe we write well. Listening is a special gift that is really needed today. People who fight against the odds, like the pupil who had difficulty in speaking and opted for drama, like the disabled people who have their own Olympics and gain records close to those of the Olympic champions, are an inspiration to the rest of us.

Sometimes we need room to cultivate our own talents, but we also need to give our friends room to cultivate theirs.

C

I will give myself and others some space to discover and develop our gifts.

Year 8:1

A

*Success is best measured by how far you've come
with the talents you've been given.*

ANONYMOUS, THE DECADES BOOK OF BIRTHDAYS

B

One of the things that stops us reaching our potential is looking at the success of somebody else. They may run faster than us, draw more artistically than us, write better, read better, obtain better grades in test and exams and so on. Thinking that we cannot achieve their attainments we do not try.

At these times we need to consider the story of the race between the Hare and the Tortoise. The Hare was faster at running, but being too confident, took things easy. The tortoise, although slower, kept going and eventually won the race. So often it is those who know what their strengths and weaknesses are and who keep trying who in the end achieve something constructive, positive and productive in their life.

C

Today I will concentrate on what I can do.

Year 8:2

A

He has achieved success who has lived well, laughed often and loved much.

BESSIE ANDERSON STANLEY, *THE DECADES BOOK OF BIRTHDAYS*

B

When a young teacher tragically lost her eldest son, her tutor group wrote to say how sorry they were. This is how she replied to their letter.

'I think most people take their health for granted. You're young and healthy – accept all the opportunities school offers you. Have a go at playing, for example, football, tennis, drama, singing or painting. If you can't do something (I can't sing for example!) then at least you can say well, I had a go, I'll try something else. Life is too precious to waste.'

C

I will make the most of the opportunities around me.

Year 8:3

A

It is only the first step which is troublesome.

MARIE ANNE DE VICHEY-CHAUMOND, *DICTIONARY OF QUOTATIONS AND PROVERBS*

B

In 1990 Anne Mackey was going to Russia for a holiday. Before she left she heard an appeal from the Russian ambassador asking for food for some Russian families. Anne Mackey's response was to empty her suitcase of clothes and fill it with tins of food, which she later delivered to a Russian family.

The next year she gave some money to a Russian hospital. When she saw the state of the hospital she appealed for other people to help. The result has meant that the hospital at St Petersburg has received two truckloads of drugs, food and equipment and an ambulance. It has also been refurbished by 250 British volunteers.

Anne Mackey is an ordinary woman who once emptied her suitcase of clothes and filled it with food.

C

Today I will make the first step towards someone in need.

Year 9:1

A

The only place where success comes before work is in the dictionary.

VIDAL SASOON, IN *THE DECADES BOOK OF BIRTHDAYS*

B

A young successful comedy writer was asked how he became a successful writer. He replied that he followed his English teacher's advice, which was: 'There are three steps to becoming a successful writer, step one, write something. Step two, send it to a publisher or media outlet. Step three, repeat steps one and two.'

Most people have dreams of being successful in some area of life, and dreams are good, but if we only keep them as dreams and do not take action, they are still only dreams.

C

Today I will take action to make my dreams come true.

Year 9:2

A

There is no failure except in no longer trying.

ELBERT HUBBARD, IN *THE DECADES BOOK OF BIRTHDAYS*

B

Tony Thomas Hall is a married man with children who works as a computer programmer for a well-known bank. There is nothing extraordinary about that until we learn that at the age of 24 he developed cancer and had to have his left leg amputated. He then developed secondary cancer of the lungs.

For most people, coping with a family and a job under such difficult circumstances would be an achievement in itself, but Tony pushes himself further. He keeps himself fit in the gym, and has put himself into athletics training, to prepare for the World Games.

Tony suffers a lot of pain when he is running, but he is determined not to give up.

C

I will continue to try, whatever my physical ability may be.

Year 9:3

A

God wants us to be victors, not victims; to grow, not grovel; to soar, not sink; to overcome, not to be overwhelmed.

WILLIAM A. WARD, IN *GATHERED GOLD*

B

In London among the homeless lived a chronic alcoholic called Carol. With help she recovered from her drink problem only to discover that she was suffering from tuberculosis. She now receives treatment to help her recover from that, but she has not allowed herself to be overwhelmed.

She spends her time counselling homeless alcoholics.

We all have a lot of potential locked away inside us. We have a choice in life, we can become victims or victors.

C

I will become a victor in life.

Year 10:1

A

The man who makes no mistakes does not usually make anything.

EDWARD JOHN PHELPS, IN *THE DECADES BOOK OF BIRTHDAYS*

B

Often the one thing that stops us reaching our full potential is fear. There is the fear of failing. Maybe we cannot do what we set out to do. Maybe others around us will do better. Sometimes it feels safer not to even try, so we cannot be said to have failed. We may fear looking like a fool to our friends and classmates. We worry that if what we do goes wrong they will laugh at us, and remember the incident.

There is also the fear of succeeding. What would that lead to? Would we get a lot of unwelcome attention?

By not reaching out and extending ourselves we are not only limiting ourselves but we are also denying those around us the gift that we have to offer.

C

Today I will risk making mistakes.

Year 10:2

A

Don't be afraid to take big steps. You can't cross a chasm in two small jumps.

DAVID LLOYD GEORGE, IN *THE DECADES BOOK OF BIRTHDAYS*

B

In 1983, sixteen-year-old Ffyona Campbell set out to walk from Caithness to Lands End to test her endurance. When she reached her destination she decided to continue. Eleven years and 19,586 miles later she walked into the record books as the first woman to walk around the world.

It was not easy. She often walked through difficult terrain, or met people who were unfriendly. At times she had no back-up team and she had to be totally self-supporting. A lot of the journeys were incredibly lonely. On top of this were all the physical problems like blisters and aching muscles. However, she persevered and she accomplished it.

Now she can continue with the rest of her life, knowing that already at the age of twenty-seven she has courageously taken big strides in her life.

C

Today I will be courageous and step out boldly.

Year 10:3

A

It isn't how long you stick around but what you put over while you are here.

GEORGE ADE, IN *THE DECADES BOOK OF BIRTHDAYS*

B

On 5 November 1994, George Forman made history when he

became the World Boxing Association and International Boxing Federation heavyweight champion of the world – at the age of 45.

As a child he was given little love and used only as a farmhand. In addition he grew up with a great deal of bitterness and hatred. When he turned to boxing he was known as a 'stone cold thug', and reportedly wished to kill his opponents.

When he lost the championship at the age of 25 he went downhill, he turned to drink, and his body deteriorated. At one point he needed sticks to walk.

His life changed dramatically in 1977 when, after a religious experience in Puerto Rico, he became a Christian. He trained to be a Baptist minister and eventually had his own church. He wanted to help the youth in the community; he wanted to provide some decent facilities for them, but no one would help with the finance, so he decided to get back into the ring.

People tried to stop him. How could a 45-year-old fight a young fit 26-year-old champion who had never lost a fight? Nobody knows – but he did!

C

I will remember that all things are possible.

Year 11:1

A

South Africa belongs to all its people, black and white, coloured and Indian, and the message we're putting forward is of nation-building and reconciliation. What is happening in South Africa is a miracle.

NELSON MANDELA, IN *MARIE CLAIRE*, APRIL 1995

B

The term 'miracle' has been used many times when people see

the changes in South Africa. Many people expected a blood bath as one group would seek to usurp the power of another. Instead we see a democracy, and different cultures working together for the good of the whole.

Many names will be recorded in the history books when South Africa's transition from apartheid to democracy is re-counted, but top of the list will probably be the name of Nelson Mandela. He spent 27 years in prison under the old regime, entering as a young man and coming out an old man. In an article in *Marie Claire* magazine, his housekeeper says of him, 'The longer I've worked for him, the more impressed I am. He just has this wonderful outlook on life and, amazingly for someone who has spent all those years in prison, has no anger in him.'

Nelson Mandela's attitude of peace and forgiveness has led the way in South Africa, and is helping the bitterness of the past to be overcome.

C

There will be times when to achieve peace I must give up my natural feelings of revenge.

Year 11:2

A

Unless you have been there you cannot understand how it feels.
YEAR 11 PUPIL SUFFERING FROM DEPRESSION

B

I once knew a young vicar who had worked in a children's ward of a big hospital. It was a special ward where few of the children would recover and many died.

At Christmas he noticed that the parents who had lost children were hanging around the hospital. He understood what it was like to lose a loved one, because as a young man he was involved in a car accident in which all of his family were killed, except him.

When he saw the parents at the hospital he gathered them together. He explained that grief is a powerful emotion, and they could, if they wanted, use it. The result was a national organization, where parents who had lost their children, helped other parents going through the same suffering.

All emotions are powerful and we have the opportunity to use them positively.

C

I will use my experiences to help others.

Year 11:3

A

Aim at the sun, and you may not reach it;
but your arrow will fly far higher than if
aimed at an object on a level with yourself.

J. HAWES, IN THE DECADES BOOK OF BIRTHDAYS

B

So often we limit ourselves with the phrase, 'I could never do that', but until we try something how do we know?

A woman once filled in an application form for a job. Her daughter encouraged her to list all of her positive qualities. The application was much more positive than she would normally write about herself. The result was she was given an interview. She did not get the job she applied for, but one at a higher level.

We have a choice in life, to aim for the sun and try to do the things that we would normally only dream about, or to watch others as they work out their dreams and ambitions.

C

Today I will think about what I really want out of life and go for it.

29 PRODUCTIVE WORK

Year 7:1

A

Work will win. Wishing won't!

ED B, IN *DAYS OF HEALING, DAYS OF JOY* (6 NOVEMBER)

B

There is a time and a place for everything – wishing is one of them. It is fun to wish upon a star. In those moments, we can conjure up the most delicious situations and events.

There are times, however, when wishing is not enough. There are times when the only appropriate response is work. There are times when all the wishing in the world will not do the work that needs to be done.

Wishing alone does not get our homework done or give us the important insights gained from actually sitting down and working through relationship problems. Wishing alone does not let go of resentments, start new friendships or improve our physical condition.

Wishing and work can both be beneficial. Our task is to know the difference between the two and decide which one is called for.

ADAPTED FROM *DAYS OF HEALING, DAYS OF JOY* (6 NOVEMBER)

C

I will think about the difference between dreams and action plans.

Year 7:2

A

Whatever your life's work, it will feel natural and right. It will feel like coming home. Our work – whether paid, unpaid or voluntary – will enable us to radiantly express our inner self. All we need to become is who we are.

GILL EDWARDS, LIVING MAGICALLY – A NEW VISION OF REALITY

B

Every one of us has a purpose, a mission, a unique role to play in the world – our life's work. Perhaps it will be based upon artistic or musical talent, or a love for children or the ability to teach, or skill for organization, or being good at cooking, or an affinity with nature, being a diplomat, or having a mechanical skill. Perhaps we are drawn towards a social, political or environmental cause of some kind. Or maybe we have an extraordinary passion for china dolls or medieval poetry. Each of us has a gift to give to the world – the gift of our own uniqueness.

By pursuing our hobbies and doing what we love doing, we can find our uniqueness and discover our life's work. This is the work where we are most productive, where we can shine and feel truly alive.

ADAPTED FROM *LIVING MAGICALLY – A NEW VISION OF REALITY*

C

Today I will reflect on what I most love doing.

Year 7:3

A

The more I want to get something done, the less I call it work.

RICHARD BACH, IN *MEDITATIONS FOR MEN WHO DO TOO MUCH* (31 JANUARY)

B

Work doesn't have to be a ball and chain. Work can be, and often is, quite fulfilling. When work begins to enslave you, you know it. You are overtired – short-tempered, prickly.

If you're passionate about your work – or, to be less dramatic, you enjoy what you do – you don't call it work!

Work and play are the same. When you're following your energy and doing what you want all the time, the distinction between work and play dissolves. Work is no longer what you have to do or play what you want to do. When you are doing what you love, you may work harder and produce more than ever before, but it will feel like play.

ADAPTED FROM *MEDITATIONS FOR MEN WHO DO TOO MUCH* AND *LIVING IN THE LIGHT*

C

I will keep my mind open to what motivates me to work and examine what that work is.

ADAPTED FROM *MEDITATIONS FOR MEN WHO DO TOO MUCH*

Year 8:1

A

Action, to be productive, has need of contemplation.

MOTHER TERESA, *PRAYER – SEEKING THE HEART OF GOD*

B

Each day Mother Teresa gets up at 4.30 am and then: prays, washes, loves, serves, prays, works, loves and serves again. This pattern is repeated daily and yearly.

The power and strength to serve, love and work is drawn from her life of prayer and contemplation. When she prays, she asks to receive the light from Jesus which makes us shine. Mother Teresa says:

'Penetrate and possess our whole being so utterly
that our lives may only be a radiance of yours.
Shine through us
and be so in us
that every soul we come in contact with
may feel your presence in our soul.'

The light which Mother Teresa receives in silent contemplation is shared with those she serves: the poor, homeless and dying people of Calcutta. Her life in the world is prayer in action. 'Action, to be productive, has need of contemplation.'

ADAPTED FROM *MOTHER TERESA* AND *PRAYER – SEEKING THE HEART OF GOD*

C

Times of stillness and contemplation can help me to work productively.

Year 8:2

A

Whatever you can do or dream you can, begin it.
Boldness has genius, power and magic in it.
Begin it now!

GOETHE (1749-1832)

B

To achieve what we want to do, to turn our plans into action, to bring about changes in life, rests upon the decision to begin; and that decision can be made in an instant.

C

I can bring about change in my life by making decisions – NOW!

Year 8:3

A

I never did anything worth doing by accident, nor did any of my inventions come by accident: they came by work.

THOMAS A. EDISON, IN *THE DECADES BOOK OF BIRTHDAYS*

B

In September 1869, Thomas Edison arrived in New York with only one dollar in his pocket. Thirteen years later, in September 1882, he pulled the switch that caused 900 houses to be lit by electricity, the first electrically lit area in the world.

The light bulb was only one of his many inventions, which included early versions of the microphone, record player and cinema film. Some of his inventions were rejected, some were never used, but overall he patented 2,500 new ideas.

Once he had an idea he worked at it until it was finished. His staff worked shifts while he developed a project, living at the laboratory, taking only short breaks. His work not only brought fame and fortune, it also brought him happiness. He enjoyed his work, and he continued to work even when there was no need, other than the need to fulfil himself.

C

I will look for fulfilment and enjoyment when working hard.

Year 9:1

A

Productive work, love, and thought are possible only if a person can be, when necessary, quiet and alone with himself.

ERICH FROMM, *MAN FOR HIMSELF*

B

To be forever on the go – always busy doing something –

compulsively active or overactive, is not necessarily what productive work is about. It is so very important to enjoy being at ease; to have quiet periods of rest; so that we can listen to our thoughts and get in touch with our feelings inside. Out of this can come a clear idea of what we want to do and achieve in life. Although nothing is produced, we are in fact productive.

C

To work productively, I will find times to be quiet and alone with myself.

Year 9:2

A

Talk does not cook rice.

CHINESE PROVERB, IN *PROVERBS FROM AROUND THE WORLD*

B

Talking about and then planning what we are going to do is of value. If we are going to travel a long way it can take time to organize, gather maps, plan routes and pack; so that we are well prepared for the journey. When writing a story or doing project work, we may take time collecting our materials and deciding how best to present our work, so that when we put pen to paper or use the word processor, the writing goes smoothly.

Sometimes, however, we can focus too much on the groundwork and resist getting the job done. At these times we need to take the plunge and put our thoughts and plans into action. Otherwise, at the end of the day, all that we are left with are ideas.

C

I will put plans into action.

Year 9:3

A

I am of the opinion that my life belongs to the whole community and as long as I live, it is my privilege to do for it whatever I can. I want to be thoroughly used up when I die, for the harder I work the more I live.

GEORGE BERNARD SHAW, IN *FEEL THE FEAR AND DO IT ANYWAY*

B

There is great satisfaction to be found in work. When we work productively we can feel vibrant and truly alive. It is a joy to be productive in whatever way we can – whether it's putting effort into a school project; being moved by a poem; helping others; experiencing the beauty of nature rather than just looking at it, or making something beautiful.

We can feel fantastic when what we've done makes a difference to our lives and to others'.

C

May I be truly active so that I can feel my 'aliveness'.

Year 10:1

A

There's no better medium in the world than film. I mean, my God, you can do anything with it. The only thing is to find out what it is that's worth doing.

JOSEPH CAMPBELL, IN *THE HERO'S JOURNEY – THE WORLD OF JOSEPH CAMPBELL*

B

Whatever good ideas we have, however talented and accomplished we are, it is of no value if our skills lie unused.

We may discover that we have a certain flair in a particular area – maybe we are good with computers, writing poetry, painting or listening to people. We can spend time developing and nurturing our skills and gifts. Like the pupa in the chrysalis, to feel our true potential and splendour, we need eventually to emerge and put our brilliance to good use.

Great peace of mind and joy can be found in our lives when, at some point, we discover what, to us, is worth doing – and we do it.

C

I will enjoy developing my abilities, knowing that one day I can do something worthwhile.

Year 10:2

A

Many times our automatic reaction when faced with an uncomfortable or confusing situation is to thrash around trying to change it immediately. We attempt to swallow the whole predicament at once and spit it out, solved ... thoughtless, quick action is often more frustrating than productive.

SUE PATTON THOELE, *THE WOMAN'S BOOK OF COURAGE*

B

When we are faced with a mountain of school work, our first response can be to feel overwhelmed by the amount of work that we have to do. We may panic and run around in circles trying to cope with it all.

One way to deal with this is to take a breather and get some distance from the problem. Next we need to break down the task ahead of us into manageable-sized pieces. We can then tackle one thing at a time until we have completed all that we have to do.

Jumping in at the deep end and 'thrashing' about without direction, will not help us solve our problems or work productively. Organizing ourselves and doing one thing at a time will!

C

I will take time to organize and plan my work.

Year 10:3

A

Stop freewheeling, get into gear, and do something with your life. There are many avenues to explore, so why not explore them? Never be afraid to step out into the unknown, into the new. Do it fearlessly, always expecting the very best as you do so.

EILEEN CADDY, IN *BAG OF JEWELS*

B

We work most productively when we work with a spirit of adventure and discovery. By being creative and trying new things we can achieve a great deal.

For example, if we often find it difficult to complete all of our homework on time, we can think of new ways to organize our time and tackle the assignments.

New inventions and discoveries come about when people look at things differently, and break limits. The more creatively that we look at our work, the more likely we are able to work productively and achieve new goals.

It can be helpful to explore new avenues with a sense of eagerness, excitement and a feeling that everything and anything is possible.

C

I will work with an adventurous and creative spirit.

Year 11:1

A

When my life is coming to an end,

how many experiences shall I look back to and say,
'To have experienced that alone
would have made my life worthwhile'?

And of how many of my actions shall I say,
'To have done this thing alone
would have made my life worth living'?
ANTHONY DE MELLO, WELLSPRINGS

B

Can we measure how productive we have been when it comes to living our lives? What is a productive life?

Throughout our lives, we build up 'rich stores' of experiences, which we are able to experience thoroughly at the time and look back on and treasure. But also in life we can create 'unfinished business' – those things which we always wanted or needed to do, but never got round to doing.

Perhaps productive work is about building up our 'rich stores' and reducing our 'unfinished business'; so that at the end of our lives, we can say: 'Doing these things has made my life worth living. I have few regrets.'

C

What are *my* 'rich stores'?

Year 11:2

A

See that nothing occupies your thoughts except an utter determination to reach out to God.
THE EPISTLE OF PRIVY COUNSEL, *THE CLOUD OF UNKNOWING AND OTHER WORKS*

B

In whatever we do, we are most successful and productive if we focus our attention with utter determination.

It is less effective to say, 'I might play well in that game of hockey' or, 'I'll see if I feel like revising for the test on Friday'. These are phrases which contain an attitude of indifference and will not help us to achieve our goals.

We need to tackle things with commitment. We need to stride out with a conviction to do our best. It is the reaching out and stretching ourselves in an unwavering way that enables us to be fulfilled.

C

I will bring unwavering determination to whatever I do.

Year 11:3

A

We're so engaged in doing things to achieve purposes of outer value that we forget that the inner value, the rapture that is associated with being alive, is what it's all about.

JOSEPH CAMPBELL, *THE POWER OF MYTH*

B

We can be caught up in the pursuit of our goals. We can try to achieve more and more success for the pleasure of the applause and approval of others. If our lives follow this pattern, we are only alive on the outside.

We also have an inner life which can feed our outer life, helping us to work happily and productively. Our inner life is of supreme importance because it is through developing our values and understanding of ourselves that we are guided in our choices for action in the world.

C

Today I will pay attention to my inner life.

30 LEARNING FROM EXPERIENCE

Year 7:1

A

If we add observation to what we see and reflection to what we read, we are on the right road to knowledge.

ADAPTED FROM CALEB COLTON, IN *TOUCHSTONES* (23 JULY)

B

We are not just feathers blown on the winds of a powerless life. We bring ourselves to our experiences. The dynamics of learning include, first, what happens – what we see or read or hear – and, second, what we make of it. So in our observations and reflections we consider what an event means to us.

As young people growing up, we need some time to think and reflect in order to make sense of the changes and experiences in our lives, whether at school or at home.

We need time and space away from interruptions and work; so that we can let ourselves learn and grow from our experiences.

This time to reflect might happen when travelling on the bus or train, or by going for a walk or by sitting in a quiet room at home. Through time, we deepen and grow stronger as we grow older, rather than only collecting more experiences.

ADAPTED FROM *TOUCHSTONES* (23 JULY)

C

Today I will reflect on the events I experience.

Year 7:2

A

We learn as much from sorrow as from joy, as much from illness as from health, from handicap as from advantage – and indeed perhaps more.

PEARL S. BUCK, IN *MEDITATIONS FOR MEN WHO DO TOO MUCH*
(23 DECEMBER)

B

We have the ability to learn from almost every life experience – but we must be open to it. If we see some situations as bad luck or in a totally negative way, then we miss the other half of the experience.

Through the loss of a friend, we may come to value our friendships with others. Getting a low mark in a test can help us to improve our study skills.

How much would we learn if everything in our lives always went right?

ADAPTED FROM *MEDITATIONS FOR MEN WHO DO TOO MUCH*
(23 DECEMBER)

C

Today I will value the opportunities to learn from my experiences.

Year 7:3

A

For the first time today
I opened my eyes and saw

a whole new world a silent translucent expanse
of jagged tiled white a luminous encounter
of blue and green where blurred figures
glided without sound about me as I held my bubbled breath

For the first time today
I opened my eyes and saw – under water

For the first time today
I trusted
Starfished on that same water I had just explored
supported by water which once I had feared so passionately
I drifted human flotsam
mind and body lost in watery equilibrium

For the first time today
I floated –
and trusted an alien element.

MAGGIE HOLMES

B

However old you are, there will always be an occasion which will count for you as a 'first':

- the first time you've felt a certain way;
- a new experience;
- a turning point in your life.

The range of feelings about these first time experiences can be very varied. What they all have in common is the opportunity to learn from them. Learning from experiences can help life become richer and more satisfying.

C

Today I will reflect on the value of learning from experience.

Year 8:1

A

Don't try to be perfect; just an excellent example of being human.

ANTHONY ROBBINS, *AWAKEN THE GIANT WITHIN*

B

Throughout life, we can experience, learn and grow.

Learning from our experiences can be an exciting and fascinating aspect of living; so be adventurous and taste what life has to offer. Make discoveries and mistakes by the dozen and enjoy the process.

The more that we experience and understand ourselves, the more natural and human we can be. We don't reach a state of perfection on this earth, where we never need to change again; so enjoy the constant changes and growth that human beings live through – and be an excellent example of being human.

C

I will welcome change and growth in my life.

Year 8:2

A

I challenge you to learn from other people's experiences as often as you can, and to utilize whatever you learn.

ANTHONY ROBBINS, *AWAKEN THE GIANT WITHIN*

B

By learning about others' experiences, discoveries and ways of living, we can save ourselves a great deal of time and effort. We don't need to find out everything from scratch, by trial and error, but can put to good use what we learn from both the good and bad experiences of others.

Our time at school offers wonderful opportunities to learn more about people and the world that we live in. If we choose to listen to and utilize what others have learnt in their lives, we can grow in our own knowledge and understanding of ourselves and our world.

C

I will save time by learning from the mistakes and discoveries of others.

Year 8:3

A

When the mouse laughs at the cat there is a hole nearby.
NIGERIAN PROVERB

That which is loved is always beautiful.
NORWEGIAN PROVERB

What breaks in a moment may take years to mend.
SWEDISH PROVERB

If you don't crack the shell, you can't eat the nut.
RUSSIAN PROVERB

ALL FROM *PROVERBS FROM AROUND THE WORLD*

B

Proverbs are sayings that carry with them advice about life. They are found all around the world and are gems of wisdom from the experience of those who have gone before us.

Sometimes we can reflect upon the meaning of proverbs and relate their guidance to situations in our own lives. At other times we will find that there is no substitute for going through an experience for ourselves – even if it means we 'learn the hard way'.

C

I will listen to the wisdom of other peoples' experience.

Year 9:1

A

A recipe for happiness.
Look at the past;

Learn from the past;
Let go of the past;
And live in the present.

S.E-W.

B

Learning from experience is all about reflecting on what has happened and then moving on. If we constantly live in the past – thinking about what happened or what might have been; we are clinging to the past and missing out on the present.

We can learn from every single thing that we experience, but if we hold the experience to us, preciously guarding it, we cannot benefit from it. If we let go of the experience – give it wings – we can set it free.

C

Today I will release the past so that I can experience what is happening now.

Year 9:2

A

Our habits form our future. Just as a train is directed by the rails it rolls on, our lives are directed by our habits.

EARNIE LARSEN AND CAROL LARSEN HEGARTY, *DAYS OF HEALING, DAYS OF JOY* (26 SEPTEMBER)

B

Our habits are the ways we have learned to behave in particular situations. Some habits are helpful, such as cleaning our teeth morning and night. Others are less helpful, like leaving the cap off the toothpaste tube so that the toothpaste dries up.

If, every time we meet a dog, it barks and growls at us, we may come to the conclusion that all dogs are unfriendly. This is what our experience so far has taught us. Our survival instinct triggers a response and we become very wary of dogs, expecting them all to be unpleasant.

Sometimes we need to look beyond what we have learned from experience. By seeing past our habits, and the way we usually react to things we can expand our horizons, freeing ourselves to discover a world with new possibilities.

C
Today I will look beyond my habits.

Year 9:3

A
The old saying, 'If at first you don't succeed, try, try again' is so true. It doesn't mean beat yourself up and try the same old way again. It means recognize your error and try another way – until you learn to do it correctly.
LOUISE L. HAY, *YOU CAN HEAL YOUR LIFE*

B
When we are trying to do something new, or learn a skill, we may have a set idea about how we are supposed to achieve success. Our minds can get fixed on looking at the situation in a certain way. If this way doesn't work we may feel frustrated because we are stuck in a pattern and are repeating the same mistake again and again.

Sometimes we need to be more flexible with ourselves and step outside the situation, looking at it from a different angle. This will help us to see more clearly the way we were trying to operate. We can then recognize our errors and try a different way.

C
If at first you don't succeed, try, try again.

357

Year 10:1

A

I am not discouraged, because every wrong attempt discarded is another step forward.

THOMAS EDISON, IN *AWAKEN THE GIANT WITHIN*

B

In our lives, we all make decisions that in hindsight, we may feel were wrong. However, all is not lost, for we can learn from the experience and use the lessons to make a 'better' decision the next time.

Remember: Success truly is the result of good judgement. Good judgement is the result of experience, and experience is often the result of bad judgement!

ANTHONY ROBBINS, *AWAKEN THE GIANT WITHIN*

C

I will welcome my mistakes as good experience.

Year 10:2

A

You're not a failure if you don't make it;
you're a success because you try.

SUSAN JEFFERS, *FEEL THE FEAR AND DO IT ANYWAY*

B

We may not accomplish all of our goals, but the process that we go through in trying, can be our success. The very fact that we try is commendable, because we have stretched and expanded our horizons, and learnt much along the way.

If we 'reach for the stars', we open ourselves to the possibility of new experiences and achievements. We may not end up where we originally intended, but our lives will be enriched for the experience. It is the reaching out and having a go that is the important thing!

C

I am a success because I try.

Year 10:3

A

It was a very hot morning, that morning on August 6th, 1945. The sun was shining brightly. I was polishing a pair of sunglasses. Suddenly there was a flash – a blazing light – that turned the sky into a furnace. For a moment, I could not open my eyes. Then I grabbed my helmet and ran to the window, thinking that it was a small bomb. I looked out and saw a boy – a 16-year-old boy – begin to melt – his skin crumbling off from the head down. His eyes were still open in horror.

At first I thought the bomb had only hit our plant. Then the blast pushed me back into the room, which began to cave in on top of me … I crawled out from under the rubble and shouted, 'I'll help you, I'll help you.' But there were very few who could be helped. About 1500 of the workers were already dead, another 500 would die the next day.

Within an hour there were between 10,000 and 30,000 charred bodies floating in the river. Parts of the bodies were moving because schools of fish began feeding on the corpses.

I was then 31. Today I am 60, but still I see the effects of the bomb throughout Japan where thousands of people suffer and die from radiation diseases. They also worry about the health of their children and grandchildren.

MASAHIRO SADANAGA, IN *PRAYERS FOR PEACEMAKERS*

B

There are thousands of nuclear weapons in the world today. We now know the devastation that one small bomb can cause.

Let us hope that the nations of the world who possess nuclear weapons have learned from the experiences of Hiroshima and Nagasaki.

C

I will do what I can to make the world a safer and more peaceful place.

Year 11:1

A

Failure is success if we learn from it.
MALCOLM S. FORBES, IN *THE DECADES BOOK OF BIRTHDAYS*

B

Nobody likes to fail. It makes us feel foolish and inadequate. However, we all 'fail' at different times of our life. The secret is to learn from the experience, turning weakness into a strength.

In everyday life there are so many things to learn; how to get along with various people, how to cope with different situations. None of us comes equipped with automatic knowledge of these things. It is through the failed attempts that we learn. But if we do not even make an attempt, then how can we progress?

It is the same with our gifts and talents. We cannot develop them until first we have the courage to test them out.

C

Today I will look for my talents and see how I can develop them.

Year 11:2

A

Courage, unused, diminishes.

Commitment, unexercised, wanes.
Love, unshared, dissipates.

ANTHONY ROBBINS, *AWAKEN THE GIANT WITHIN*

B

Whatever we discover on life's journey is of its greatest value when we put the knowledge to good use.

You could stick up helpful sayings or pearls of wisdom like:

'Each day is a new beginning'
'Live in the moment'
'I am a worthwhile and lovable person'

on your kitchen cupboards or your bedroom mirror, to serve as a constant reminder and inspiration to you. This will enable you to keep the things that you've learned and treasure the most in the forefront of your mind – constantly reminding you to live your beliefs; be true to yourself and make good use of all that you've learned.

C

I will make good use of the things that I've learned in my life.

Year 11:3

A

The loftiest towers rise from the ground.

CHINESE PROVERB, *PROVERBS FROM AROUND THE WORLD*

B

We all need to learn in order to grow. Some of us learn quickly from our experiences, while for others it can be a gradual process. However quick we are to learn, we all need to start at the beginning and build on our experiences and knowledge, step by step.

Our time at school can offer us opportunities which give us a good grounding in general knowledge and useful skills. We can use this firm foundation to help us as we develop and build our special interests and find our direction in life.

C

I will build on each experience.

31 COURAGE/MEETING CHALLENGES

Year 7:1

A

The hero is no braver than the ordinary man, but he is brave five minutes longer.

RALPH WALDO EMERSON, IN *DAYS OF HEALING, DAYS OF JOY*
(30 DECEMBER)

B

Simon Weston was 20 years old when he was terribly burnt during the Falklands Campaign. He was a soldier waiting to leave a ship when an enemy missile set the ship on fire. Many of his friends died and Simon was close to death. Even after plastic surgery he was badly scarred and horribly disfigured.

However, Simon did not hide away from the world, but faced it. All who saw him could see his courage, his acceptance of what had happened, and his determination to fight back to life.

C

Today I will think about the words being strong and tough, which describe an attitude of mind.

Year 7:2

A

God grant me the serenity

To accept the things I cannot change,
The courage to change the things I can,
And the wisdom to know the difference.

REINHOLD NIEBUHR, IN *DAYS OF HEALING, DAYS OF JOY*
(1 APRIL)

B

We are social beings and care about what our friends think about us. Sometimes this stops us saying or doing what we really feel we should, for fear of being laughed at or rejected.

Once a wealthy man was being congratulated on his 80th birthday. Everybody thought that he had had a good life, but he admitted that when he was young he wanted to do something completely different, but lacked the courage. Nothing else ever satisfied him.

We all need courage when faced with new opportunities.

C

Today I will have the courage to do what I think is right; fear will not hold me back.

Year 7:3

A

Courage is the price that life exacts for granting peace.

AMELIA EARHART, IN *EACH DAY A NEW BEGINNING* (2 APRIL)

B

When we think of courage we often think of someone who accomplishes a brave and daring deed. Rescuing someone or taking part in a death-defying stunt. Every day there are incidents in our life where we need courage. Maybe it means having the courage to speak up for what we believe, the courage to stand with someone who is unpopular, the courage to tell the truth, the courage to be different.

When we do face up to a difficult task we experience a wave of peacefulness. Courage has its reward.

ADAPTED FROM *EACH DAY A NEW BEGINNING* (2 APRIL)

C

I will have courage to go forward and to handle whatever confronts me.

ADAPTED FROM *EACH DAY A NEW BEGINNING* (2 APRIL)

Year 8:1

A

When I moved from one school to another, I hid behind my mum and dad. I was shy and to see thirty pairs of eyes looking at me felt like a crowd of people in the classroom. Then one boy invited me to sit down. He gave me courage and friendship.

CARLEY, AGED 12

B

Meeting new people can be difficult. We can all recall our first day at school as it usually makes such a major impression on us. As we move on through the school system and we make friends who travel with us, it becomes easier to cope with the changes in classes and schools.

A real challenge faces us when we move to a totally different situation, like a new school or on to a job. There will come a point when we will meet the experience of having to enter a room full of new faces. It can be very intimidating to be stared at by 30 pairs of eyes. These are the times that we can support those in need of courage.

C

I will reach out to those who need extra help today.

Year 8:2

A

The ability to accept responsibility is the measure of a person.

ROY L. SMITH, IN *DAYS OF HEALING, DAYS OF JOY* (23 AUGUST)

B

'Life is full of challenges. These can take many forms. Temptation is one. Many of us will be tempted to smoke, drink or to take drugs. It will take courage to meet these challenges and a strength of character to turn our backs on the temptations.' (Gemma Evans, aged 12)

Courage is needed in every part of our life, not only when we are faced with a major challenge.

This is a time of our life when we are 'finding our feet' and sometimes this means that we do not act in a way that our parents find acceptable. It is also a time when many of us can find it difficult to go against our peers. To be part of a group is important. The challenge is to be part of a group while still maintaining our standards.

C

I will accept the challenge to be the person that I want to be.

Year 8:3

A

Courage is absolutely necessary for goodness.

RICHARD GLOVER, IN *GATHERED GOLD*

B

We never know when we are going to need courage. Life does not wait for us to be adult, or physically strong before facing us with the unexpected. This is the experience of 12-year-old Hayley Thomsen:

'I've had to show lots of courage in the past few years, when my Mum died. It took me totally by surprise because I always thought my Mum was going to be around. So when my Dad came in and told me that Mum had passed away I just couldn't believe it. I cried for a while, but then I realized that my Mum wouldn't want me to be sad, she would want me to be happy. So this is where I showed courage, by thinking about how she would be out of her misery and pain. I still think about her, but I think about her in a happy way. If I hadn't shown courage then I wouldn't be able to talk about her now.'

C

I will be inspired by the courage of others.

Year 9:1

A

Courage is fear that has said its prayers.
ANONYMOUS, IN *GATHERED GOLD*

B

Sometimes the barrier that stops us helping in a difficult situation is the fear that we might make a mistake or make it worse. When this happens we can think or pray about what we should do.

Some situations though are life-threatening and require an immediate response. There is a common fear of using resuscitation techniques in case we damage the unconscious person, but if they are going to die without our help, what more damage could we do?

Five-year-old Georgia Cribbin saw her diabetic father unconscious and went to great lengths to get sugar and ease it into his mouth. It was over a year since she had seen her mother do this, but alone in the house she remembered. She saved her father's life.

Surely this is the secret, when we truly love and care for

people we can overcome our fears to help them. Courage is an outworking of our love.

C

I will use my courage to help others.

Year 9:2

A

Bravery is not the absence of fear, but the mastery of it.
ANONYMOUS, IN *GATHERED GOLD*

B

So often when volunteers are required people tend to step back rather than step forward. This happened recently in a school when two volunteers were required to be interviewed by an industrialist. Not only would it be the first time the participants had been interviewed, but they would also be watched by their peers.

It took a lot of courage to participate, but there were some who were willing to give it a try.

After the interviews the pupils said they had found it really helpful and good preparation for the future. Many others then said that in hindsight they would have liked to have taken part.

Sometimes to gain from life's experiences we must be willing to master our fear, take a deep breath and go for it. Courage is the antidote to fear.

C

I will look for new challenges today.

Year 9:3

A

Courage consists not in hazarding without fear, but being resolutely minded in a just cause.
PLUTARCH, IN *GATHERED GOLD*

B

Martin Luther King was aware of racism at an early age. He wanted equal rights for all people, no matter what the colour of their skin. He said:

'I have the audacity to believe that peoples everywhere can have three meals a day for their bodies, education and culture for their minds, and dignity, equality and freedom for their spirits ... I still believe that we shall overcome' (in *Christianity: an approach for GCSE*).

His challenges to the status quo were always peaceful. He was not given peace in return. His house was bombed, he was stabbed, and he received abusive letters and phone calls. Eventually he was shot by a sniper and died, a relatively young man. Thanks to the courage, strength and will-power of Martin Luther King, others have been set free to continue the struggle for justice and equality.

C

I will have courage when seeking fairness and justice.

Year 10:1

A

A man of courage is also full of faith.

CICERO, IN *DAYS OF HEALING, DAYS OF JOY* (10 NOVEMBER)

B

Why are so many rides at the fairground frightening? Why do we bother to go on rides that whizz us around at high speeds, turn us upside down, and give us the impression that we are going to crash at any moment?

Deep down we know that the rides have passed safety inspections, but there is always the possibility that something can go wrong, and so they still give us a sense of danger – we are taking a risk. They cause the adrenalin to pump around our body and when the ride is over we are left feeling exhilarated and excited. We have faced our fear and have a sense of achievement.

In life there are constant challenges. How we respond to them decides whether our life is going to jog routinely along or whether it is going to be exciting and give us a sense of achievement.

C

I will have faith in my ability to cope with challenges.

Year 10:2

A

Speak up for those who cannot speak up for themselves.

PROVERBS 31:8

B

Dietrich Bonhoeffer was a minister in the German Lutheran Church when Adolf Hitler came to power.

He was horrified by the treatment of the Jewish population. He preached against it, he trained his students to be prepared to 'stand up and be counted'.

He was in America when the war broke out, a safe haven, but he returned to Germany. He said, 'I will have no right to participate in the reconstruction of Christian life in Germany after the war if I do not share the tribulations of this time with my people.'

He did not survive the war. He was hanged for being involved in a conspiracy against Hitler, but he inspired many others to carry on his cause.

There are many people in this world who, through exploitation and oppression, do not have a voice. Those of us who enjoy freedom can meet the challenge of speaking out for them.

C

I will speak up for others.

Year 10:3

A

One person with courage makes a majority.

ANDREW JACKSON, IN *MORE GATHERED GOLD*

B

In the late eighteenth century, the trade of slaves was still being conducted, as humans were shipped from Africa to America. Not only was freedom taken away from people, they were also treated in the most inhumane manner.

Many people were opposed to the slave trade, but there were big profits involved and money can sometimes speak louder than words. However, William Wilberforce was one person who was not influenced by money. He spoke to his friends about the issue and then proposed a resolution against the trade in the House of Commons.

While he waited for a change in the law, he took part in schemes that improved the life of the slaves. He had to devise various strategies to ban the trade, first in Britain, then Europe, then the British colonies. Shortly before he died a law was passed freeing the slaves.

Courage gives us the power to challenge the status quo.

C

I will be active and speak out when I see injustice.

Year 11:1

A

There is a time for all, when a great something-else is needed – not later, not earlier, but then. And these qualities make up the contents of courage.

LEO, *DEAR DRAGON*

B

When we come upon a problem that hurts us and upsets us, we should not look upon it as a stick to beat us down, but as a challenge that is going to help us to grow and shape our character.

Problems can be like buses – they are nowhere to be seen, then two or three come along together. This is when we need courage. We need to take each problem and deal with it. For example, if we suffer a loss or bereavement, our courage can help us to share with and support others in the future.

Courage can bring the best out in us and open the door to patience, wisdom and kindness.

C

I will embrace the future for I have courage.

Year 11:2

A

Show when you are tempted to hide, and hide when you are tempted to show.

A. B. BRUCE, IN *MORE GATHERED GOLD*

B

I remembered sitting on a train bound for Oxford where I was to attend an interview for a college course. This course would mean a completely new career change for me.

Suddenly the implications of what I was about to do descended upon me. I would be years older than anyone else on the course; I lacked a vital qualification; I might not like the new career, or even get a job in that profession.

The train was still in the station and I had the chance to get off it before I made a complete fool of myself – but I realized that by running away I would never know if I could have done it. So I gritted my teeth and stayed on the train. I attended the interview, gained the vital qualification, completed the course and got a job in my new career, which I really enjoy.

I am so happy that I found the courage to have a go.

J.A.H.

C

I will not let my fears limit me.

Year 11:3

A

Courage is in the sense of being correct and causing no delay in doing what must be done.

LEO, DEAR DRAGON

B

Sometimes we need courage to do something totally different or unexpected. Like giving up a good career to care for the homeless. To delay going to university in order to help in a school in Malaysia or look after orphans in Mexico.

It is like swimming against the tide. Our friends may be going in one direction and we are going in the opposite. We may feel self-doubt and there are the enquiring looks from friends and relatives to deal with. It is a difficult time because in these situations we may feel that we are putting ourselves above the parapet and fear that if we fail there will be many onlookers to say 'I told you so'.

However, sometimes we need to take the risks and try something new or different in order to have a deeper, richer life, a fuller understanding of the world.

C

I will consider why I am doing, what I am doing.

32 FAITH

Year 7:1

A

Now faith is being sure of what we hope for and certain of what we do not see.
HEBREWS 11:1

B

Often people say that they only believe in what they can see, despite the fact that we cannot see the wind, yet we know that it exists; we cannot see electricity yet we rely on its power; we cannot see love but all wish to experience it. It is not unreasonable to believe in the wind, or electricity, or love, because we see the results of their power every day. It is the same for those with faith, they also see the results of its power.

Just as a little child has to take a first step, just as a young bird has to take a first flight, each one setting out into the unknown, so to gain faith one must take a first step. As the child learns to walk and the bird learns to fly, so the person with faith finds that first step is only the beginning of a whole new experience.

C

Today I will look beyond the material things around me.

Year 7:2

A

Faith is like the air in a balloon.

If you got it you're filled.
If you don't you're empty.

PEGGY CAHN, IN *EACH DAY A NEW BEGINNING* (29 NOVEMBER)

B

The famous tight-rope walker, Charles Blondin, used to walk above Niagara Falls on a tight-rope as the crowd watched in awe. He would push a wheelbarrow over the Falls on the tight-rope. He then approached the onlookers and asked if they believed that not only could he push the wheelbarrow on the tight-rope, but a wheelbarrow with somebody sitting inside. They all believed that he could. Blondin would then invite a member of the crowd to get inside the wheelbarrow to be taken across the Falls. This offer was declined.

Only someone with real faith in Blondin would actually put their life into his hands by allowing him to take them across Niagara Falls on a tight-rope.

True faith demands action.

C

Today I want to consider where I am placing my faith.

Year 7:3

A

Be still, and know that I am God.

PSALM 46:10

B

For many years Jennifer Rees Larcombe had been confined to a wheelchair. She was very ill and on four occasions had almost died. She had been treated by many doctors but there was nothing that they could do. She had often prayed for healing but nothing had happened.

In June 1990 she was at a church in Haslemere when a

376

young woman openly declared that she thought Jennifer was going to be made well. Jennifer asked the young woman to pray for her, but she was reluctant, being new to faith and not even sure how to pray. The young woman was eventually persuaded to pray for Jennifer – Jennifer explains what happened next by saying, 'I simply stood up'. She entered the church in a wheelchair and left walking, a fit and healthy person.

ADAPTED FROM *UNEXPECTED HEALING*

C

I will be open to all possibilities.

Year 8:1

A

So far as Anna was concerned, being good, being generous, being kind, praying and all that kind of stuff had little to do with Mister God. They were, in the jargon of today, merely a 'spin off' … No! Religion was all about being like Mister God.

FYNN, *MISTER GOD THIS IS ANNA*

B

Anna was a red-headed five-year-old child living in the East End of London. She was no angel, yet she had an easy relationship with 'Mister God'. She marvelled at the beautiful creation that Mister God had made. She talked easily about Mister God to everyone she chatted to, as a part of normal conversation.

Her simple, yet profound understanding of Mister God made several adults re-think the old fashioned image they held about God. For Anna 'the whole point of being alive was to be like Mister God and then you couldn't help but be good and kind and loving, could you?'

C

I will come to God with the heart and mind of a child.

Year 8:2

A

'Please, please, Mister God, teach me how to ask real questions. Oh! please Mister God, help me to ask real questions.'

ANNA, IN *MISTER GOD THIS IS ANNA*

B

One night Fynn, Anna's guardian, heard Anna's tear-filled voice asking for help with the 'real questions'. When she was calm he asked her what she meant. She explained that people should get wiser as they grow older – but they don't.

She felt that we put the questions of life and death into small boxes and the answers we receive fit the size of the box. Consequently, we put Mister God into a box. Anna wanted to ask real questions, to understand fully Mister God, not to make him fit the box we have made for him.

C

I will ask real questions and leave enough space for big answers.

Year 8:3

A

'I found God more real, more strongly than ever before'

FYNN, IN *MISTER GOD THIS IS ANNA*

B

At the age of seven Anna climbed into a tree and fell out, badly injuring herself. A few days later she was dead. Fynn, her guardian, was devastated and wanted so much to hate God, yet he found God more real. He said:

'It slowly began to make sense, the bits began to fall into place. Something was happening and it made me cry, for the first time in a long, long time I cried … Anna's life hadn't been cut short, far from it, it had been full, completely fulfilled.' *(Mister God This Is Anna)*

C

I will have faith when I face the unknown.

Year 9:1

A

'Faith is to believe what we do not see, and the reward of this faith is to see what we believe.'

AUGUSTINE, IN *GATHERED GOLD*

B

We show faith in many areas of life. When we first learn to walk, swim or ride a bike, we must come to a point where we stop relying on other people and see if we can cope without support. When the first step is taken our faith is rewarded. What was once an act of faith is now a part of life.

It is the same in the spiritual world. We may not be sure there is 'anyone out there', but we will only find out if we are willing to take a step of faith.

C

I will overcome my doubts and take a step of faith.

Year 9:2

A

God will wait as long as it takes for us.

THE REVD. R. WALTERS, IN *DAYS OF HEALING, DAYS OF JOY* (13 JANUARY)

B

C.S. Lewis, the writer of *Chronicles of Narnia*, was for many years a convinced atheist. He preferred books written by atheists and the company of atheists. He was sometimes surprised to find that a book he enjoyed was by a Christian, or that a fellow academic was a Christian. He formed many arguments against the existence of God, until one night. He said:

'I gave in and admitted that God was God, and knelt and prayed; perhaps that night, the most dejected and reluctant convert in all England ...

The hardness of God is kinder than the softness of men and this compulsion is our liberation.' *(Surprised by Joy)*

C

I will keep my mind open to the things that I do not yet understand.

Year 9:3

A

Be still and know that I am God.

PSALM 46:10

B

In the book *Mister God This Is Anna*, young Anna observes Fynn check a radio on the outside, to measure the voltage and on the inside to measure the current. Anna concludes that people are like this: they measure God on the outside.

We can talk about God, go to a place of worship, study the scriptures, but never know God. Anna believed that we need to get inside and experience God, then the meaning of life will unfold before us.

C

I will be still and listen with my heart.

Year 10:1

A

It requires not only a power, but an almighty power, to raise the heart of man to believe.

RICHARD SIBBES, IN *GATHERED GOLD*

B

In 1986, David Verdegaal's heart stopped. He almost died and the experience he encountered while balanced between life and death changed his life. He said, 'From the moment I died, I had the sense of God being there, and I immediately asked him to forgive me for the shambles of my life, the fact that I wasn't living anywhere near how I ought to have been.

'Then a long tunnel of light came towards me and enveloped me. I had the most phenomenal sense of being transformed. I was the being overwhelmed by love. All the frictions, all the doubts, all the negative side of life was washed away. It was a complete cleansing of the past, the shedding of everything superfluous.

Next I had the equally wonderful sensation of being taken into God's arms. If you could remember what it was like when you were born, the first time you were picked up and cuddled, it was like that must have been – a complete comforting and reassuring. In a way, I saw God, in a way I didn't – His essence was in the light – but what I felt was definitely a fatherly embrace.' *(Daily Mail, 28 February 1995)*

C

I will learn from the experience of others.

Year 10:2

A

We walk by faith not by sight.

2 CORINTHIANS 5:7

B

Faith is jumping off a wall expecting to be caught. Faith is being led around blindfolded expecting to be guided. Faith is sharing a confidence expecting it to be kept. Faith is part of our everyday life. It gives us freedom, the opportunity to test new possibilities and gives a sense of adventure to life.

If we lack faith we will lessen our horizons. We will withdraw into the familiar and comfortable.

We can see the physical world all around us. There is also a spiritual world, but it may take a step of faith to find it.

C

I will consider what faith I have in my life.

Year 10:3

A

Your faith should not rest on the wisdom of men, but on the power of God.

1 CORINTHIANS 2:5

B

There is a lot of scepticism about near death experiences, but for the people who experience them there are no doubts.

David Verdagaal completely turned his life around after one such experience. He gave up his job and his home and completely changed his lifestyle.

His family totally believe his experience by observing the change in his life. It has also increased their faith and trust. But they will never fully understand what David saw. His wife says:

'David has had a vision which I can't possibly share. It's like someone who's been on holiday. They can tell you about it, but you can't experience it yourself.' *(Daily Mail,* 28 February 1995)

C

I will look for the higher wisdom.

Year 11:1

A

One grain of faith is more precious than a pound of knowledge.

JOSEPH HALL, IN *MORE GATHERED GOLD*

B

Science is based on facts, but facts are born from suppositions. The scientist must first have a hypothesis, which might be based on experience or it could be on assumption. To find out if the hypothesis is true, experiments must be conducted.

This is the way science moves forward and discovers more about the laws of nature. Faith is discovered the same way. When we being to wonder, 'Is there someone or something out there?', we will only find out by making it our hypothesis and testing it.

A man was thinking about life and what it was all about. His concluding thoughts were, 'If you're out there God, you've got to get me.'

The following day he met a stranger who said, 'I've come to get you,' and proceeded to share his faith. Nobody knew of the words the man had said in his heart. This experience shook the man. It seemed too improbable to be true.

Unless we are willing to test the theory we will never find out.

C

I will have the courage to look beyond my personal experience.

Year 11:2

A

There are more things in heaven and earth, Horatio,

Than are dreamt of in your Philosophy.

WILLIAM SHAKESPEARE, HAMLET

B

When eight-year-old Simon Teece was struck by scaffolding, he was not expected to live. If he did he would probably suffer brain damage. His parents were told that his chances of survival were slim. The members of a local church prayed constantly for Simon. Slowly he recovered and there was no brain damage.

It could just have been the medical care that helped him to recover so well, but his family saw it as an answer to prayer. An experiment in San Francisco involving 400 patients gave evidence to suggest that prayer can play a significant part in healing the sick.

C

I will be aware that there are experiences in life that I have yet to understand.

Year 11:3

A

But someone may well say,
'You have faith, and I have works',
Show me your faith without the works,
and I will show you my faith
by my works.

JAMES 2:18

B

Faith is not a priceless antique that is stored away and only brought out on special occasions.

It is 'living organism' that lights our spiritual life. The

amazing thing about faith is, it is not limited. It increases every time we use it.

Sometimes it is the light that shines in the darkness of difficulties. Sometimes it is the light that highlights the path we can take in life. A care and concern for others is the natural out-working of faith, and faith can be a beacon to help guide others in life.

C

I will look for faith in my life.

33 LIVING YOUR OWN LIFE

Year 7:1

One cannot have wisdom without living life.

DOROTHY MCCALL, IN *EACH DAY A NEW BEGINNING*
(22 JANUARY)

B

Once during an upper school PSE lesson on self-awareness, the pupils had to think of one thing about themselves of which they were proud. As they considered the task, each pupil came up with a different answer. For one it was their success at school work, for another their ability to listen to others. However, the answer that was particularly interesting was from Lucy, who said, 'I am proud of my individuality'.

Her individuality set her apart from the others. Whatever the issue she would work out her own moral values in relation to it and stick by them. She would never go along with the crowd in order to be accepted or liked. She had the strength of character to trust her own judgment and to stand by what she believed.

When asked what being an individual meant to her Lucy replied, 'Freedom'.

C

Today I will stand by what I believe.

Year 7:2

A

One doesn't recognize in one's life the really important moments – not until it's too late.

AGATHA CHRISTIE, IN *EACH DAY A NEW BEGINNING* (4 JULY)

B

There is a story of an Indonesian fisherman who sat one afternoon resting in the sunshine. He was approached by a friend who asked him why he was not out fishing. 'But I have all I need for today,' replied the fisherman. 'But,' enthused his friend, 'you could fish for more and make more money.' 'Why?' enquired the fisherman. 'Well,' replied the friend, 'you could buy an engine for your boat and go out more often and get more fish. Then you would make more money, and you could buy more boats and employ people to fish for you, and you could spend your time in leisure.' 'What do you think I am doing now?' replied the fisherman.

It is easy to get caught up in the way of life around us, but we all need to stop and consider what we really want from life.

ADAPTED FROM *EACH DAY A NEW BEGINNING*

C

Live all you can; it's a mistake not to. Live your moments to the fullest.

Year 7:3

A

When I slow down long enough to smell the roses, I usually see the beauty and all else that is ours to share.

MORGAN JENNINGS, IN *EACH DAY A NEW BEGINNING*
(25 MARCH)

B

There is a story of a big black crow that would look at the

beautiful white doves, and wish that he could be such a sleek, attractive bird. One day the crow almost achieved his aim when he found a pot of white paint and managed to cover his feathers with the paint. He proudly joined the doves, eating where they ate, and flying where they flew. It was not long before he realized that he did not like the food that they ate, neither did he like living in the trees. Being a crow did not seem such a bad thing after all.

Life would be dull if we were all the same, each one of us has our own unique contribution to make to the community. There is no point in pretending to be what we are not, when we are valuable just as we are.

C

Today I will be happy to be myself.

Year 8:1

A

A lion met a tiger
as they drew beside a pool.
Said the tiger, 'Tell me why
you're roaring like a fool.'
'That's not foolish,' said the lion
with a twinkle in his eyes.
'They call me king of all the beasts
because I advertise!'
A rabbit heard them talking
and ran home like a streak.
He thought he'd try the lion's plan
but his roar was just a squeak.
A fox came to investigate –
had luncheon in the woods;
So when you advertise, my friend

be sure you've got the goods!

FROM STEPHEN GAUKROGER AND NICK MERCER, *FROGS II*

B

The moral of the story is to be yourself.

It is good to have people that we admire, but we need to take what we admire about them and apply it to our own life – we must not try to be them.

We have our own personality, abilities and experience to offer the world. If we try to be a carbon copy of someone else we usually end up a poor imitation and look foolish.

When we value what we have to offer, we can stop being a rabbit pretending to be a lion, and instead be glad to be ourselves.

C

I will carefully consider what is special about me.

Year 8:2

A

Do all the good you can
By all the means you can
In all the ways you can
In all the places you can
At all the times you can
To all the people you can
As long as ever you can.

JOHN WESLEY, IN *RULE OF CONDUCT*

B

Sometimes at school a disorientated bird gets trapped inside a classroom. It will fly around terrified trying to find a way out. Pupils usually have three reactions to this event. Some ignore it as they are too busy to stop and get involved. Some try to chase the bird and increase its panic, and some do all they can to help the bird escape calmly.

It is the same all through life: we are faced with decisions as to how to react to different situations. Do we ignore what happens around us, make it worse or try to help as constructively as possible?

C

I will do all the good I can.

Year 8:3

A

Life is not a solo but a chorus.
We live in relationships from the cradle to grave.

ANONYMOUS, IN *MORE GATHERED GOLD*

B

Whilst living our own lives, we still need to remember that we do not live in isolation. Many of us do not live in small communities where everybody knows each other, and people look out for one another, and so we can lose our sense of belonging. It is easy to fall into the way of 'looking after number one', making sure that we do not miss out on anything.

How pleasant our life would be, and the lives of those around us if we looked after one another. For example, we could make sure that the person next to us was comfortable, had enough to eat, and we could listen to their problems. We would not miss out, because they would probably do the same for us. We would be living in harmony with one another.

C

I can make a positive contribution to society around me.

Year 9:1

A

Single-mindedness
Don't grumble, don't bluster,
don't think of your worries,
Don't think of your worries,
but think of your work.
The worries will vanish,
the work will be done;
no man sees his shadow,
who faces the sun.
STEPHEN GAUKROGER AND NICK MERCER, *FROGS II*

B

How much time do we spend dreaming about what might be and worrying about what could be? To be told to spend this time concentrating on work seems to be a strange request. Work is so often given a bad press today, and we are led to believe that work is not to be enjoyed – but to be avoided. In reality, work is a positive activity, it gives a sense of self-worth and achievement. As we go on through life a lot of our time will be spent doing some form of work – so why not enjoy it?

The happiest people are those who wake up in the morning looking forward to the tasks ahead.

C

I will have a positive attitude towards my work.

Year 9:2

A

Man made in the image of God, has a purpose – to be in relationship to God, who is there. Man forgets his purpose and thus he forgets who he is and what life means.
FRANCIS SCHAEFFER, IN *MORE GATHERED GOLD*

B

There is a purpose in life for all of us and when we realize this, we can accept the nobility of our own life. Sometimes we may feel that we do not 'come up to the mark' when we compare ourselves to others, but when we realize that we each have a purpose, we have no need to feel inferior. Finding meaning and purpose in our lives can be an exciting adventure.

C

I will look for the purpose in my life.

Year 9:3

A

For they sow the wind
And they reap the whirlwind.

HOSEA 8:7

B

We have the whole of our life spread before us like an open book. We decide what will be written on the pages by the decisions we take. Rather than being so caught up with the whole process of living we need to stop – and think about the direction that we want our life to take. We need to decide what is important and what is unimportant to us.

If we do not do this we could spend the rest of our life putting our energies into worthless projects, never understanding our reason for being.

C

I will live my own life by thinking about what direction it will take.

Year 10:1

A

Life is either a daring adventure or nothing.

HELEN KELLER, IN *EACH DAY A NEW BEGINNING* (29 AUGUST)

B

Each day we are faced with new opportunities. We can look forward to them as an exciting challenge or just regard everything as ordinary and boring.

When we face up to life as a challenge we grow as a person. We can become aware of new opportunities, new experiences and new ways of using our talents. But if we withdraw from life, we lessen ourselves. Life becomes monotonous and we can become depressed. Not only does life seem to be boring – we become boring! How we live our life is a choice that each of us can make each new day.

C

I will look forward to the new opportunities that face me today.

Year 10:2

A

We have not passed that subtle line between childhood and adulthood until we move from the passive voice to the active voice – that is, until we have stopped saying, 'It got lost', and say, 'I lost it'.

SYDNEY J HARRIS, IN *THE DECADES BOOK OF BIRTHDAYS*

B

Living our own life means taking responsibility for what we do. We cannot say that we are living our own life if we choose to blame others for our mistakes. When we take responsibility for our mistakes we are in a position to admit that we are wrong. We can then say 'sorry', make amends and learn from the incident.

When we are young we are usually made to say sorry. As we grow older we sometimes use the word as an easy way out of trouble. But truly to live our own life, we must be prepared to take responsibility for our actions and rebuild the broken bridges.

C

I will be responsible for my actions.

Year 10:3

A

I don't know what your destiny will be but one thing I know, the only ones among you who will be really happy are those who have sought and found how to serve.

ALBERT SCHWEITZER, IN *FROGS II*

B

Albert Schweitzer was truly qualified to speak these words. He was brought up in a good home and given many opportunities. He became an exceptional musician, author, minister and also the principal of a well-known theological college. As a young man he decided that he should help others in return for all the happiness he had enjoyed. So he trained as a doctor and for 50 years he worked in Africa tending the sick.

We all have choices as to how we want to live our lives. Serving others is one way of finding real happiness. Schweitzer gave up a good life and found an even better one.

C

I will carefully consider what I want to do with my life.

Year 11:1

A

Pain is inevitable, but misery is optional.

BARBARA JOHNSON, *SO, STICK A GERANIUM IN YOUR HAT AND BE HAPPY*

B

We are all going to encounter some form of pain as we travel along the path of life. Sometimes it will be physical, at other times mental, spiritual or emotional and sometimes all of these. Some of you will already have suffered some form of pain, others have yet to reach that milestone.

How we live our life will determine how we react to the pain. We can mope around, moaning, deciding that nobody has suffered like us – or we can look for the positive points in the suffering and keep our spirits lifted. Pain and misery do not have to be inextricably linked.

C

When I experience pain I will try not to be miserable.

Year 11:2

A

Life is easier than you think –
All you have to do is
Accept the impossible,
Do without the indispensable,
Bear the intolerable and
Be able to smile at anything.

ANONYMOUS, IN *SO, STICK A GERANIUM IN YOUR HAT AND BE HAPPY*

B

The author, Barbara Johnson, has suffered much pain in her

life. Of her four sons, one was killed at war, one in a road accident and a third son left home and disowned the family, even to the extent of changing his name. Her husband suffered severe brain damage and she was diagnosed diabetic.

She had an awful lot of unhappiness in her life for one person. After severe depression, she reached a point where she decided to kill herself. Fortunately, before she took the final plunge, she realized that she must accept all the things that had happened to her. As a result she has written several books about her experiences and they are all incredibly funny. Being miserable does not make the problems better, but being cheerful makes them easier to bear.

C

I will remember that dark moments are often short corridors leading to sunlit rooms.

SO, STICK A GERANIUM IN YOUR HAT AND BE HAPPY

Year 11:3

A

Life isn't always what you want –
but it's what you've got.

BARBARA JOHNSON, SO, STICK A GERANIUM IN YOUR HAT AND BE HAPPY

B

The perfect life, the life we have always wanted may seem to be beyond our reach. We feel that if we were more intelligent, richer, more beautiful, taller, shorter, fatter, thinner, our life would be just right – but even when we achieve these things, it never is.

One writer said, 'Don't take life so seriously – you'll never get out of it alive.' If we can learn to laugh in spite of the circumstances that surround us, we will enrich others and enrich ourselves.

It is said that laughing is like juggling on the inside. Not only does it exercise the heart, it alters our mood and refreshes us. Life isn't always what we want – but it can be good for a laugh.

C

I will look at the funny side of life today.

34 SERVICE (GIVING)

Year 7:1

A

A farmer whose corn always took the first prize at the state fair had the habit of sharing his best corn seed with all the farmers in the neighbourhood. When asked why, he said, 'It is really a matter of self-interest. The wind picks up the pollen and carries it from field to field. So if my neighbours grow inferior corn, the cross-pollination brings down the quality of my own corn. That is why I am concerned that they plant only the very best.'

ANTHONY DE MELLO, *THE HEART OF THE ENLIGHTENED*

B

There is a seed of hope in this story, which perhaps shows a way forward for communities, small or large, all over the world. Anthony de Mello, who wrote the story, describes the key message as: 'All that you give to others, you are giving to yourself.' (*The Heart of the Enlightened*)

C

Today I will give to others the gifts I want to accept for myself.

Year 7:2

A

Once upon a time the members of the body were very annoyed with the stomach. They were resentful that they had to obtain food and bring it

*to the stomach while the stomach itself did nothing but devour the fruit
of their labour.*

*So they decided they would no longer bring the stomach food. The hands
would not lift it to the mouth. The teeth would not chew it. The throat would
not swallow it. That would force the stomach to do something. But all they
succeeded in doing was make the body weak to the point that they were all
threatened with death. So it was finally they who learned the lesson that in
helping one another they were really working for their own welfare.*

ANTHONY DE MELLO, *THE HEART OF THE ENLIGHTENED*

B

'It is impossible to help another without helping yourself, or
harm another without harming yourself.' (*The Heart of the
Enlightened*)

Everybody in school has a part to play in creating and shaping the quality of life in the tutor group, in the houses and in
the school as a whole.

C

Today I will think about what I want to give my school and what I
want to get from It.

Year 7:3

A

*Most of us need help at times. Most of us can offer help at other times.
The need to feel needed, to feel that we have a contribution to make, is
part of our human nature. Any service that is to be of any real value must
be offered in such a way that it preserves a person's dignity – her sense
of her own worth. The relationship between the helper and the helped,
if it is to be real, must be a two-way relationship.*

ADAPTED FROM KEN PRIDEAUX-BRUNE, *A TICKET FOR A
JOURNEY*

B

As we help the elderly and the handicapped we find we learn from them and that we gain at least as much from the relationships as they do.

A young volunteer took a blind person for a walk. The need to describe the passing scene to her blind friend made her look at things in quite a new way. A blind person had in fact taught her to see.

ADAPTED FROM *A TICKET FOR A JOURNEY*

C

We make a living by what we get. We make a life by what we give.

Year 8:1

A

Someone will ask, 'What can I do to help?' Her response is always the same, a response that reveals the clarity of her vision … 'Just begin … Begin at home … Begin by helping someone in need in your community, at work or at school. Begin by making whatever you do something beautiful for God.'

FROM AN INTERVIEW WITH MOTHER TERESA IN *WORDS TO LOVE BY*

B

Mother Teresa never worried that the money to do her work would not come. She was sure that it would. From governments, from the rich, and from the poor countries in which poverty is not nearly as desperate as it is in Calcutta. For her, every opportunity to help the poor in any way was another chance to do something for God.

CHARLOTTE GRAY, IN *MOTHER TERESA*

C

Today I will help someone in need in my local community.

Year 8:2

A

In Korea, there is a legend about a warrior who died and went to heaven. 'Before I enter,' he said to the gatekeeper, 'I would like you to take me on a tour of hell.' The gatekeeper found a guide to take the warrior to hell. When he got there, he was astonished to see a great table piled high with the choicest foods. But the people in hell were starving. The warrior turned to his guide and raised his eyebrows.

'It's this way,' the guide explained. 'Everyone who comes here is given a pair of chopsticks five feet long and is required to hold them at the end to eat. But you just can't eat with chopsticks five feet long if you hold them at the end. Look at them. They miss the mouth every time, see?'

The visitor agreed that this was hell indeed and asked to be taken back to heaven post-haste. In heaven, to his surprise, he saw a similar room, with a similar table laden with every choice of foods. But the people were happy: they looked radiantly happy.

The visitor turned to the guide. 'No chopsticks, I suppose?' he said. 'Oh yes,' said the guide, 'they have the same chopsticks, the same length and they must be held at the end just as in hell. But, you see, these people have learned that if a man feeds his neighbour, his neighbour will feed him also.'

KOREAN LEGEND, IN *PRAYERS FOR PEACEMAKERS*

B

The story illustrates the benefits and beauty of living a life where sharing, co-operating and giving are natural reactions between people. The thoughtful sharing of our gifts and resources with others enriches everybody. We are fulfilled and happy when help and support are given freely.

Cutting ourselves off from each other, ignoring others needs and refusing to share, benefits nobody. Our survival and happiness depend upon people sharing, giving and supporting each other.

C

Today I will take the opportunity to share.

Year 8:3

A

'What is real?' asked the Rabbit one day, when they were lying side-by-side near the nursery fender, before Nana came to tidy the room. 'Does it mean having things that buzz inside you and stick-out-handles?' 'Real isn't how you are made,' said the Skin Horse. 'It's a thing that happens to you. When a child loves you for a long time, not just to play with, but really loves you, then you become real.'

'Does it hurt?' asked the Rabbit.

'Sometimes,' said the Skin Horse, for he was always truthful. 'When you are real you don't mind being hurt.'

'Does it happen all at once, like being wound up,' he asked, 'or bit by bit?'

'It doesn't happen all at once,' said the Skin Horse. 'You become. It takes a long time. That's why it doesn't often happen to people who break easily, or who have sharp edges, or who have to be kept carefully. Generally, by the time you are real, most of your hair has been loved off, and your eyes drop out and you get loose in the joints and very shabby. But these things don't matter at all, except to people who don't understand.'

MARGERY WILLIAMS, IN *PRAYERS FOR PEACEMAKERS*

B

Love makes you 'real'. Loving and being truly loved by another is a wonderful feeling. However, in becoming 'real', we also risk becoming vulnerable and being hurt.

Allowing ourselves to be loved takes courage. Perhaps more challenging and frightening than accepting love, is giving your love to another. It takes courage to love someone without expecting love back.

There are many people in the world who are waiting to become 'real'.

C

The gift of love can bring people to life.

Year 9:1

A

Jesus went about doing good. And we are trying to imitate Him now because I believe that God loves the world through us. I see so many people in the street. People unwanted, unloved, uncared for, people hungry for love. They are Jesus. Where are you?

MOTHER TERESA, *PRAYER – SEEKING THE HEART OF GOD*

B

Mother Teresa began her work with the poor, the homeless, the forgotten people, the outcasts and the dying in 1948 in Calcutta, India. Helping the needy and poor is Mother Teresa's way of serving and loving God. In fact she sees Jesus in each needy person – 'Whenever you did this for one of the least important of these brothers of mine, you did it for me!' (Matthew 25:40). Jesus spent a lot of his time in the company of the poor: teaching and healing them.

The hallmark of Mother Teresa's life has been compassion and service to others. She challenges us by asking a very uncomfortable question: 'What are we doing for the needy and poor?'

C

Today I will consider what I can do for those who are in need.

Year 9:2

A

A Sister was telling me that just two or three weeks ago she and some

*other Sisters picked up a man from the streets in Bombay and brought
him home. We have a big place donated to us which we have turned
into a home for the dying. This man was brought there and the Sisters
took care of him. They loved him with dignity. Right away they discovered that the whole of his back had no skin, no flesh. It was all eaten up.
After they washed him, they put him on his bed, and this Sister told me
that she had never seen so much joy as she saw on the face of that man.
Then I asked her, 'What did you feel when you were removing those
worms from his body; what did you feel?' And she looked at me and
said, 'I've never felt the presence of Christ; I've never really believed the
word of Jesus saying, "I was sick and you did it to me". But his presence
was there and I could see it on that man's face.' This is the gift of God.*

DAILY PRAYER WITH MOTHER TERESA

B

The man was treated with gentleness, kindness and concern.
He wasn't treated with disgust, but as a special person who
needed love and compassion.

There is a lot of talk about the poor in Britain today, but
talk is easy, loving and serving the poor is much harder. It
doesn't matter what a person says about leading a good life –
what matters more is what a person actually does – how a
person lives. Actions speak louder than words.

C

I will see everyone as a special person needing love and compassion.

Year 9:3

A

*Everybody can be great.
Because anybody can serve.
You don't have to have a college degree to serve.
You don't have to make your subject and your verb agree to serve.*

You don't have to know about Plato and Aristotle to serve.
You don't have to know the second theory of thermo-dynamics in
physics to serve.
You only need a heart full of grace.
A soul generated by love.

MARTIN LUTHER KING, IN *PRAYERS FOR PEACEMAKERS*

B

Everybody can serve another person. For example, we can serve people by: listening to a person who needs to talk; running an errand for a house-bound neighbour; paying attention to small children and treating them with respect or taking part in a charity event. All it takes is a bit of courage, a willingness to give, respect for those we are serving and a loving heart.

Serving others is a natural thing to do.
Service dissolves barriers between people.
Service is our practical responsibility towards each other.
Service is love in action.

C

Today I will look for opportunities to serve others.

Year 10:1

A

If all your 'giving' is about 'getting', think how fearful you will become.
SUSAN JEFFERS, *FEEL THE FEAR AND DO IT ANYWAY*

B

Most of us think of ourselves as generous and giving, but do we really give, or just exchange one favour for another? Do we give to charity because it makes us feel less guilty? Have we been nice to our parents because then they may be more likely to let us go to a party?

If we only 'give' to receive, we will feel less able to give generously – in case we don't get enough back! When we start to measure out carefully how much we hand over, we are not really giving. We have stopped the spontaneous flow. The flow which moves from our hearts and reaches out to others.

C

May I freely give, for the sake of giving.

Year 10:2

A

To love is to be able to give. And now is the time to begin … Giving is about outflow. It is about letting go of your crouched, withholding self and standing tall with outstretched arms. When we really feel this sense of abundance, we truly understand the saying 'My cup runneth over'.

SUSAN JEFFERS, *FEEL THE FEAR AND DO IT ANYWAY*

B

There is no end to the amount of love that we can give, or that can flow through us. Sometimes, however, we hold back from giving, from a sense of lack and fear that we don't have enough to share. At other times we may feel that what we have to offer to others is not of much value or worth; so we curb our desire to be of service to others.

Instead of focusing on how little we have to give, we can decide to stop holding back, open up and give freely from our hearts.

C

My cup runneth over

Year 10:3

A

Sit down right now and make a list of people to whom you would like to give love and appreciation, and think of a way that you can do so to each one within the next week ... Practise speaking more words of thanks, appreciation, and admiration to people.

SHAKTI GAWAIN, *REFLECTIONS IN THE LIGHT*

B

Showing our admiration and appreciation to others can have many benefits. Not only will we help others to feel good about themselves, but we can also take pleasure giving, and feel that we have something to share and offer.

When our compliments and thanks are freely given, without thoughts of what we will get in return, or what people will think of us, we can feel really alive. We can see ourselves as a channel that love flows through.

C

I will practise speaking more words of thanks and appreciation.

Year 11:1

A

Do you always expect to be rewarded for what you do? He who has understood the secret of love asks for nothing: he gives freely.

OMRAAM MIKHAËL AÏVANHOV, *GOLDEN RULES FOR EVERYDAY LIFE*

B

Our hearts must be full of love for human beings, because they are all our brothers and sisters. We must think of them and help them without expecting the slightest reward, for, in reality, our reward is already given to us in that inner sense of expansion, that extraordinary sensation of warmth that fills us when we love.

OMRAAM MIKHAËL AÏVANHOV, *GOLDEN RULES FOR EVERYDAY LIFE*

C

Today I will give without expectation.

Year 11:2

A

In the sphere of material things, giving means being rich. Not he who has much is rich, but he who gives much.

ERICH FROMM, IN *TOUCHSTONES* (25 DECEMBER)

B

Material possessions have high status value in our world today. The things that we own make statements about us, for example: the clothes we wear, the electronic gadgetry we have and where we go on holiday.

Material things only enrich us when we use them and share them to improve our lives and the lives of others. We don't need to be well-off to share what we have with others. It's the act of sharing that nourishes us and strengthens our relationship with others.

When we respect what we own as a gift from God and share it with others, we grow richer spiritually.

ADAPTED FROM *TOUCHSTONES* (25 DECEMBER)

C

I will reflect on how willing I am to share what I have.

Year 11:3

A

We always have a choice about how to act, and when we choose to add a dash of kindness to our attitudes and actions, we bring joy and comfort not only to those on the receiving end but to ourselves as well.

SUE PATTON THOELE, *THE WOMAN'S BOOK OF COURAGE*

B

We can give a positive change to our lives by treating others with kindness. When we meet someone who is in a grumpy mood, we have the choice to be aggressive and unpleasant back, or respond with genuine kindness, maybe by smiling and making eye contact when we speak with them.

By adding 'a dash of kindness' to what we say and do, we may help those around us to feel appreciated and valued, and we will also feel good about ourselves.

C

I will bring kindness to my encounters with others.

35 TIME

Year 7:1

A

How often are we 'too busy' even to watch the sun set, or listen to the birds sing? How often do we treat today as just another day? How much of our precious lives do we waste in gentle slumbering?

GILL EDWARDS, *STEPPING INTO THE MAGIC*

B

The Buddhist teacher Thich Nhat Hanh notes that to live without awareness – for example to drink tea without knowing that we are drinking tea – is to live as a dead person. Time is not money. Time is much more precious than money. Time is life!

Now is the only time we can live. Now is the only time we can change or make decisions.

When we live in the moment, putting our heart and soul into whatever we are doing – drinking tea, smelling a rose, listening to music, washing the dishes – we begin to realize our true potential.

ADAPTED FROM *STEPPING INTO THE MAGIC*

C

Today I will be more aware of what I do with my time.

Year 7:2

A

The years of my life,

The days of my years,
The hours of my days,
They are all mine.
Mine to fill, quietly, calmly,
But to fill completely, up to the brim …

MICHEL QUOIST, *PRAYERS OF LIFE*

B

Hilary, a thirty-nine-year-old secretary, discovered a year ago that she had breast cancer. Since then, she says, she no longer frets over finding dirty socks on the bathroom floor, or missing a favourite TV show. What matters most is spending 'quality time' with her family and friends, walking down to the river, tending the garden. Simple things. 'Life has become much simpler, but somehow it's in sharp focus. The days used to blur into one another – but now, every day is precious and unique. Having faced the possibility that I would never see a daffodil again, I burst into tears of joy and gratitude when they came into bloom a few weeks ago – and I touched their petals with such tenderness. I'm not sure I had ever really seen a daffodil before.'

There is not an endless supply of 'tomorrows' and 'next years'. If we miss an opportunity, we might never have the chance again.

GILL EDWARDS, *STEPPING INTO THE MAGIC*

C

Today I will cherish each moment.

Year 7:3

A

The clock master was about to fix the pendulum of a clock when, to his surprise, he heard the pendulum speak. 'Please, sir, leave me alone,' the pendulum pleaded. 'It will be an act of kindness on your part. Think of the number of times I will have to tick day and night. So many times each minute, sixty minutes an hour, twenty-four hours a day, three

hundred and sixty-five days a year. For year upon year ... millions of
ticks. I could never do it.' But the clock master answered wisely, 'Don't
think of the future. Just do one tick at a time and you will enjoy every
tick for the rest of your life.'

And that is exactly what the pendulum decided to do. It is still ticking
merrily away.

ANTHONY DE MELLO, *THE HEART OF THE ENLIGHTENED*

B

The present moment is never unbearable if you live in it fully.
What is unbearable is to have your body at 10 am in one place
but at the same time your mind in another.

ADAPTED FROM *THE HEART OF THE ENLIGHTENED*

C

Today I will reflect on how to be fully in the present, not mourn for
the past or worry about the future.

Year 8:1

A

This morning I got kidnapped
By three masked men.
They stopped me on the side-walk,
And offered me some candy,
And when I wouldn't take it
They grabbed me by the collar,
And pinned my arms behind me,
And shoved me in the back-seat
Of this big black limousine and
Tied my hands behind my back
With sharp and rusty wire.
Then they put a blindfold on me,
So I couldn't see where they took me,

And plugged up my ears with cotton
So I couldn't hear their voices.
And drove for 20 miles or
At least for 20 minutes, and then
Dragged me from the car down to
Some cold and mouldy basement,
Where they stuck me in a corner
And went off to get the ransom
Leaving one of them to guard me
With a shotgun pointed at me,
Tied up sitting on a stool …
That's why I'm late for school!

SHEL SILVERSTEIN, IN *THE KINGFISHER BOOK OF CHILDREN'S POETRY*

B

Being on time for appointments, lessons or friends makes life more simple. There is then no need to make apologies; make up complicated excuses, or feel guilty – and above all, it means less worry and stress. If being late is part of your lifestyle, ask yourself why you need to be late. Look at the advantages of being punctual.

Give yourself enough time to walk everywhere you go, instead of rushing around. Set your alarm, so that you wake up with enough time to prepare yourself for the day ahead. Try arriving on time for a whole week – see how it feels.

C

I will take charge of my life.

Year 8:2

A

Practically speaking, if timesaving devices really saved time, there would be more time available to us now than ever before in history. But,

*strangely enough, we seem to have less time than even a few years ago.
It's really great fun to go somewhere where there are no timesaving
devices because, when you do, you find that you have lots of time.
Elsewhere, you're too busy working to pay for machines to save you time
so you won't have to work so hard.*

*The main problem with this great obsession for Saving Time is very
simple: you can't save time. You can only spend it. But you can spend
it wisely or foolishly.*

BENJAMIN HOFF, *THE TAO OF POOH*

B

We only have a maximum of twenty-fours in a day. We can fill
our lives full, rush from one activity to another, trying to save
ourselves time and cram in as much as possible. Alternatively,
we can simplify our lives and make sure that we use our time
to do something that is important to us.

Time spent in this way is quality time.

C

It is up to us to give ourselves as much quality time as we can.

Year 8:3

A

*When my Mum died, I realized that I'd never said how much I loved
her. We'd never really talked and shared our feelings for each other. In
all of her life, I'd never told her that she was kind, generous, loving,
understanding and wise – and she was all of these things.*

*So many things were left unsaid. Now she's dead, I want to tell her.
I wish we could spend half-an-hour together – even a five-minute
phone call would be enough.*

M.W.

B

It can feel like we have all the time in the world to do the things
we choose to do; to say the things we choose to say – and to speak

openly to whom we wish. But will we ever take the opportunity of doing and saying the things that really matter to us?

Expressing our feelings and thoughts about people, even if they are dead, can be helpful and healing.

C

I will ask myself: 'Is there anything that I have left unsaid?'

Year 9:1

A

Some people are forever looking over their shoulders at things gone by.
DR BRIAN ROET, *ALL IN THE MIND? – THINK YOURSELF BETTER*

B

We can spend all of today thinking or talking about what happened yesterday. But yesterday has now gone. It is in the past. What happened in the past cannot be changed.

The only opportunities for change and living is in the present moment. Although we cannot change the past, we can change the effect the past has on us today. We can deal with unfinished business from yesterday, today. We can use yesterday's experience to build a better today. We can reflect on what we've learned from yesterday.

But by dwelling too much on what was, we cut ourselves off from the opportunities in our life NOW.

C

I will focus on the opportunities of today.

Year 9:2

A

So do not worry about tomorrow; it will have enough worries of its own. There is no need to add to the troubles each day brings.
MATTHEW 6:34

B

Living each day as it comes is good advice.

Being alert to what is happening now, in the present, can be difficult. How often are our present moments filled with future worries like: 'Oh no, I've got a test tomorrow!'; 'I've volunteered to read out in assembly, but I'm dreading it now'; 'I've applied for a Saturday job, but I might not get it.'

It's important to plan and prepare for the future, but worrying won't make the future better. In spending so much of our lives dreaming about the future, we can forget that *this* moment, which will never come again, is when we are actually alive. By worrying about the future, we waste the time we already have – in the present.

C

Live each day as it comes, for NOW is the only moment we have. Life is now, not tomorrow.

Year 9:3

A

Haven't you noticed that when you become totally engrossed in something, you lose track of time? Why? Because you no longer focus upon it.
ANTHONY ROBBINS, *AWAKEN THE GIANT WITHIN*

B

We can lose track of time when we are absorbed in an activity that we enjoy. Then time has no meaning for us. We have gone beyond it in a way. We can experience a sense of liberation and freedom when we stop clock-watching, and instead really focus and concentrate on what we are doing. We are then not only living in the moment but also fully participating in life.

C

May I sometimes become so absorbed in what I do that I forget about time.

Year 10:1

A

Why is it that most people think change takes so long? One reason, obviously, is that most people have tried again and again through will power to make changes, and failed. The assumption that they then make is that the important changes must take a long time and be very difficult to make.

ANTHONY ROBBINS, *AWAKEN THE GIANT WITHIN*

B

Sometimes we may struggle for years to stop a bad habit or behave in a certain way, to no avail. We can muster every last gram of will power, to overcome our over-eating, smoking, gossiping or whatever demon we are faced with, but we end up where we started.

We tend to expect important changes to be long and difficult and a test of great will power, but in reality it can be as simple as making a split-second decision to live another way. When we are 100 per cent sure that we want a situation to change – and resolve deep within ourselves to live a different way – then we can go beyond will power and call upon the strength in our heart to follow our decision through.

C

I will make changes in life by using the power in my heart.

Year 10:2

A

This instant is the only time there is. I have often thought that we have much to learn from infants. They have not yet adapted to the concept of linear time with a past, present and future. They relate only to the immediate present, to right now ... They feel that they are joined to everything in the world as part of a whole. To me, they represent true innocence, love, wisdom and forgiveness.

GERALD G. JAMPOLSKY, *LOVE IS LETTING GO OF FEAR*

B

Imagine how simple our lives would be if we lived more in the moment, as infants do. Babies do not feel separate from their environment and so feel part of everything that is around them. Their whole world is like an enveloping blanket – a kind of unbroken wave of belonging and satisfying wholeness. They experience the security of life with no beginning and no end. We too, could experience the joy of an infant, if we let go of the past and not fear the future.

C

This instant is the only time there is.

LOVE IS LETTING GO OF FEAR

Year 10:3

A

If we can live with the knowledge that death is our constant companion, … then death can become … a source of wise counsel. With death's counsel, the constant awareness of the limit of our time to live and love, we can always be guided to make the best use of our time and live life to the fullest … When we shy away from death … we inevitably shy away from life.

M. SCOTT PECK, *THE ROAD LESS TRAVELLED*

B

That we will one day die is a fact of life. When we have faced up to the reality that we will die, we can make the best of our lives and start truly living. Living truly is living the life that we want to live – a life in which we have taken opportunities to use our talents positively.

A deep satisfaction can be experienced because we have tried to be true to ourselves and live by our values. Living with an awareness that today might be our last day to live, concentrates the mind on what is right, necessary and true for ourselves, enabling us to make wise decisions.

C

Today I will be aware that I have a limited amount of time to live and love.

Year 11:1

A

Most of us, until we feel that tight turn of the screw called the 'midlife crisis', don't pay much attention to time, for our illusion is we will live forever. In our open-ended youth we often kill time, as if it were our enemy, getting through days, weeks and years without recognizing time as our most valuable gift.

AMY BJORK HARRIS AND THOMAS A. HARRIS, *STAYING OK*

B

Do we appreciate each day of life we have? Do we ever start Monday morning wishing it was Friday afternoon? Do we ever greet Friday morning with: 'Thank God it's Friday!' Do we will the clock to move faster?

Time is a precious gift, yet we often won't appreciate it until we've nearly run out of time. Why do we take our seconds, minutes, hours and days for granted? If we were told that we only had a limited amount of time left to live, then our view of time would no doubt change – each moment becoming precious. Well, we actually do only have a limited amount of time. Our time on Earth is finite. We have no idea how long we will live. It makes sense, therefore, to use each day in rewarding ways.

C

Each day is a valuable gift.

Year 11:2

A

Most of us are far down the path before we stop and smell the roses ...
Will you do time or do life? The answer depends on whether or not you
own your life, treasure it, and plan its use.

AMY BJORK HARRIS AND THOMAS A. HARRIS, *STAYING OK*

B

Managing and making good use of our time is an important skill to develop. Our time can be taken up, stolen and organized by others – our friends, parents, teachers and other adults. Before we know it, there's no time for ourselves – no time even to smell the roses.

Giving ourselves time to think, reflect and plan will help us to live our life as we want it to be.

Draw yourself a timeline. Put on it all the things you've done and all the things you still want to do. This is a powerful exercise because it focuses our attention on what we really want, value and treasure in our lives.

C

Today I have a choice – to do time or to do life.

Year 11:3

A

How do you want to be remembered ... ?
Start acting that way now. Why wait to be memorable? Live each day
as if it were one of the most important days of your life, and you'll
experience joy at a whole new level.

ANTHONY ROBBINS, *AWAKEN THE GIANT WITHIN*

B

We sometimes have a certain idea of how we would like to be in five, ten or twenty years' time. Maybe we imagine ourself as a confident, popular and outgoing 25-year-old?

Take your courage in your hands, and be that person now. Be a sensation this very day. Let your potential and inner qualities shine out at once. Be glad to be who you are and grasp this instant to start being all of the things that you want to be.

Take hold of all the qualities that you imagine the 'future you' will have and live your dreams *now*.

C

I will start acting the way I want to be – right now.

36 OPEN-MINDEDNESS

Year 7:1

A

Lord, forgive me,
I thought that I was helping,
but I was so blinded by my own culture that I could not see theirs;
so proud of my own language that I taught that, instead of learning
theirs;
so wrapped around by love of my own immediate family
that I could not imagine such love committed to their extended family;
so sure of right and wrong, in Western terms, that I could not
recognize them
in the perspectives of another society.

D. TEMPLE, *DEVELOPMENT IS NOT OUR WORD*

B

The majority of us grow up believing that our culture is the norm. Today, we have many opportunities to mix with people of other cultures. If we cling to our familiar ways and close our minds to the perspectives of others we demean them and rob ourselves.

We all get used to the films where everything appears simple: the baddies are usually unattractive with greasy hair, and although quick on the draw or tough fighters, they are not quite as skilled as the goodie, who is usually good looking and wins by being that much stronger.

As we grow up, we learn that outward appearance is not an

indicator of inner goodness, nor is the victor of a fight or battle always on the side of right. We cannot learn unless we are willing to challenge concepts that we have held for years, and be open to new ideas.

C

Today I will be open to new ideas.

Year 7:2

A

Out West, I had filled my sketch pad with drawings of mountains, horses, people and animals .... My hands held the key to my talent as an artist. Or did they?

JONI EARECKSON, *JONI*

B

It is easy to feel threatened by change. When new ideas or new ways of working are proposed they are often given a negative response. There is a fear of the unknown, maybe we fear that we will not be able to cope with the changes, or fear that we will be shut out by them. Being open to change means being open to new opportunities.

When Joni Eareckson became a quadriplegic through a diving accident in 1967, it was suggested that she take up drawing, using her mouth to hold and control the pen. She strongly resisted this idea as demeaning, and saw nothing but obstacles – eventually she gave in and attempted to draw.

Now she loves to draw and has published books and put on exhibitions of her work. When she opened her mind to new opportunities she discovered how fulfilling life can be.

C

I will welcome new opportunities.

Year 7:3

A

Do not take advantage of foreigners in your land; do not wrong them. They must be treated like any other citizen.

LEVITICUS 19:33,34

B

Although we live in a multicultural society, it is easy to keep ourselves separate – to close our minds and hearts to those from other cultures. The less we know of others the more we generalize about them.

Jenny lives in Bradford and most of her neighbours originate from Bangladesh. Her culture is new to her neighbours and their culture new to her. So Jenny and her neighbours enjoy learning about one another, they exchange recipes, explain customs, and visit each other.

Recently she was out of the house when a burglar broke in. Realizing what had happened her Asian neighbours surrounded the house until the police arrived and caught the culprit.

Jenny's life is enriched by living in a multicultural society. We have so much to learn from one another once we cross the barriers of fear and suspicion.

C

I will look forward to meeting new people.

Year 8:1

A

It is very easy to have our own opinions and believe that we are right. This is not always the case. We would all benefit from being more open-minded, to listen to other people's opinions and ideas, to discuss and think about them.

GEMMA EVANS, AGED 12

B

To be open-minded means that we should not judge people. We should accept them for who they are and what they want to be. Even if they are different from us and act differently. If they really believe in something that we do not, we should respect them for it and not tease them.

We should allow people to be their spiritual self.

AMY BROWNRIGG, AGED 12

C

I will enjoy the benefits of being more open-minded.

Year 8:2

A

Some people do not have forty years of experience; they have one year of experience forty times.

DR BRIAN ROET, *ALL IN THE MIND? – THINK YOURSELF BETTER*

B

Have you ever been in a situation where someone is trying to open a door and it will not shift? They push it, they thump it with their fists, they kick it, then use their shoulder to give it a massive blow. It does not matter how much force they exert, the door will not open. Then somebody comes up to the door, takes the handle of the door and 'PULLS' it open.

Life is often like that, when any problem occurs we deal with it in the same manner and when that doesn't work we deal with it the same way again but louder or stronger. Often the solution is to embark upon a problem with a totally different approach.

By being open-minded to the way that we tackle our daily difficulties, we can find new and exciting means of dealing with them.

C

I will look for new ways of dealing with problems.

Year 8:3

A

The mind is good – God put it there.
He gave us our heads and it was not his
intention that our heads would function
just as a place to hang a hat.

A. W. TOZER, IN *GATHERED GOLD*

B

The mind is very powerful. We begin to realize this when we look at the 'placebo' effect. When drug companies want to test a new drug they give half the patients the new drug and the other half a 'fake' drug. It might be water or a plain pill containing no active ingredients. The patient does not know if they have the real medicine or not.

Surprisingly 60 per cent of the patients taking the placebo get better. This does not mean that they were not really ill. They believe in their mind that they have had a beneficial medicine, so the mind tells the body to get better.

This shows that it is beneficial to think positively about ourselves, as our thoughts affect our body so much. If we tell ourselves that we cannot do something, it is so much more difficult to achieve what we set out to do. Conversely we have a myriad of opportunities if we step out in confidence.

ADAPTED FROM *ALL IN THE MIND? – THINK YOURSELF BETTER*

C

I will be positive.

Year 9:1

A

All our minds are narrower than we think, and blind spots and obsessions abound in them like bees in clover.

J. I. PACKER, IN *MORE GATHERED GOLD*

B

From an early age we pick up the prejudices and opinions of those around us. Then as we go through various experiences we add our own opinions to our collection of prejudices. This collection reflects how we feel about ourselves, our capabilities, our personality and strengths and weaknesses. It also highlights our ideas about others, the categories that we place people in, the positive and negative feelings we have about certain groups.

We need regularly to have a 'spring-clean', throwing out all the negative notions, and affirming all the positive ones. Making sure that there are no blind spots.

C

I will look for the positive in everybody, including myself.

Year 9:2

A

Pray not for Arab or Jew,
for Palestinian or Israeli,
but pray rather for ourselves
that we might not divide them
in our prayers but
keep them both together
in our hearts.

BASED ON THE PRAYER OF A PALESTINIAN CHRISTIAN

B

Jonathan Bradley was adopted and brought up as an Orthodox Jew. His natural father was a Kuwaiti Arab.

When Jonathan's Jewish parents died he attempted to settle in Israel. The Israelis asked him to leave thinking that he might be an Arab spy. He then tried to work in the country of his natural father, but they refused him entry. Jonathan says, 'To Jews, I am an Arab and, to Arabs, a Jew.'

Jonathan is in a wonderful position to help bring peace and understanding to both countries, if only they had the vision and openness to accept him.

C

I will accept people for being themselves.

Year 9:3

A

Mentally handicapped
Walking
with mother,
Like it always does,
Wading through the rainy weather
It always looks for us.

Running
Towards us,
Hoping to play,
Hands wagging lifelessly,
A sign to run away.

Staring
From the steamed up window.
'Is HE looking at us?'
Eyes that never meet eyes,
Looking from the bus.

DANNY CERQUEIRA, IN *CITY LINES*

B

The whole poem was taken from memories of when I was about nine years old. A mongol boy lived across the road from me. I never used to play with him because he was different and I was afraid of that.

The second verse is dedicated to Naomi. I was with a couple of friends and we were waiting for their mother. We were laughing and having fun when Naomi saw us. Obviously she wanted to join in the fun and ran ahead of her mother towards us. I was ready to run and ran across the road. I felt terribly guilty afterwards.

Finally the last verse was again referring to a particular day; while I was waiting for the bus to go to school, the familiar blue bus stopped in the traffic. The other people at the bus stop pretended not to see the children lolling up and down in the bus.

DANNY CERQUEIRA, IN *CITY LINES*

By ignoring and running from those who are different, we close our minds to the qualities that they have to offer.

C

I will accept everyone for being themselves.

Year 10:1

A

The human mind is not a vessel to be filled but a flame to be kindled.

DR BRIAN ROET, *ALL IN THE MIND? – THINK YOURSELF BETTER*

B

In childhood a multitude of delicate feelings are tentatively trying to grow – just as young seedlings which raise their shoots above the soil. If these feelings are ignored, trampled on or made out to be bad, mad or wrong, they will wilt and shrink as seedlings would without water. In this way we learn to feel badly about ourselves. We learn we are no good, not right, worthless to express an opinion or hold a point of view.

ALL IN THE MIND? – THINK YOURSELF BETTER

Being open-minded also means being open-minded about ourselves. Too often we pick up on what we have come to think as our deficiencies and make them our boundaries. We can look at ourselves afresh, and redefine our boundaries. We can see ourselves in a new light and learn to think positively about ourselves.

C

I will reassess what I think about myself.

Year 10:2

A

You Never Took Me
When I had arrived for the job
I saw your surprise
and then you filled me
with all of your lies.

You said to me you
wanted someone older.
A lump in my throat
I shrugged my shoulder.

You said 'I hope you understand.'
Then I arose and you shook my hand.

Yes, your reason I do understand!
You never took me and that's a fact.
You never took me because I'm Black.

ENGLEY STEWART, IN *CITY LINES*

B

People are often regarded as naive and emotional if they choose a car for its colour and not the make, engine capacity and fuel consumption. How many of the people who decide this method of choosing a car are guilty of doing the same when they choose a person?

Experiments show that to be black or to have a name that

does not sound 'British' is not only sometimes an obstacle to getting a job, but even stops some people getting an interview.

We need to be open to all and accept people for the person they are inside, not having prejudices about the colour on the outside.

C

I will try to stop racism whenever I meet it.

Year 10:3

A

Equality
We have lived a painful history,
we know the shameful past,
but I keep on marching forward,
and you keep on coming last.

Equality and I will be free.
Equality and I will be free.

Take the blindness from your vision,
take the padding from your ears,
and confess you've heard me crying,
and admit you've seen my tears.

MAYA ANGELOU, *I SHALL NOT BE MOVED*

B

It can be easier to pretend that we have not seen something, because to see something that is not fair and right and to choose to ignore it makes us uncomfortable.

It is only when we admit that there are things wrong in the world that we can find out more about them and do something to bring about change. If we were being exploited or oppressed we would want someone to speak up for us. In the same way we should keep our minds open to the suffering of others.

C

I will not turn a 'blind eye' to injustice.

Year 11:1

A

A wareness is a powerful tool. Most of us think our map of the world is the way it is. We think, I know what makes me feel loved. That must be what works for everyone else. We forget that the map is not the territory. It's only how we see the territory.

ANTHONY ROBBINS, *UNLIMITED POWER*

B

Recently the National Rivers Authority used helicopters to observe the landscape and redraw the rivers that had altered their course through flooding. Maps need to be constantly redrawn as new roads, housing estates and towns change the landscape. Old maps are a hindrance to anyone trying to use them to find their way around a new area.

It is the same with the way we view life. If we have one fixed view and never bother to reassess our thoughts and feelings, or our views on certain subjects, we will find ourselves feeling alienated from those around us.

To understand others we need to be aware of how they see the territory.

C

I will try to understand the view point of someone else today.

Year 11:2

A

Colour Prejudice
Black boy meets white girl, they hold hands.

At this touch Cupid's arrow lands,
But arrow in the front, or in the back,
It doesn't matter, he's still black
her parents give the black a miss -
That, my friend, is Prejudice.

White boy meets black girl, holds her hand,
Visions of a promised land,
Takes her home to see his dad,
Surprise, surprise, his father's glad
Her mum likes him as well, you know.
Very strange, even so.
This way round they're not dismissed –
Again my friend, that's Prejudice.

PETER WILLIAMS, IN *CITY LINES*

B

Prejudice is to judge someone before we know them. It is to forget our powers of reason, our capabilities of discussion and it focuses only on differences and barriers that we have built up. When we look with prejudiced eyes, we do not accept people for being who they are, but put them into categories with labels like 'Black', 'Poor', 'Rich', 'Disabled', 'Southerner', 'Northerner' or 'Foreigner'.

The more we label people, the less we use our reason. The less we reason, the more unreasonable we can become. Not only do we do an injustice to those we label, but we also do an injustice to ourselves by limiting the possibilities in our lives.

C

I will try hard not to be prejudiced.

Year 11:3

A

Think of a major mistake you've made in the last year. You might feel an instant rush of gloom. But chances are the mistake was part of an experience with more successes than failures. And, as you consider it, you'll begin to realize you probably learned more from that mistake than from anything else you did that month.

ANTHONY ROBBINS, *UNLIMITED POWER*

B

When we think of a past mistake, we may cringe inside. Sometimes we might even blush to think about it. If we give it too much attention, as time passes, the mistake can become bigger and bigger in our mind and can affect our confidence.

If we let them, such events can dominate our life. We need to open our mind and focus on all that we learnt from the mistake. If we let our mind see the mistakes rather than the experience we gained, we will withdraw within ourselves and become afraid to try new things. If we focus on what we learned from the experience, we will happily expand our horizons.

C

I will not let past mistakes rule present decisions.

37 UNITY OF PURPOSE

Year 7:1

A

All groups function best if they have a specific purpose in mind.

JEANETTE RAYMOND, *IMPLEMENTING PASTORAL CARE IN SCHOOLS*

B

We label twenty-five or thirty pupils as a 'tutor group' or 'form' but of course being given a particular room in school for registration periods and lunchtimes does not automatically turn these pupils into a working group.

What is the purpose of a tutor group? Does everybody realize the potential of belonging to a tutor group for several years?

It is within the tutor group that pupils can learn about personal and social development – it gives a practical experience of working together as a group – and it is in everybody's interests to create a happy, comfortable, supportive and safe atmosphere.

One indicator of a successful tutor group is the reception and support given to a new pupil. A new person joining the group is an opportunity for everybody to gain – but everybody needs to realize this!

C

Today I will reflect on how we work together as a tutor group.

Year 7:2

A

Bohunt School exists to meet the educational needs of all its pupils. Central to the school's philosophy is a belief in the individual as a member of the community. The aim is to seek the fullest personal, social and academic development of each student by their participation in the richness of opportunities created within the whole school curriculum. Bohunt works towards the achievement of each person's maximum potential.

BOHUNT SCHOOL PROSPECTUS

B

Like most schools, Bohunt School aims to provide a calm environment, but for this to happen everybody needs to show care for others and their surroundings. Pupils should be encouraged to express feelings, and to develop confidence and independence. At the same time everybody needs to be sensitive to others and aware of personal and group responsibilities.

Good communications are vital within a large community; so that understanding and tolerance can grow. When school communities work together; so much can be achieved – and everybody benefits.

C

Today I will think about my contributions to the life of my school.

Year 7:3

A

Together we must learn to live as brothers,
or together we will be forced to perish as fools.

MARTIN LUTHER KING

B

Sometimes, when things go wrong, we need to chat about our problems.

Talking things over helps, too, when things are OK. It helps us to make sure that we are working along the right lines. Nations are like this, too, and the United Nations provides opportunities for nations to talk things over.

The United Nations was set up in 1945, following World War II, by people who asked themselves very similar questions. They came from a variety of nations and shared the common background of war and destruction. They saw the only hope for people lying in nations being able to meet together to discuss differences and to decide upon united action, both social and political, wherever it was needed.

GWYNETH WINDSOR, *EXAMINING CITIZENSHIP*

The three main aims of the United Nations are:

- *to maintain international peace and security*
- *to develop friendly relations among nations – based on respect for the principles of equal rights and self-determination of peoples*
- *to co-operate internationally in solving economic, social, cultural and humanitarian problems and in promoting respect for human rights and fundamental freedoms.*

JOHN FOSTER, *ISSUES 5 – THE CROSS-CURRICULAR COURSE FOR PSE*

C

I will become more aware of current world issues.

Year 8:1

A

We are here to create our personal and global Dreams – and we inspire others by 'walking our talk'. If we overflow with joyful exuberance ... love and respect others, serve the world in ways that delight us ... then we pave the way for others to do so.

GILL EDWARDS, *STEPPING INTO THE MAGIC*

B

Picture a world where the people are united by their love and respect for each other – with everyone serving the world in ways that thrill, delight and inspire them. When we are true to ourselves, we set an example for others to follow. It can then be easier for them to live their dreams. When we 'walk our talk', we 'practise what we preach'.

Imagine the joy in a world where everyone endeavours to work for the happiness and fulfilment of themselves and each other.

C

United through love and respect for each other, we can create 'Peace on Earth'.

Year 8:2

A

Pollution

Pollution in our seas and skies,
On the beaches and through the towns.
Litter, junk and chemical waste,
Spoiling our earth all around.
Now it's time to pull together,
Time to make sure that something is done.
To neglect this cause could be disastrous,
But if people unite the battle is won.

ALISON BAWN, AGED 11, IN *GO GREEN*

B

The sound of many voices calling for change can make people in power, stop, listen and act. For example the number of recycling facilities for paper, glass and aluminium which are now available, came about through people running campaigns to pressurize their local councils into providing these facilities.

Although it's fun and exciting to bring about change on a large scale, we also need to look at our own 'back-yard'. For instance, what are the pressing environmental challenges in our school and what can we, as a school community, do about them?

C

I will pull together with others to change my environment.

Year 8:3

A

A New person in this world. All of us are excited about it.
It is a nice thing.
Everyone shout Hooray.

ALEC, AGED 7, ON THE BIRTH OF HIS SISTER

B

There are so many things in our lives for us to celebrate. The birth of a much wanted baby is indeed something to 'shout Hooray' about. On how many other occasions can we join together and shout with joy and excitement?

We are surrounded by marvels and miracles – the food on our plate, the rising and setting of the sun, our friendships and families and our opportunities to learn and grow at school. All of these are good enough reasons to 'throw a party' and share our pleasure and enthusiasm with others.

Inviting others to celebrate with us makes us all feel good as we unite together and rejoice.

C

Today I will make time for celebrating with others.

Year 9:1

A

So many people feel powerless and insignificant when it comes to social issues and world events ... Such people fall into the mindset of thinking, 'Even if I get my own life and the lives of my family in order, what good will it do? Some nut in a position of power could accidentally push the button and blow us all up anyway!'

ANTHONY ROBBINS, *AWAKEN THE GIANT WITHIN*

B

It often feels more comfortable to bury our heads in the sand like an ostrich, and leave the decision-making about the world in which we live, to other people. Society's problems may seem impossible to solve and so because we feel powerless, we don't even bother trying.

Each of us *can* make a difference. If our individual voice goes unheard, then we can join with other voices to express how we want our lives and our world to be. We can become involved in organizations like Friends of the Earth, Christian Aid, Oxfam or Amnesty International and shape the fortune of individuals and future generations.

When, as individuals, we decide to take responsibility and unite together, almost anything can happen.

C

When I feel powerless to make changes in the world, I will unite with others.

Year 9:2

A

It's fun and creative to take some time to visualize a more perfect, enlightened world.

SHAKTI GAWAIN, *REFLECTIONS IN THE LIGHT*

B

In order change our world and make it a better place, we first need to have a vision of how we would like it to be. We then need to share this vision with others, inspiring them to work towards this goal and dream as well. Maybe there is bullying going on in the class, and you want it to stop and be replaced with peace and mutual respect.

If we share what we want and hope for with others, we will find that, by uniting together, the situation can change. When we share our dreams, they can often become reality.

C

I will develop my dreams for a better world and then share them with others.

Year 9:3

A

Our Earth
The earth we live on is a delicate place,
Under constant threat from the human race.
The need is clear to find a solution,
To save this planet from pollution.

Rivers, streams and forests are dying,
Innocent creatures are suffering and crying.
What have they done to deserve such a fate?
This destruction must stop before it's too late.

People aren't friends even to their own kind,
Look out to the streets and you will find,
Scenes of squalor, misery and starvation,
Is there no hope for the earth's salvation?

People who care please make a stand,
To stop the destruction of our land.

So join as one, and start the fight,
To save the world and make it right!

CLAIRE RUTHERFORD, AGED 14, IN *GO GREEN*

B

Through radio, television, magazines and lessons in school, we are more aware than any previous generation of the need to care for the damaged environment. This awareness can be readily seen by the number of 'environmentally friendly' products which are now on sale in shops and supermarkets.

Saying, 'I care about my world', or being aware of environmental issues, problems and solutions is one thing; doing something practical, individually, as a tutor group or as a school community, is quite another. 'What can I do on my own?' 'What more could I do by joining up with others?'

Ask yourself, 'What is stopping me?' 'Why do I hesitate?'

C

I will take pleasure in joining with others to care for our Earth.

Year 10:1

A

The nations of the world resemble today a pack of mountaineers tied together by a climbing rope. They can either climb on together to the mountain peak or fall together into an abyss.

MIKHAIL GORBACHEV

B

In 1985, Mikhail Gorbachev became leader of the Soviet Union. Within five years his courageous policies had revolutionized life in the Soviet Union and Eastern Europe. A gifted politician with a clear vision, he brought 'freedom' to millions of people. In 1990, he was awarded the Nobel Peace Prize for his part in ending the Cold War between the Soviet Union and the West.

Gorbachev was a practical and realistic politician with a deep awareness and understanding of global situations and problems. He saw clearly how the nations of the world are linked and connected with each other. But if nations are like mountaineers climbing together, then communications, respect and trust are surely the tools which will help them survive and safely reach the summit.

C

With strength and unity of purpose, all things are possible.

Year 10:2

A

A single arrow is easily broken,
but not ten in a bundle.

JAPANESE PROVERB

When spider webs unite,
they can tie up a lion.

ETHIOPIAN PROVERB

PROVERBS FROM AROUND THE WORLD

B

On our own we may be weak and vulnerable, but when we unite with others, our power increases, and so much more can be possible. If we all share the responsibility of looking after our tutor room, for example, it will be an easy task.

Sometimes we find strength in numbers when we band together with those to whom we are similar. At other times it is our combined differences that make us strong as a group. For example, when performing a tutor group play, we can all use our individual strengths. Some will excel at writing, some at performing, whilst others will help behind the scenes. Everybody can unite together and contribute in different ways in order to produce a successful play.

C

I will enjoy working together as a group.

Year 10:3

A

He who builds to everyman's advice will have a crooked house.

DANISH PROVERB, IN *PROVERBS FROM AROUND THE WORLD*

B

It is not enough to unite with others to tackle a problem or project. There also has to be a common goal in mind and a willingness to co-operate.

Whenever we work with others we need to find ways of allowing everybody to contribute to the common vision, rather than all pulling in our own individual direction. There needs to be a meeting of minds so the group can work in a single-minded way. Sharing out the tasks helps to bond people into a team.

When we learn how to work with others, we often find that the outcome is richer than it would have been if we'd tried to work alone.

This is the magic of uniting with others with a common purpose in mind.

C

A group works best when its members are pulling in the same direction.

Year 11:1

A

A cool drink is as refreshing to someone who is thirsty, as a friendship is to an aching heart.

MARCIA

B

When people unite, for whatever purpose, a bond is formed between them. If it is a connection that feels positive and up-lifting, we can choose to develop and cultivate it. When we unite as friends, we can regularly phone or write to each other, or offer invitations to spend time together, and share in the things that we like to do.

When we join with another in friendship, we both feel good because we are in a two-way relationship, both sharing, caring and supporting each other.

Old pain, sadness and loneliness can dissolve as we feel the joy that the new alliance brings.

C

I thankfully unite with others in friendship.

Year 11:2

A

Do not take the blame or feel guilty for the world's problems. None of us is truly responsible for the lives of others. We are all co-creating this world together ...

SHAKTI GAWAIN, *REFLECTIONS IN THE LIGHT*

B

Trying to change everything on our own, or expecting others to take on the responsibility for the care of this world, are not effective ways to bring about solutions to world problems. To make our world the way we want it to be, we need to co-operate with each other and work together.

Those of us with money, for example, can help others to help themselves, by giving to charities and organizations like Oxfam, Comic Relief and Christian Aid. Part of their work involves not only supplying meals to the hungry, but also the means for them to grow more food for themselves.

C

We can work together to build a better world.

Year 11:3

A

Differences need not divide us. They do in truth enrich our lives. As one of my teachers said 'Diversity is God's gift – disunity is what we do with it.'

BOB KNIGHT, *AN HONEST TEST*

B

We are united in that we are all human beings. We are united in the fact that we share the same home – planet Earth. Individual and cultural differences are reasons for celebration. Differences between people are natural. Different thoughts, feelings, beliefs, attitudes, behaviour and views of life will be found in every age group, family, school, town and country. These differences, however, do not have to mean divisions.

In team games, the players will have a variety of individual skills and talents, which are pulled together by team spirit. In this way, the whole team benefits. It is the same in the game of life, in which all people in the world are team members. We can be united by everybody respecting, appreciating and celebrating the fact that we are not all the same.

C

I will appreciate the diversity of human beings.

38 ONE GENERATION TO ANOTHER

Year 7:1

A

They taught me to trust in the words that they said;
They taught me to walk; they taught me to talk;
They taught me to pray when I went to bed;
They taught me a lot – my parents.

GORDON BAILEY, *PLASTIC WORLD*

B

When we are small our parents are always right, and we rely on them totally. When we first start school our teachers replace our parents as the ultimate authority. As we move on from the infant stage to juniors our friends become very important and by our teenage years our parents appear out of touch, our teachers authoritarian, but our group of friends are our support, guide and help.

It is usually as we reach the upper part of our teenage years that we again turn to our parents. As we mature we realize that they are not so out of touch, that they have some good ideas, that they can become our friends. Parents want the best for us. They want us to learn from their mistakes and so avoid some of the more painful pitfalls in life. Life is too short to cut them out of what is going on in our life.

C

Today I will be open to suggestions from those who care for me.

Year 7:2

A

My mother gave me and my brother a strong sense of our own value.
PATRICIA ROUTLEDGE

B

If you watch the Antiques Roadshow on television, you will see anxious-faced members of the public look intently at the experts to see if the article that they have brought in is worth much. They are usually asked how they came by the object, and often the reply is, 'It's been passed down through the family'. Sometimes it is worthless in terms of economic value, but holds a lot of sentimental value.

Recently a young man approached the experts with a plastic bag of silver objects that his father had collected. It was obvious that the son did not rate his father's 'treasures' as they had been stuffed in a bag at the bottom of a wardrobe, but his ideas soon changed. It was clear his father had a shrewd mind and a lot of knowledge about silverware. Without the family realizing it, when he died he left them, not a plastic bag of rubbish, but an inheritance worth over £80,000.

We are not all so fortunate to inherit great wealth, but we all inherit something from our parents whether it is the colour of our eyes or the shape of our feet.

There are other aspects of our parents that we can inherit, that can be more valuable than any material object. These are things like their values, their experience and their love.

C

Today I will consider the values that I hold dear.

Year 7:3

A

You shall give due honour and respect for the elderly, in the fear of God.
LEVITICUS 19:32

B

'I have a valued first birthday card from my grandmother. For me it is a link with my past. Both my grandmothers died when I was a small child and I feel that I have been deprived. I would have loved the opportunity to talk to them about their life and about our family history.' (J.A.H.)

Many cultures have a great reverence for the old people in their family and in their community. They respect them because they have lived a long time and have learnt much and therefore have much wisdom to offer.

They also respect them because they brought up their children with care and now it is time for the children to care for them. Some societies consider it shameful to put their old people in a home. They would feel that they were failing in their family duty if they did so. We can learn a lot from this attitude. Respect for the older generation costs us nothing and we might find that they have some interesting things to say if we have the time to listen.

C

I will value every member of my family.

Year 8:1

A

An old lady once said to me that parents should not be taken for granted. I didn't really take any notice at first, but when I got home I realized that she was right. Parents aren't just a source of money or just there to buy clothes and sweets.

We should treat our parents the way we want them to treat us.

RACHEL JEFFERY, AGED 12

B

If we are in a situation where we see our parents every day, we can accept this as being the norm, and grow to expect this as a right. Also, because our experience tells us that they are going to be there for us, we can start to take advantage of them. We may find that by nagging, sulking or by being rude we can wear them down until we get what we want. We may fall into the habit of considering only our wants and find that we disregard the needs of our parents.

Our parents will not always be there for us. It is helpful to both our parents and ourselves if we can learn to treat them well, appreciating all they do.

C

I will treat my parents as I would like to be treated.

Year 8:2

A

The Child

Your thoughts are simple and straightforward,
So what if they say it's untoward?
But, alas you do have a narrow view,
Not enough scope to realize what they'll do to you.

For contaminated you have been born,
There's but one restricted way for you to form;
You must, one day, become all they are,
Yes, those things you watch being wicked from afar.

The gradual change will happen every day,
You'll feel your attitudes start to sway.
You'll feel it happen, but you'll be helpless, you know.
Your old emotions are things you'll be frightened to show.

DAVID UPSHALL, IN *CITY LINES*

B

When I was ten, I didn't want to get any older, but I was determined that I'd always understand the feelings of a child when I grew up. I've not even finished growing up yet, and already I cannot identify with a ten-year-old and deep down I know that ultimately I'll be like all the adults who sometimes don't understand me now. I'll lose contact as I get older and become something different.

DAVID UPSHALL, IN *CITY LINES*

The generation gap creeps up on us gently and silently. Maybe it is by storing away our images of childhood that we will one day be able to communicate with and understand our own children.

C
I will treasure the experiences of my childhood.

Year 8:3

A
Teenagers today are self-centred without respect for parents and older people, impatient about rules and responsibilities. They think they know everything, and as for the way the girls dress …

PETER THE MONK, IN *THE TIMES EDUCATIONAL SUPPLEMENT*, 10 MARCH 1995

B
Peter is describing the teenagers of 700 years ago! It is unpleasant for both the teenagers of yesterday, as well as today, to be stereotyped in such a way. Many teenagers show consideration to others, are respectful, responsible, and patient. When we put an age group into a box and label them as all having certain ways of behaviour, we are ignoring the individuality of each person in that group. This is stereotyping.

It is not only teenagers that get stereotyped, The young can do the same to the older generation. When we accept each other for who we are as individuals, then we can respect and learn from one another. Unless we are willing to see the person rather than the label, things will never change,

C

I will choose to see people of different generations as individuals instead of stereotypes.

Year 9:1

A

I've learnt that if I do something wrong an adult will always teach me the right thing to do. But I have also learnt that adults sometimes do the wrong thing, which is weird for me as I have always looked up to my mum, dad and teachers.

NINA, AGED 12

B

It is often a hard lesson when we discover that those we respect make mistakes. There are times, for example, when we know what we could do in a certain situation, but we do not do it. We are all fallible human beings and we all make mistakes.

We can accept this in ourselves for we know we still have weaknesses – we're still growing up. However, we need to realize that when we are adults, we will still make mistakes and might not live up to others' expectations of us. When we are older the only difference is that we will have more knowledge and experience of life.

C

Adults are human too.

Year 9:2

A

Wisdom

There had never been any argument about it: Fred was
the wisest and shrewdest man in town. One day a young
lad in the community questioned him about it.

'Fred, what is it that makes you so wise?' he asked.

'Good judgment,' replied Fred readily, 'I'd say it
was my good judgment.'

'And where did you get your good judgement?'

'That I got from experience.'

'Where did you get your experience?'

'From my bad judgment.'

STEPHEN GAUKROGER AND NICK MERCER, *FROGS II*

B

There are many things in life that we have to experience for ourselves, but we can alleviate ourselves from a lot of pain by learning from the mistakes of those who have gone before us.

It is easy to ignore what appears to be a rambling older person as they recount tales from the past, but if we carefully listen, they may be showing us how to avoid the mistakes that they once made.

C

I will try to learn from others.

Year 9:3

A

Old Folks Laugh

They have spent their
content of simpering,
holding their lips this

and that way, winding
the lines between
their brows. Old folks
allow their bellies to jiggle like slow
tambourines.
The hollers
rise up and spill
over any way they want.
When old folks laugh, they free the world.
They turn slowly, slyly knowing
the best and worst
of remembering.
Saliva glistens in
the corners of their mouths,
their heads wobble
on brittle necks, but
their laps
are filled with memories.
When old folks laugh, they consider the promise
of dear painless death, and generously
forgive life for happening
to them.

MAYA ANGELOU, *I SHALL NOT BE MOVED*

B

An ageing rock and roll star played a piece of music and commented, 'I didn't like that tune, I mean it, I'm too old to lie.'

Sometimes it isn't until old age that we feel we have the freedom to be ourselves, to say what we really think and do what we feel like doing, even to being a rebel. Maybe that is why, so often, young people get on well with their grandparents. When older folk reach this relaxed stage of their lives, they can look back and laugh at the things that have happened – becoming a tonic to all they meet.

C

I will try to be more like the older people that feel the freedom to be themselves.

Year 10:1

A

There is a wealth of wisdom and experience that could be shared by the people of our community.

S.E-W.

B

Our western culture is sometimes referred to as a 'Youth Culture', as great store is placed on the images of the young, agile, fresh and energetic. The qualities of the young are inspiring and beautiful, but there is also the 'glory' of the older generations.

Parents and grandparents have their own loveliness born of their experience of life. Each wrinkle and attitude that older people wear has been won in their battles of life.

The knowledge and insight that our parents, grandparents, aunts, uncles and neighbours possess, are like national treasures – to be cherished, appreciated and shared by all.

C

Today I will see older people as 'experienced people'.

Year 10:2

A

O generations of freedom remember us – the generations of the vision.

LIAM MAC UISTIN

B

These words are taken from an unusual monument in a park

in Dublin. The design of the monument is tiered. At the bottom there are children crouching, above them children sitting, the next tier has children kneeling and at the pinnacle a child stands with its arms outstretched. The arms turn into swans about to fly away.

The children have moved from fear to freedom, but it has not happened in an instant. Generation after generation have worked towards this goal.

C

I am willing to plant seed that will be reaped by the next generation.

Year 10:3

A

We Saw a Vision

In the darkness of despair we saw a vision
We lit the light of hope and it was not extinguished.
In the desert of discouragement we saw a vision
We planted the tree of valour and it blossomed.
In the winter of bondage we saw a vision
We melted the snows of lethargy and the river of
resurrection flowed from it.
We sent our vision aswim like a swan on the river.
The vision became reality.
Winter became Summer.
Bondage became Freedom.
And this we left to you as your inheritance.
O generations of Freedom remember us –
    the generations of the Vision.

LIAM MAC UISTIN, FROM A MONUMENT IN DUBLIN

B

So many of the good things around us are the result of the

struggles of previous generations. For example, the stopping of the slave trade and the right to vote came about because of people protesting and campaigning for the fair and equal treatment of all.

We are entitled to education and medical care, but this has not always been so. In the past, people with vision have recognized injustice, endeavoured to improve people's lives and in the process they have revolutionized the thinking of their day.

Some died in their struggles, never seeing the changes themselves, but they were content that future generations should gain from their work. Our visions must not be limited by our own horizons – we need to consider the sort of works we wish to leave to the next generation.

C

I will think about the society I wish to leave for my children.

Year 11:1

A

Experience is a comb which nature gives us when we are bald.

CHINESE PROVERB, IN *DECADES BOOK OF BIRTHDAYS*

B

Every day we experience something new about life. If we collect all these experiences by the time we are old, we will have quite an accumulation. Very often, older people may not remember what they had for breakfast, but can describe in minute detail an incident that happened fifty years ago.

Life changes so rapidly. The experience of the older generation is important, because they can explain where, as a society, we have come from. Understanding our roots can give us more confidence and freedom to branch out into new experiences.

C

I will appreciate the experience of older people.

Year 11:2

A

I speak to you as a man who fifty years and nine days ago had no name, no hope, no future and was known only by his number A70713.

ELIE WIESAL, *THE GUARDIAN*, 28 JANUARY 1995

B

As a boy, Elie Wiesal suffered in the death camps of Auschwitz and Buchenwald. On the 50th Anniversary of the liberation of the camps he said these words:

'I speak as a Jew who has seen what humanity has done to itself by trying to exterminate an entire people and inflict suffering and humiliation and death on so many others.

In this place of darkness and malediction we can but stand in awe and remember its stateless, faceless and nameless victims. Close your eyes and look; endless nocturnal processions are converging here, and here it is always night. Here heaven and earth are on fire.' (*The Guardian*, 28 January 1995)

Because Elie Wiesal survived and was able to recount the horror so vividly, we can listen and say we will not let this happen again.

C

I will build on the experience of others.

Year 11:3

A

Experience is not what happens to you, it is what you do with what happens to you.

ALDOUS HUXLEY, IN *MORE GATHERED GOLD*

B

Elie Wiesal used his terrible experience of the concentration camps to inform future generations. All he asks of us is to listen:

'Close your eyes and listen. Listen to the silent screams of terrified mothers, the prayers of anguished old men and women. Listen to the tears of children, Jewish children, a beautiful little girl among them, with golden hair, whose vulnerable tenderness has never left me. Look and listen as they quietly walk towards dark flames so gigantic that the planet itself seemed in danger.

All these men and women and children came from everywhere, a gathering of exiles drawn by death.' (Elie Wiesal, *The Guardian*, 28 January 1995)

Surely we owe it to him and to everyone who suffered through man's inhumanity to man to respond with, 'We have heard, we will not let this happen again.'

C

I will pass the message on to the next generation.

39 INDEPENDENCE

Year 7:1

A

We indigenous peoples, though impoverished and feeble because of the oppression we have had to bear on our shoulders for centuries, do not want to be treated with the paralysing paternalism that reduces us to the category of children that are not able to take care of themselves. We are adult and demand to be treated as such by society and by the churches.

MEXICAN PRIEST

B

Independence is a precious gift. Some people never receive this gift, they may need physical help, economic help or emotional support.

Independence is a form of freedom, a freedom to live the way we wish, a freedom to spend our money as we wish, to wear what we wish, to eat what we wish. With independence comes a responsibility to use our independence wisely; a responsibility to guard the independence of others.

Some people have economic, emotional and physical independence but not independence of mind. We see from the passage above that although the natives of Mexico had been made dependent on others, they still had the dignity of an independent mind.

C

Today I will value the areas in my life where I am independent.

Year 7:2

A

Freedom is not the right to do as you please;
it is the liberty to do as you ought.

ANONYMOUS

B

Having an independent mind can be costly. Think of the conscientious objectors at the time of World War I. They believed strongly that to fight in the war was wrong. They were not greeted with 'Live and let live', or 'I disagree but I respect your opinion'. Instead they were often physically attacked, abused and even jailed.

Many people find it difficult not to go along with their friends, when all their friends carry the same point of view. We do not know if the friendship is strong enough to stand a disagreement. However, we should be willing to share our viewpoint, whatever it costs, because it is only when we all share together that we learn, understand and help each other.

C

Today I will quietly and clearly share my point of view.

Year 7:3

A

There are times when we all need others, this does not mean that we lose our independence, but that we have the wisdom to know that at times it is important to give it up.

J.A.H.

B

A year 11 pupil wrote, 'Independence to me as a person is the freedom to decide for myself. We need the ability to become self-reliant and self-supportive. Independence does not mean cutting myself off from help; just not depending on it! To be independent is my own decision and therefore independence comes from within.'

When we have that independence we can choose not only to help ourselves, but to use it to help others.

C

Today I will think of those around me and how I can help them.

Year 8:1

A

When my Mum was 18, she found a job, and that was in the Co-op, and she was working in the fish and chip shop. And when my Mum was asking the customer what she wanted, my Nan – (my Nan was working there as well) my Nan barged in, and said 'Excuse me, what do you want?' And my Mum started crying because she wanted to say it for the first time.

KELLY, AGED 8, IN *BACKWARDS AND FORWARDS*

B

Independence does not happen all of a sudden. It is a gradual process and sometimes each step of the way has to be negotiated. There are times when we feel that we are responsible enough to make our own decisions in some areas, but our parents disagree. Sometimes they are right, sometimes we are right. Hopefully, as we show responsibility in small things, we will be given opportunities with bigger decisions in our lives. When we are parents we will realize that 'letting go' of our children is a painful but necessary process.

C

I will look for ways in which I can show that I am a responsible person.

Year 8:2

A

Make a point of always standing upon your own two feet, and simply strive to succeed with what you have, what you possess, what brain power, what physical strength, what knowledge.

ALLAN FORSTER, IN *BACKWARDS AND FORWARDS*

B

In recalling his youth, Allan Forster tells of the time a friend promised to get him a holiday job on the trawlers. On the appointed day Allan was up early, ready, looking forward to the new experience. As the day wore on it became evident that the friend was not going to turn up, and his offer of a job was only boastful talk. He was really miserable but his mother gave him good advice, telling him to stand on his own two feet. Taking her advice Allan fearfully made his way to the port, made his own enquiries and consequently was employed to work on the trawlers during the holidays.

C

I will stand on my own two feet and make the most of my talents.

Year 8:3

A

If ever you want anything in this life, you have to depend upon your own efforts. Then the only person who can really let you down is yourself. You can't blame other people, because you will always know that in the last resort it is you yourself who have failed to take personal responsibility for your own future.

ALLAN FORSTER, IN *BACKWARDS AND FORWARDS*

B

How many times a day do we blame other people for the

things that go wrong in our life. Our friends can become a prop to lean against – 'I didn't do this because she had my book', 'I didn't make a noise, he made me laugh'. We can always blame our actions on somebody else. As we mature and begin to take responsibility for our own actions, we realize that others are not responsible for what we do. When we reach this point we can begin to decide how we want to behave and we can begin to give our life direction.

C

I will take responsibility for my actions.

Year 9:1

A

A family settled down for dinner at a restaurant. The waitress first took the order of the adults, then turned to the seven-year-old. 'What will you have?' she asked. The boy looked around the table timidly and said 'I would like to have a hot dog.'

Before the waitress could write down the order, the mother interrupted, 'No hot dogs,' she said. 'Get him a steak with mashed potatoes and carrots.' The waitress ignored her. 'Do you want ketchup or mustard on your hot dog?' she asked the boy.

'Ketchup.'

'Coming up in a minute,' said the waitress as she started for the kitchen.

There was a stunned silence when she left. Finally the boy looked at everyone present and said 'Know what? She thinks I'm real!'

ANTHONY DE MELLO, *HEART OF THE ENLIGHTENED*

B

It can be very difficult for a parent who is used to taking care of a child's needs for many years, to realize that the child is of an age, where they can in some matters, make their own decisions and choices.

In the story above, the waitress helped the boy to feel that he was 'real' and independent. The family were not intending to be unkind, but were carrying on in their usual custom, a custom that was rapidly becoming out-dated.

Sometimes, like in this story, a few words can make people readjust their position, quite painlessly.

C

I will value each step of independence.

Year 9:2

A

Take it for granted that they will go. This isn't rejecting them or making them feel that you want them to go, but just accepting that this is the way life is, and that they should feel no hesitation about leaving you.

ELIZABETH FENWICK, *ADOLESCENCE*

B

Everyone needs independence at some time in their life. This usually causes arguments, as we usually want more freedom than our parents are prepared to give us. We will also want to visit places of which our parents will disapprove.

The big step of independence is when we leave home. Our parents will naturally think that we are too young to look after ourself. But we have to look after ourself at sometime in our life as our family will not always be there. It will be hard at first, but we will soon get used to it.

JO KNIGHT, AGED 12

C

I will value the years I have with my family.

Year 9:3

A

Responsibility walks hand in hand with capacity and power.

JOHN G. HOLLAND, IN *MORE GATHERED GOLD*

B

To be our own person we need to be independent of our friends and family. It means knowing how we want to spend our time, what books we like to read, what hobbies interest us, what our favourite foods are. It means working out what our personal responsibilities are and carrying them out.

There will be times when we will need and depend on others. There will always be joint responsibilities, or times when we need someone who has more experience than ourselves in certain areas of life. But, working and sharing with others should never negate our independent identity.

ADAPTED FROM *EACH DAY A NEW BEGINNING* (23 JANUARY)

C

I will think about the person I am.

Year 10:1

A

One bird cannot fly to heaven
with another bird's wings

THOMAS ADAMS, IN *MORE GATHERED GOLD*

B

Each person is an individual in their own right. As a child we express our individuality with the words 'I'll do it myself', and as the child struggles to button up a coat or tie a shoe lace they learn to be independent.

As we develop and grow we will be different from our

parents and we will want the differences to be tolerated and encouraged. We also need to respect and love our parents for who they are, and not wish them to be an idealistic image of what we imagine a parent should be.

Each day the things that we do independently increase until we are ready to fly from the nest. Then we can put all our practice and experience to good use. Our wings of experience will help carry us through each daily challenge.

C

I will see each new day as another step towards my independence.

Year 10:2

A

If a little tree grows in the shade of a larger tree, it will die.

SENEGALESE PROVERB, IN *PROVERBS FROM AROUND THE WORLD*

B

For some people the idea of leaving home is a frightening prospect, while for others, it is an exciting thought.

Some families cannot wait for their children to 'leave the nest', while others want them to stay forever. There comes a time when we must all eventually step out on our own. The age will be different for each person, but it is necessary for us to become an individual and lead an independent life from our family.

Sometimes when a bird is reared by hand it takes the human to be its parent. It follows the human everywhere and relies on it totally for its provision. The bird will never fly away, fend for itself, find its own food, or live with other birds. In fact, apart from its physical appearance, it can hardly be called a bird. It hasn't experienced independence and freedom.

To be an independent human being we must reach a point where we are willing to make our own way in the world.

C

When the time is right, I will find my own space to live and grow.

Year 10:3

A

So he returned home to his father.
And while he was still a long distance
away, his father saw him coming, and was
filled with loving pity and ran and
embraced him and kissed him.

LUKE 15:20

B

Sometimes our efforts to be independent go drastically wrong. There are centres in London and in other big cities up and down the UK that give day-time care for the homeless. They also try to find accommodation for them, but many of the clients sleep on the streets. Most of the families of these people are totally unaware of the situation, and the homeless people are too ashamed to admit their circumstances to their families.

However, sometimes when the homeless person has had the courage to contact their family, they have been happily re-united.

When we are ready for independence we must also be mature enough to know when we need support. To go back home does not mean failure, it means the opportunity of a fresh beginning.

C

I will remember that independence does not mean isolation.

Year 11:1

A

You can't solve the past, the past is no longer here, instead look to the future and search for opportunities to put things right.

ELISA GRAY

B

Part of being independent is taking responsibility for our actions. Part of being mature and growing up is admitting to ourselves when we have done something wrong. Taking responsibility means accepting our mistakes and problems as ours and then dealing with them.

There will always be people to offer advice, but we need to think for ourselves and see it only as advice. We have grown beyond the point where we blame others for our failings. When faced with problems and challenges we need to consider ways of dealing with the situations, consider any advice and then make our own decisions. This is all part of the process of being independent.

C

As an independent person I will look for opportunities to find solutions to challenges and problems.

Year 11:2

A

We the Peoples of the United Nations determined …
to reaffirm faith in fundamental human rights,
in the dignity and worth of the human person,
in the equal rights of men and woman and
of nations large and small.

CHARTER OF THE UNITED NATIONS

B

To be independent we need to believe in our own dignity and worth as a human being. If we cannot accept ourselves as being someone of value we can never truly be independent. We will rely on other people to tell us how good we are and we will be in constant need of people who can affirm us as being worthwhile. Once we can accept ourselves for being who we are we have a freedom of independence. We will not need the approval of others.

Once we accept ourselves as being a person of dignity and worth we will be able to give the same respect to others.

C

I am a person of dignity and worth.

Year 11:3

A

We hold these truths to be self evident,
that all men are created equal,
That they are given by their creator
certain unbreakable rights,
That among these are life, liberty,
and the pursuit of happiness.

TAKEN FROM THE AMERICAN *DECLARATION OF INDEPENDENCE*

B

Some people are more outspoken about claiming their rights than others. Some people have more power to demand their rights than others. The majority of us in this country have the right to life, liberty and the pursuit of happiness.

With this independence comes responsibility and we must make sure that our independence does not infringe upon the rights of others.

This means that we use our liberty to walk where we wish without blocking the path for others. It means that we enjoy a joke but not at the expense of someone else.

On a global scale it means paying a fair price for the goods from other countries; so that people in those countries may also enjoy freedom and independence.

C

I will enjoy my independence but not at the expense of others.

ACKNOWLEDGEMENTS

The publishers would like to thank the following for the use of extracts from copyright material.

Amnesty International United Kingdom for extracts from their *Suggested Assembly*; Bantam Doubleday Dell Publishing Group Inc for *Wellsprings* by Anthony de Mello; Mary Batchelor for *Mary Batchelor's Everyday Book*, published by Lion Publishing Ltd; Alison Bawn for the poem 'Pollution' on p. 438; BBC Worldwide Limited for *Assertiveness – The Right To Be You* by Claire Walmsley; The Bible Societies/HarperCollins Publishers Ltd, UK © American Bible Society, 1966, 1971, 1976, 1992, for the extracts from the *Good News Bible*; Cambridge University Press for *Get Together* by Frank Cooke and for extracts from the Authorized Version of the Bible (The King James Bible), the rights in which are vested in the Crown, and are reproduced by permission of the Crown's Patentee, Cambridge University Press; Conari Press for *The Woman's Book of Courage* by Sue Patton Thoele; Darton, Longman and Todd Ltd for *The Joy of Being – Daily Readings with John Main* selected by Clare Hallward, and for *The Dart of Longing Love* by Robert Llewelyn; Dorling Kindersley Ltd for *Adolescence* by Elizabeth Fenwick and Dr. Tony Smith; Eden Grove Editions for *Living in the Light* by Shakti Gawain, and for *You Can Heal Your Life* by Louise L. Hay; Ebony Elliott-Wildmane for the poem 'Do you care?' on pp. 309–10; Exley Publications Ltd for *The Dalai Lama* by Christopher Gibb and for *Mother Teresa* by Charlotte Gray; Faber and Faber Ltd for extracts from *Collected Poems 1909-1962* by T. S. Eliot; Siedah Garrett and Glen Ballard for their song 'Man in the Mirror' from the album *Bad* by Michael Jackson, © Epic CBS Inc./MJJ Productions Inc., on p. 95; Mark Gibson for the poem 'The Hunt' on pp. 285–6; Gill Macmillian for *Prayers of Life* by M. Quoist; Victor J. Green for *Festivals And Saints Days* published by Cassell; HarperCollins Publishers for *Strength To Love* by Martin Luther King, *You Can't Afford the Luxury of a Negative Thought* by John Roger and Peter McWilliams, *I Want to Change But I Don't Know How To* by Tom Rusk and Randy Read, *Surprised by Joy* by C. S. Lewis, *The Heart of Enlightened* by Anthony de Mello, *Mister God, This is Anna* by Fynn, and *The Tiny Book of Hugs* by Kathleen Keating; Hodder Headline plc for *Blue Horizons* by Rabbi Lionel Blue, *The Bible – the New International Version*, © the International Bible Society, *Christianity: An Approach for GCSE* by Kevin O'Donnell, *Up to Date* by Steve Turner, and *Travelling In* by Monica Furlong; Rebecca Hopkins for the poem 'Tropical Rain Forests' on p. 308; The Hunger Project for *A Shift in the Wind 5*; Impact Publishers, Inc., San Luis Obispo, California for *Teen Esteem: A Self-Direction Manual for Young Adults* ©1989 Pat Palmer and Melissa Alberti Froehner, and for *Liking Myself* ©1989 Pat Palmer, reproduced by permission, further reproduction prohibited; Susan Jeffers for *Feel the Fear and Do It Anyway*, published by Arrow Books Ltd; Barbara Johnson for *So, Stick a Geranium in Your Hat and Be Happy*; Brian Keenan for *An Evil Cradling*; Carol Owens for 'Christmas Isn't Christmas' from *Cantata Glory of Christmas* by Jimmy and Carol Owens, © 1980 Lexicon Music Inc; Kevin Mayhew Ltd for *Prayers for Peacemakers* by John Ansell et al.; Longman Group Ltd for *New Methods in RE Teaching – An Experiential Approach* by Hammond, Hay, Moxon, Netto, Raban, Straugheir and Williams; Merlin Press for *It Doesn't Have To Be Like This* by David Icke; Methodist Church (Division of Social Responsibilities) for *Act Together for Tomorrow's World*; New World Library for *Reflections in the Light – Daily Thoughts and Affirmations* and *Creative Visualisation* both by Shakti Gawain; Norman Vincent Peale for *The Power of Positive Thinking*, published by World's Work Ltd; Alan Paton for the prayer on pp. 111–2; Penguin UK for *A Book of Friends and Friendship*, © Celia Haddon, reproduced by permission of Michael Joseph Ltd; John Pepper for *How to be Happy*, published by Gateway Books; Judy Piatkus (Publishers) Ltd for *Living Magically* and for *Stepping Into the Magic* both by Gill Edwards; Queen Anne Press (Lenoard Associates) for *The Illustrated Family Hymn Book*; Quest International for *Changes – Becoming the Best You Can Be* by Gary R. Collins et al., and for *Skills for Adolescence*; Robert Frederick Ltd for *The Decades Book of Birthdays*; Scripture Union for *Frogs in Cream* and *Frogs in Cream II* by Stephen Gaukroger and Nick Mercer; Idries Shah for *Caravan of Dreams*, published by Octagon Press Ltd (London); Simon & Schuster, London for *Awaken the Giant Within* and *Unlimited Power* both by Anthony Robbins, copyright ©1986 Robbins Research Institute; Joanna Smith for the poem 'Destruction' on p. 110; Souvenir Press Ltd for *Joy – Expanding Human Awareness* by William C. Schutz; Sphere Books Ltd for *To Have or To Be* and *Beyond the Chains of Illusion* both by Erich Fromm; Stanley Thornes Ltd for *Assemblies* by Rowland Purton; Tear Fund for *Tear Times*; D.C. Thomson & Co. Ltd for *The Friendship Book of Francis Gay*; Toc H for *A Ticket for a Journey – Some Thoughts on Toc H Today* by Ken Prideaux-Brune, and for *An Honest Test* and *Joyful Journey – Patterns of Prayer in Toc H* both by Bob Knight; Virago Press for the poem 'Equality' by Maya Angelou; Debora Wilson for the poem 'The Hurt World' on pp. 110–11;

The publishers have made every effort to trace copyright holders. However, if any copyright material has not been acknowledged or has been acknowledged incorrectly we will be pleased to put this right at the first opportunity.

The publishers would like to acknowledge the following books as the source of many of the quotations used in this book.

Days of Healing Days of Joy: Daily Meditations for Adult Children, second edition, Earnie Larsen and Carol Larsen Hegarty, Hazelden Meditations, Hazelden Foundation, 1992; *Each Day a New Beginning: Daily Meditations for Women*, second edition, Hazelden Meditations, Hazelden Foundation, 1991; *Gathered Gold* and *More Gathered Gold*, compiled by John Blanchard, Evangelical Press and Services Ltd, 1984 and 1986 respectively; *Touchstones: A Book of Daily Meditations for Men*, Hazelden Meditation Series, Harper & Row Publishers Inc, 1987.